THE PIONEER MINISTRY

THE LIBRARY OF HISTORY AND DOCTRINE

The aim of this international Library is to enable scholars to answer questions about the development of the Christian tradition which are important for an understanding of Christianity today

THE
PIONEER MINISTRY

The Relation of Church and Ministry

ANTHONY TYRRELL HANSON

Philadelphia
The Westminster Press

© SCM PRESS LTD 1961

Library of Congress Catalog Card No. 61–6386

PRINTED IN GREAT BRITAIN

CONTENTS

To Michael and Cordelia Hollis

*

Pro tanto quid retribuamus?

PREFACE

I WISH to acknowledge the help I have received in writing this book in the form of useful advice from a number of friends. Dr Norman Snaith has kindly helped me with his advice on some of the material in Chapter Two. Professor S. L. Greenslade has offered several most useful suggestions after reading the whole book in typescript; and I have received valuable suggestions at various times from my brother, Dr R. P. C. Hanson, from the Rev. D. L. Edwards, Editor of the SCM Press, and from the Rev. T. S. Garrett, my former colleague on the Liturgy Committee of the Church of South India. To all these I would like to express my sincere thanks. I would also like to mention particularly the Ormeau Road Branch of the Belfast Public Library for the way in which they procured for me two important books at relatively short notice. Such efficient service deserves acknowledgement.

St Anne's Cathedral   A. T. H.
Belfast

NOTE

Quotations from the English Bible are from the Revised Version unless otherwise indicated. Quotations from the LXX are from A. Rahlfs' edition, Stuttgart, 1950. Quotations from the Greek New Testament are from the Bible Society's edition, ed. E. Nestle and G. D. Kilpatrick, London, 1958.

ἰσχυρὰν παράκλησιν ἔχωμεν οἱ καταφυγόντες κρατῆσαι τῆς προκειμένης ἐλπίδος· ἣν ὡς ἄγκυραν ἔχομεν τῆς ψυχῆς ἀσφαλῆ τε καὶ βεβαίαν καὶ εἰσερχομένην εἰς τὸ ἐσώτερον τοῦ καταπετάσματος, ὅπου πρόδρομος ὑπὲρ ἡμῶν εἰσῆλθεν Ἰησοῦς, κατὰ τὴν τάξιν Μελχισεδεκ ἀρχιερεὺς γενόμενος εἰς τὸν αἰῶνα.

Hebrews 6.18–20.

I

Introduction

THE LAST fifty years have probably seen more discussion and debate in Britain about the doctrine of the ministry than has any other period since the seventeenth century. This debate seemed to culminate in the publication in 1946 of *The Apostolic Ministry*, edited by the late Bishop Kirk (London, 1946). This book was a comprehensive attempt on the part of the leading Anglo-Catholic scholars of the day to prove from the New Testament and the early Fathers the necessity of the doctrine of the Apostolic Succession as they conceived it. At the time of its publication it was hailed by many as providing the decisive proof from history of this doctrine. In the years which have elapsed since its publication it may be fairly said that the book has proved decisive, but not in the sense in which its authors hoped it would. It has shown decisively that the doctrine of the Apostolic Succession cannot be proved from history. The *coup de grâce* to the arguments most emphasized in *The Apostolic Ministry* seems to have been given by A. Ehrhardt's book *The Apostolic Succession* (London, 1953). He has succeeded in showing that the conception of the *shaliach* which is the linchpin of the arguments put forward by Dr Kirk and his colleagues will not bear the weight of what is made to depend upon it. Dr Ehrhardt writes: 'We are therefore forced to conclude that unless Dr Kirk abandons Rengstorff's theory that the apostle was the *shaliach* of Christ, he cannot very well maintain the doctrine of the apostolic succession.'[1] In other words, whatever a *shaliach* was, or was able to do, he could not commission a successor. Dr Ehrhardt also points out that another essential link in the argument will not hold—it is impossible to trace a satisfactory succession between the apostles and the first bishops: 'What cannot be proved is that any of the Twelve instituted a particular succession of bishops, or that the particular ministerial succession which, according to the Pastoral Epistles, was instituted by St Paul, has been followed down to our own time.'[2]

[1] *Op. cit.*, p. 20.   [2] *Op. cit.*, p. 21.

It is true that recently Dr Austin Farrer, in a Foreword to a new impression of *The Apostolic Ministry*,[1] has undertaken to answer the critics of the book (London, 1957) and in particular to defend the *shaliach* theory, but it does not seem likely that he will make many new converts to his theory by his arguments. He admits that the use of *shaliach* in the sense which he requires is not found till well after our Lord's time, but he still looks on it as affording an analogy for the sending of the apostles: 'Christ's commissioning of the Twelve is to be viewed rather as his own adaptation of a commonplace business arrangement.'[2] One of the aims of the present work is to show that a loftier lineage than a commonplace business arrangement can be found for the apostolate of the Church, and one intimately bound up with the people of God in the Old Testament. Dr Farrer does also admit that the function of *shaliach* could not be passed on; a *shaliach* can appoint no deputy. But he seems to reassure himself by the thought that the apostles were not exact replicas of Christ, they were not meant to be Messiahs, he says, just as the bishops or others whom they in their turn commissioned were not meant to be exact replicas of the apostles. Something, at any rate, was passed on. He does not seem to see that this admission entirely destroys the force of his argument about the *shaliach*: the only point in quoting the *shaliach* analogy was that the *shaliach* was a deputy. The *shaliach* function in Judaism has no other relation at all to either the Old Testament or the New. But it is precisely in this characteristic that his analogy fails: Dr Farrer argues that our Lord intended to appoint a succession of men by which his authority could be handed down in the Church, and we are given as an analogy (claimed to have influenced our Lord's mind) an arrangement by which authority could be handed on from a man to his deputy, but to no one else after that. If this proves anything, it proves that the apostles did not have any successors at all.

The breakdown of the Anglo-Catholic attempt to prove their particular doctrine of the ministry from Scripture has left something of a vacuum. Does it mean that the New Testament has not got a doctrine of the ministry? Is Streeter's epigram correct—'All have won and all shall have prizes'? Were the writers of the New Testament not interested in the ministry? Certainly it is true that the writers of the New Testament were not interested in answering the questions about the ministry which

---

[1] For an effective criticism of some vital aspects of this book see also W. H. Vanstone in *The Historic Episcopate in the Fullness of the Church*, ed. K. M. Carey, London, 1954. Note especially his effective treatment of Dr Farrer's peculiar interpretation of Titus 1.5-7.
[2] *Op. cit.*, p. viii.

Western theologians have been putting to them ever since the Reformation. Was the ministry instituted by Christ? To whom did our Lord give his authority? If he instituted a ministry, when and how did he do it, and did he distinguish any grades of orders in it? How is the ministry perpetuated and what authority does it bear? These are not questions to which clear and definite answers will be found in the New Testament. The consequence has been that theologians have tended to read into the New Testament their own theories of the ministry, theories already formed on *a priori* grounds. One of the most instructive instances of this can be seen in two editions of the Pastoral Epistles which were published about the turn of the century. Both were written by distinguished scholars, and the authors of both were sincerely convinced that what they believed about the ministry was what was taught in the Pastorals. Consequently J. H. Bernard in his commentary represents St Paul as an old-fashioned Anglican of the Tractarian school,[1] while R. F. Horton gives us a St Paul who was a Congregationalist with a leaning towards Liberal theology.[2] From each we learn something about the author of the commentary, but no very convincing picture of St Paul's doctrine of the ministry emerges.

Perhaps in this *a priori* approach lies the fault; a number of people who have written about the ministry during the last two generations have not only begun with the determination to find their own theories vindicated in the New Testament, but they have also approached the New Testament evidence itself in an indirect fashion. They have begun by considering the position of the apostles as reflected in the Synoptic Gospels, but after that they have jumped to some period more or less early in the second century AD, and only after that have they considered the evidence of the Epistles. This is true of two books published within the last fifty years which have had a considerable influence on the current debate concerning the ministry in the New Testament. These are Bishop Gore's *The Church and the Ministry*,[3] and Kirk's *The Apostolic Ministry*, already referred to. No doubt good reasons can be brought forward for adopting this method: the paucity of clear evidence in the Epistles on the points at issue is perhaps the most convincing reason. It is safer to argue from the known to the unknown, and what we find in the second century must have had its origin somewhere. But this method of arguing back from the second century to the first has one disadvantage: it relies too much on the argument from silence. This excessive reliance on the argument from

[1] J. H. Bernard, *Pastoral Epistles* (Cambridge Greek Testament), 1899.
[2] R. F. Horton, *The Pastoral Epistles* (Century Bible), London, 1901.
[3] 5th ed., London, 1913.

silence is also evident in another book, which is in some ways a more effective and convincing plea for the Anglo-Catholic point of view than either of the two books mentioned above, R. C. Moberly's *Ministerial Priesthood*.[1] His treatment of Clement in particular (pp. 183–89) relies very much on the argument: 'it must have been thus, therefore it was thus.'

Now that so many theories about the doctrine of the ministry have been conjured out of the New Testament with very little result as far as establishing an agreed doctrine of the ministry is concerned, it may seem extremely rash to venture on yet another book on the subject. Would it not be better to agree that the New Testament does not offer us a doctrine of the ministry? I believe that it is indeed true to say that the New Testament does not contain the sort of doctrine of the ministry which it has been required to give—that is, a doctrine which will enable us to pass judgement on the various forms of the ministry possessed by the Church today, labelling some as legitimate and others as illegitimate.[2] But it need not follow that the New Testament has no doctrine of the ministry at all. This book represents an attempt to approach the question in a slightly different way. It originated in a certain amount of Bible study undertaken at the request of the Church Missionary Society with the purpose of finding out what exactly the New Testament says about the unity of the church. As a result of that study two things seemed to stand out: the first was that the doctrine of the apostolate in the New Testament is connected in some way with the doctrine of the Remnant. And the second was that Paul does have a doctrine of the ministry, but that it is not to be found in the place where it is generally sought, and it is expressed in terms quite different from those which we are accustomed to use in expounding the theology of the ministry today. The realization that there was a doctrine of the ministry in the New Testament came most appropriately, for it seemed to fill a gap: for one who had started out from the Tractarian doctrine of the ministry, and had then been convinced by some years' experience in the Church of South India that such a theory failed to fit the facts of experience, it was a relief to find that we are not left without any guidance in the New Testament about the nature of the Church's ministry.

---

[1] 2nd ed., London, 1899.

[2] Compare Moberly, *op. cit.*, p. xlvi, where non-episcopal ministries are described as 'wrong in practice and inferior in privilege'. Some modern Anglicans are just as emphatic as Moberly on this point. E. L. Mascall, *The Recovery of Unity*, London, 1958, p. 189, quotes with approval the following from the well-known Roman Catholic ecumenist Père Bouyer: 'Only a man who has validly received the divine commission through the apostolic succession can validly perform the Eucharist. Any other Eucharist is empty of reality, because empty of significance; it is not Christ's own Eucharist.'

The next step was to examine the doctrine of the Remnant in the New Testament. This inevitably led back to the Old Testament. The first chapter, therefore, of this book deals with the question: did the Remnant in the Old Testament have a mission? Reason is shown to believe that, in the prophecies of the Second Isaiah at least, the Remnant was thought of as having a mission. This is then brought into connection with the mission of the Remnant in the New Testament, and the conclusion emerges that the apostolic mission passed from the faithful Remnant in the Old Testament through the Messiah to the apostles and first disciples in the New Dispensation. We then turn to a close examination of St Paul's doctrine of the ministry, which is to some extent set forth in I Cor. 4 and 10, as well as in the *locus classicus* for the ministry, ch. 12. But the main exposition of Paul's doctrine of the ministry is found in II Cor. 3–6, a section which has received little attention from those who have sought a doctrine of the ministry in the New Testament, and yet one which gives a much fuller theology of the ministry than either I Cor. 12 or Eph. 4. In the next chapter Paul's doctrine of the ministry is shown to fit in with the function of the apostolic Remnant, and some conclusions are drawn about the apostolate of the Church. The rest of the book contains a comparison of this New Testament teaching with what has been said about the relation of the ministry to the Church by some of the sub-apostolic writers, and also by four significant theologians of the Reformation period. The doctrine is then viewed in the light of what some modern writers, from Maurice to Torrance, have said on the subject, and the book ends with some conclusions about the apostolate of the Church and the nature of the ministry, with special reference to those insights which we have gained in the course of our ten years' experience in the Church of South India.

We are really more concerned in this book with the relation of the ministry to the Church than with the actual question of ministerial succession. Indeed the attempt has been made to avoid asking those questions about succession which have so often been asked with such inconclusive results. The conclusion of this book would stand even if the main contentions of *The Apostolic Ministry* were proved correct. One of the principles asserted in the following pages is that the ministry is in fact related more closely and (if the expression may be allowed) more theologically both to Christ and to the Church than many writers, whether Anglo-Catholic or otherwise, have claimed. If this discussion has the effect of concentrating the debate more on the theology of the ministry and less on its pedigree, this book will have achieved its object.

2

The Mission of the Remnant

NEARLY ALL that we can learn about the mission of the Remnant in the Old Testament comes from the Book of Isaiah. Naturally, as we examine it we must take it in its historical order, examining passages from Isaiah's pen first, and then those of the time of the Exile, and so on. But we must always bear in mind that what chiefly concerns us is the interpretation which our Lord, and after him the writers of the New Testament, put upon the Old Testament. They thought of the Book of Isaiah as one work issuing from one mind. Hence the fact that, for example, some scholars today think that the 'Servant Songs' in chapters 40–55 are by a different hand from that which wrote the rest of these chapters will not be so very important from our point of view. What the prophets who wrote these chapters meant is not to be disregarded, but more important is what these chapters meant to Jesus and his disciples. Thus there will be no disingenuousness involved in stressing that the Suffering Servant in chapters 40–55 is sometimes presented as a group and sometimes as an individual. It may be that one writer is responsible for the group meaning and another for the individual meaning. But our Lord accepted both meanings as the mind of God, since both were found in the text; and for our purpose our Lord's meaning is decisive. Indeed this is surely a case where the deeper truth lies in the recognition that both individual and group interpretations are true. If two prophets are behind chapters 40–55, and not only one, their messages are complementary and not mutually exclusive.

In Isa. 8.16–20 the prophet apparently consigns his teaching to his disciples, as representing the faithful Remnant:

> Bind thou up the testimony,
> Seal the law among my disciples.
> And I will wait for the Lord, that hideth his face from the house
>   of Jacob,
> And I will look for him.

Here the 'testimony' and 'the law' refer to the same thing, Isaiah's teaching about the coming disaster. Since Israel would not listen to him, he consigns it to his disciples, who are to bring it forth when the day of disaster comes. It is not clear whether the teaching is written or oral. Skinner assumes that it is written,[1] but Gray thinks that 'among my disciples' means 'in the hearts of my disciples', and that therefore 'law' and 'testimony' are figures for oral tradition.[2] Wade comments: 'He (Isaiah) expected the disciples to form the nucleus of the Remnant that is to survive the judgements.'[3] Here then is the conception of a faithful Remnant that will survive the coming crisis and after it disclose the true teaching. Compare 30.8, also from Isaiah's pen, which rather suggests a written document.

When we turn to the Second Isaiah we find a great deal of material about the mission of the Servant. In 42.1-6 we have what is generally called the First Servant Song. The servant has a mission to the nations:

> Behold my servant, whom I uphold;
> my chosen, in whom my soul delighteth:
> I have put my spirit upon him;
> he shall bring forth judgement to the Gentiles . . .
> he shall bring forth judgement in truth.
> He shall not fail nor be discouraged,
> till he have set judgement in the earth;
> and the isles shall wait for his law . . .
> I the Lord have called thee in righteousness,
> and will hold thine hand, and will keep thee,
> and give thee for a covenant of the people,
> for a light of the Gentiles.

North says that the last verse here, from 'I the Lord have called thee', is 'an oracle originally relating to Israel, and subsequently transformed into a Servant Song'.[4] But we may treat it as a homogeneous passage, for that is the form in which the message reached our Lord. There is considerable doubt as to what exactly 'judgement' means here (*mishpaṭ*). In v. 4 the parallel to *mishpaṭ* is *tōrāh*. This is translated 'law' in both RV and RSV, but of course at that period the word could easily mean 'oral instruction' rather than 'written code'. George Adam Smith repudiates the idea of a juridical sentence and describes *mishpaṭ* as 'coterminous with national virtue'[5] and 'the ordinance and will of God'. Similarly Whitehouse,[6]

---

[1] J. Skinner, *Isaiah I-XXXIX* (Cambridge Bible), 1896.
[2] G. Buchanan Gray, *Isaiah I-XXVII* (International Critical Commentary, hereafter cited as ICC), Edinburgh, 1912.
[3] G. W. Wade, *Isaiah* (Westminister Commentaries), 2nd ed. rev., London, 1929.
[4] C. R. North, *The Suffering Servant in Deutero-Isaiah*, London, 1948.
[5] *The Book of Isaiah* (Expositor's Bible) Vol. II, London 1890; new and rev. ed., 1927.
[6] O. C. Whitehouse, *Isaiah* (Century Bible), Vol II, London, 1900.

Skinner,[1] and H. H. Rowley[2] translate it as 'true religion', and Skinner adds the translation 'revealed religion' for *tōrāh*. Some recent scholars seem to have reverted to 'judgement' for *mishpaṭ*, e.g. North in the work already quoted. He translates *tōrāh* here as 'instruction'. A recent writer on the subject claims that the two words here contain 'the suggestion of an instruction in judgement and right . . . which is rooted in the divine execution of judgements in history'.[3] This fits in very well with the task to which the first apostles were called by our Lord. So far then the Servant is to be perhaps judge and certainly teacher of Gentiles as well as Jews. But v. 6 carries the idea further: 'I . . . will . . . give thee for a covenant of the people.' The original meaning is obscure: *berith 'am* is a strange, unparalleled phrase. The LXX translator, one may suspect, was anxious to restrict the application to the Jews, and translates it: ἔδωκά σε εἰς διαθήκην γένους. If North is justified in believing that the passage originally referred to Israel, and not to the Servant as an individual, Ewald's suggestion may have been right, that it means 'a covenant people'. Whitehouse, Wade, and Torrey[4] all support this interpretation. But v. 6 suggests that the work of the Servant is connected with the work of a people. The Servant, judge and teacher as it appears, was to be connected with a people in his task of mediating God to the nations.

In 42.19 the apostolate of the Remnant comes out very clearly, despite some obscurities in the text:

> Who is blind, but my servant?
> or deaf, as my messenger that I send?
> Who is blind as he that is at peace with me,
> and blind as the Lord's servant?

Here the Hebrew actually uses the root *shalach* from which the much disputed word *shaliach* is derived. Unfortunately the LXX is defective here and gives nothing corresponding to the phrase 'my messenger that I send'. The phrase 'he that is at peace with me' is a notorious difficulty: all sorts of conjectures have been made, varying from Wade's *moshlam*, 'he who has received his full pay and is therefore faithful',[5] to Palache's bizarre Meshullam, a post-exilic figure, son of Zerubbabel (I Chron. 3.19). A very recent authority, Koehler and Baumgartner's Hebrew Lexicon (Leiden, 1953), simply gives the word up as an insoluble mystery. How-

[1] *Isaiah XL-LXVI (RV)* (Cambridge Bible), 1917.
[2] *The Biblical Doctrine of Election*, London, 1950, p. 117.
[3] W. Zimmerli in Zimmerli and J. Jeremias, *The Servant of God*, ET (Studies in Biblical Theology 20), London, 1957, p. 28.
[4] *The Second Isaiah: a New Interpretation*, Edinburgh, 1928.
[5] An idea less akin to Second Isaiah's theology it would be difficult to find.

ever, the important point as far as our present purpose is concerned is
that here the Servant is surely a people (blind and deaf as Israel so often is)
and yet is also an apostle.[1]

The next passage links up even more directly with the apostles in the
New Testament. In 43.10 we find:

> Ye are my witnesses, saith the Lord,
> and my servant whom I have chosen:
> that ye may know and believe me,
> and understand that I am he.

The thought is continued in v. 12:

> I have declared, and I have saved, and I have shewed,
> and there was no strange god among you:
> therefore ye are my witnesses, saith the Lord.

With this we should put one other passage, 44.8:

> Fear ye not, neither be afraid:
> have I not declared unto thee of old, and shewed it?
> and ye are my witnesses.
> Is there a God beside me?

The scholars of the last generation tended to think of the witness to God's
power as being borne at the time of the prophet's speaking. Israel is called
on to witness now. But in view of the modern emphasis on the eschatological element in Second Isaiah, it is likely that many scholars today would
think rather of the witness as yet to be given when the day of God's
righteousness comes. The prophet looks forward and warns the Jews
that they will be called on to give witness to God's power when it is presently displayed. The faithful among them will give ear now and be ready
to witness then.

In the light of the New Testament emphasis on the role of the apostles
as witnesses, this is a very important passage. The faithful Remnant in
Second Isaiah are to be witnesses to God's acts when those acts are fulfilled among them in the coming eschatological crisis. In the Book of
Acts especially we find the apostles witnessing to God's acts in Jesus
Christ which have themselves inaugurated the last days. The LXX in
both the above passages translated the Hebrew 'edim as μάρτυρες. Compare Acts 1.8: 'Ye shall be my witnesses';[2] cf. also I John 1.2; Acts 1.22.

---

[1] Rudolf Kittel in his *Biblia Hebraica* (Stuttgart, 1949) actually suggests reading
מִשְׁלָחִי for the obscure word, which is extraordinarily close to ἀπόστολος.

[2] ἔσεσθέ μου μάρτυρες; cf. γένεσθέ μοι μάρτυρες, Isa. 43.10, and μάρτυρες ὑμεῖς ἐστε,
44.8. See also Acts 2.32; 3.15; 10.39, 41; 13.31.

B

Another very interesting connection between this passage and the New Testament is that here the Servant also is to be a witness. Both in John's Gospel and elsewhere in the New Testament it is claimed that our Lord is a witness. In John 8.14 he says: 'Even if I bear witness of myself, my witness is true.' Compare also John 3.11: 'We . . . bear witness of that we have seen; and ye receive not our witness.' See also John 3.32; 8.18; and compare 18.37: 'To this end have I been born, and to this end am I come into the world, that I should bear witness unto the truth.' This last sentence is a strong reminder of the central place which witness bears in the Son's mission. In the Fourth Gospel the Father also bears witness, e.g. 5.32–37. In 8.18 these two witnesses are brought together: 'I am he that beareth witness of myself, and the Father that sent me beareth witness of me.' This is very much what we should expect of the peculiar technique of the author of the Fourth Gospel: the Son's and the Father's functions are interchangeable to a large extent, and we find a function of the Son apparently being predicated of the Father; cf. 17.1–2.

In the rest of the New Testament also our Lord is sometimes described as bearing witness. Compare I Tim. 6.13, where it is said of Jesus Christ that 'before Pontius Pilate [he] witnessed the good confession'. Theologically more profound is Rev. 1.5, where Jesus is called 'the faithful witness' (ὁ μάρτυς ὁ πιστός), no doubt in reference to his having fulfilled the prophecies and to his revelation of God the Father. The same thought occurs in Rev. 3.14, where he is described as 'the Amen, the faithful and true witness'. Hence we may claim that the function of both the Messiah and his apostles as witnesses derives from the witness which the Servant and the faithful Remnant were to bear in the days of the revelation of God's salvation.

But there is an even more intimate connection between the passage in Isa. 43 and 44 and the New Testament. Isa. 43.10 appears to be echoed by our Lord in the Fourth Gospel. We must compare Greek with Greek here if we wish to see the correspondence clearly. The second clause of Isa. 43.10 is rendered by the LXX as:

ἵνα γνῶτε καὶ πιστεύσητε καὶ συνῆτε ὅτι ἐγώ εἰμι.[1]

The Greek of John 8.24 is:

ἐὰν γὰρ μὴ πιστεύσητε ὅτι ἐγώ εἰμι, ἀποθανεῖσθε ἐν ταῖς ἁμαρτίαις ὑμῶν.[2]

[1] '. . . that ye may know and believe and understand that I am' (my translation, as also in the next four citations).
[2] 'For if you do not believe that I am, you will die in your sins.'

Compare also John 8.28:

"Ὅταν ὑψώσητε τὸν Υἱὸν τοῦ ἀνθρώπου, τότε γνώσεσθε ὅτι ἐγώ εἰμι.[1]

We might also compare what is not quite as close a parallel: Isa. 44.8 in the LXX runs:

οὐκ ἀπ᾽ ἀρχῆς ἠνωτίσασθε καὶ ἀπήγγειλα ὑμῖν; μάρτυρες ὑμεῖς ἐστε, εἰ ἔστιν θεὸς πλὴν ἐμοῦ.[2]

With this compare John 8.25:

Σὺ τίς εἶ; εἶπεν αὐτοῖς ὁ Ἰησοῦς, τὴν ἀρχὴν ὅ τι καὶ λαλῶ ὑμῖν.[3]

C. K. Barrett in his commentary on St John has noticed the connection between Isa. 43.10 and John 8.24; he calls it 'a remarkably close parallel'.[4] He points out that ἐγώ εἰμι (in itself a meaningless phrase in Greek) is meant to translate the Hebrew 'ani hu', and that in the Greek as in the Hebrew it is probably an allusion to the divine name. In the context of John 8.24 it indicates the eternal being of Jesus and puts him in the category of God. Similarly Barrett concludes that the phrase in John 8.25, τὴν ἀρχὴν ὅ τι καὶ λαλῶ ὑμῖν, must mean, 'I am from the beginning what I tell you'. So far then we may fairly suggest that in this discourse John is looking back to the function of the Servant in Second Isaiah and identifying Jesus with him, and Jesus' faithful disciples with the faithful Remnant, who are themselves to be associated with the Servant at the revelation of God's righteousness or salvation. At the same time however Jesus is also identified with God, who in the Second Isaiah passage calls on both Servant and Remnant to witness. This is quite in John's style: Jesus is both witness to God and he is God who calls on others to witness. We have noted above how often he is described as witness, e.g. 8.14. In 8.24 f. however he appears as God appears in Isa. 43.10; 44.8, and calls on his faithful disciples to witness to his being.

The Greek of John 8.28 is even closer to the LXX of Second Isaiah (see above where Isa. 43.10b and John 8.28 are compared). Barrett's comment on John 8.28 is illuminating: 'The subject of γνώσεσθε is apparently the Jews, but John cannot mean that they will recognize the truth of Jesus' claims after the Crucifixion, since it is well known to him that this had not happened. He is addressing his readers.' Here then Jesus tells his

---

[1] 'When you shall lift up the Son of Man, then you shall know that I am.'
[2] 'Have you not given ear from the beginning, and I have announced it to you? You are my witnesses whether there is any god but me.'
[3] 'Who art thou? Jesus said to them, Originally what I say to you.'
[4] *The Gospel according to St John*, London, 1955, pp. 282 f.

faithful disciples that they will eventually know the truth about him, know the secret of his nature, just as in Second Isaiah the prophet says that when they are able to witness to the fulfilment of God's purposes, then they will know God's true nature. In John 8.28 Jesus is still speaking from the point of view of God, but his role as Servant-Witness is not forgotten. The verse ends: 'As the Father taught me, I speak these things.' And in the passage which John is echoing here it is not only the faithful in Israel who are to witness, but also 'my servant whom I have chosen'. John does not actually use the word 'witnesses' for the disciples anywhere. We can suggest two reasons for this: the first is that he wanted to keep the name 'witness' for the Messiah, who came to bear witness to the truth. Compare his refusal to use 'apostle' for the disciples for the same reason. The other reason we may suggest is that, when John wrote, μάρτυς had acquired its technical meaning of 'martyr'. But there can be little doubt that John had Isa. 43.10; 44.8 in mind, and that he meant to identify the faithful disciples with the faithful Remnant, and Jesus with both the Servant and God.

This in itself is important evidence, and helps us to see how the role of the faithful Remnant in the Old Testament was assumed by the apostles and disciples in the New Testament. It gives us evidence as to what John thought the apostles were in relation to our Lord. But can we go any further than that? Can we say that this was what was in the mind of our Lord? The problem of how to discern in the Fourth Gospel what is the author's own reflection and what is the tradition which he received is one which has baffled scholars so far, and seems today as far from solution as ever. Indeed some modern editors seem to insist that this is the question which must not be asked about John's Gospel. But we can at least say this: we assume on sufficient evidence that Jesus did study the prophecy of the Second Isaiah. There he would find a doctrine of a Servant who is sometimes an individual and sometimes a group. This Servant was to witness to God's action in the coming crisis, and the group, the faithful Remnant, was also to witness. Our Lord did call a group of disciples around him, of which the Twelve were at least the nucleus. John presents us with a discourse in which all these ideas are present, though expressed in language which seems to belong to the time of writing rather than to our Lord's own period, and expressed through the medium of a Christ who speaks more like the Jesus of present Christian experience than the Jesus of the Synoptic Gospels. Further than this the evidence will not permit us to go with certainty. But it does not seem unreasonable to conclude that John was not inventing ideas of himself and attributing them to Jesus, but was clothing in the language of his own day teaching which our Lord did actually give, though he expressed it within the limits of the consciousness that was possible to him in the days of his flesh.[1]

A little further on in Isa. 43 (vv. 20 f.) occurs the following passage:

> Because I give waters in the wilderness,
> and rivers in the desert,
> to give drink to my people, my chosen:
> the people whom I formed for myself,
> that they might set forth my praise.

As this passage is quoted in the New Testament we must pay attention to the Greek. In the LXX v. 21 runs:

> τὸ γένος μου τὸ ἐκλεκτόν,
> λαόν μου, ὃν περιεποιησάμην
> τὰς ἀρετάς μου διηγεῖσθαι.

It seems likely that the prophet is looking forward to the coming deliverance, because of his reference to waters breaking out in the desert. This was to be one of the accompaniments of the revelation of God's righteousness in the deliverance of his people. The chosen people here may refer to Israel as a whole, or more likely to those who had the faith to believe Yahweh's promise made by his prophet. This passage is quoted specifically in I Peter 2.9:

> ὑμεῖς δὲ γένος ἐκλεκτόν,
> βασίλειον ἱεράτευμα,
> ἔθνος ἅγιον,
> λαὸς εἰς περιποίησιν,
> ὅπως τὰς ἀρετὰς ἐξαγγείλητε τοῦ ἐκ σκότους ὑμᾶς καλέσαντος εἰς τὸ θαυμαστὸν αὐτοῦ φῶς.

> But ye are an elect race, a royal priesthood (or 'a palace, a priesthood'), a holy nation, a people for God's own possession, that ye may shew forth the excellencies of him who called you out of darkness into his marvellous light.

Most commentators seem to agree that the author of I Peter in using γένος ἐκλεκτόν and λαὸς εἰς περιποίησιν etc. is consciously quoting Isa. 43.21; e.g. Bigg,[2] Beare,[3] Selwyn.[4] Our author here must have understood the prophet to have been speaking of the faithful Remnant, a very likely

---

[1] With this whole discussion cf. Zimmerli (*op. cit.*, p. 30 n. 92): 'The proclamation of salvation to the peoples radiates from this revelation through history to which Israel, by its experience of grace, remains the true witness.' In this work Jeremias has not included John 8 in his list of New Testament references to Second Isaiah applied to Jesus (pp. 88–92).
[2] C. Bigg, *Peter and Jude* (ICC), 1901.
[3] F. W. Beare, *The First Epistle of Peter*, Oxford, 1947.
[4] E. G. Selwyn, *The First Epistle of St Peter*, London, 1946.

interpretation, as we have seen. In the coming deliverance the faithful Remnant would carry out their mission of proclaiming the praise of God. These words he unhesitatingly applies to the Christian Church as a whole. The prophecy, he believes, has been fulfilled in the Christian Church. The full significance of this we will try to bring out later. For the moment it is sufficient to notice that here quite unmistakably the Christian Church is identified with the faithful Remnant, and the mission of the Remnant is the mission of the Church. Whether this Epistle was written by Peter or not,[1] all are agreed that it was written when the apostles and first disciples were dying out. What the Epistle does not tell us is how the mission of the Remnant passed over from the first apostles to the Church.

Isa. 49.5 f. is the famous passage where the Servant is described as 'a light to the Gentiles, that thou mayest be my salvation unto the end of the earth'. It is interesting to note that his task is also 'to restore the preserved of Israel'. The Hebrew is $n^e ts\bar{u}r\bar{e}$, which refers no doubt to those of Israel who would still be alive and faithful when God's coming deliverance would take place. This confirms the suggestion that the passage in 43.21 refers to the faithful Remnant rather than to the people as a whole. The LXX gives the word a connotation more suitable to its own day by translating διασποράν τοῦ 'Ισραήλ, thus referring to the Jews scattered all over the Greek world. Possibly the Greek translator has also tried to suggest that the Servant here, despite his many individual characteristics, is really the Jewish people, for he has inserted εἰς διαθήκην γένους before εἰς φῶς ἐθνῶν, thus giving the sense:

> Behold, I have given thee for a covenant of a people, for a light to the nations.

The passage shows clearly the evangelistic mission of the Servant. But our Lord and his first disciples would have read it in the context of the other Servant passages (not the so-called 'Servant Songs' only), and it would have spoken to them of a mission undertaken by one that he might pass it on to the group whom he had called around him.

One more passage in Second Isaiah deserves brief attention, 55.4:

> Behold, I have given him for a witness to the peoples, a leader and commander to the peoples.

Those who, like North, hold that the Servant Songs refer to an individual and are by one author, while the rest of the Servant-references are by another author and signify Israel or the Remnant, point out that this is not

---

[1] If it was by Peter, his use of Isa. 43 in this way rather strengthens the likelihood of that chapter having been used by our Lord himself as John represents it to have been.

a Servant Song, so the reference is to the people. There must also be a
reference to David, as v. 3 of this chapter refers to him. Wade sums it up
thus: 'The pronoun refers to David, but to David as represented by, and
perpetuated in, the people.'[1] Skinner and Torrey refer it to the Messiah.
Here then is another reference to the Servant which also contains, we may
be sure, an implied reference to the group. And here also the function of
the Servant is to be a witness.

Three probably post-restoration prophecies, all more or less dependent
on the Second Isaiah, seem to echo his conception of the mission of the
Remnant. The first is Isa. 2.3:

> And many peoples shall go and say,
> Come ye, and let us go up to the mountain of the Lord,
> to the house of the God of Jacob;
> and he will teach us of his ways,
> and we will walk in his paths:
> for out of Zion shall go forth the law,
> and the word of the Lord from Jerusalem.

This prophecy is also found in Micah 4.1–4, so many editors (e.g. Gray)
have suggested that it was an anonymous, floating, post-exilic prophecy
that was later fixed at this point in the collection of Isaiah's prophecies.
Both Skinner and Wade think that the 'teaching' ('law' here is *tōrāh*) will
be done by agents, not directly by God. The latter speaks of the Jewish
people as 'a source of spiritual enlightenment to mankind'. Skinner (who
attributes the fragment to Isaiah of Jerusalem) thinks the agents are to be
prophets. In any case we see the faithful Remnant exercising a teaching
ministry.

The second passage is Isaiah 12.4 f.:

> And in that day shall ye say,
> Give thanks into the Lord,
> call upon his name,
> declare his doings among the peoples,
> make mention that his name is exalted.
> Sing unto the Lord, for he hath done excellent things:
> let this be known in all the earth.

The Hebrew of 'let this be known' is doubtful. The Hebrew as read by
the Massoretes would mean 'this is made known'; the LXX seems to have
read 'make this known'.[2] There seems little doubt from the liturgical

---

[1] *Isaiah* (Westminster Commentaries).

[2] The Q're is מוּדַעַת, Hoph'al partic. fem.='a thing made known'. LXX
ἀναγγείλατε presumably implies הוֹדִיעוּ. R. Kittel conj. מִי יָדַע עֹאת, 'who has
known this?'

form and cross-connections with late Psalms in this passage that it is well
post-exilic (so Cheyne, Gray, Skinner, Wade). Whether the author intended the Remnant to make known God's praises with an evangelistic
intent or not is doubtful. But it could certainly be taken in that sense by
later readers.

THE REMNANT AS JUDGES

In the rest of the Old Testament and in the intertestamental literature
there is no hint of the mission of the Remnant. Such a thought is confined
to the Book of Isaiah. But we do find something, though not very much,
about the role of the Remnant as judges or rulers. This may be significant
for the New Testament interpretation of the Remnant, for the saints in
the New Testament did expect to judge the world (see I Cor. 6.2). Also
certain scholars have recently claimed that the apostles were appointed
as judges and rulers over the Church, which would dispose one to look
for the suggestion in the Old Testament or later Jewish literature that
certain members of the Remnant would be judges or rulers over the rest of
the Remnant.

There is an interesting passage in Micah where there is some suggestion
of subordinate rulers under the Messiah. Micah 5.5 f. runs:

> And this man shall be our peace:
> when the Assyrian shall come into our land,
> and when he shall tread in our palaces,
> then shall we raise against him seven shepherds,
> and eight principal men.
> And they shall waste the land of Assyria with the sword,
> and the land of Nimrod in the entrances thereof:
> and he shall deliver us from the Assyrian,
> when he cometh into our land,
> and when he treadeth within our border.

All scholars seem to agree that this is not from Micah. J. M. P. Smith puts
it in the post-exilic era;[1] C. W. Wade argues for a time a few years before
the fall of the city in 586 BC;[2] The RV translation is unsatisfactory: 'this
man' should probably be 'this', referring to the leaders. And 'he shall
deliver' should probably be plural, also indicating the leaders (so RSV).
The two numbers seven and eight are of course an Hebrew idiom meaning a sufficient quantity of leaders for all emergencies. They are to be
subordinate rulers under the Messiah; the Hebrew word *naṣik* means

---

[1] *Micah, Zephaniah, Nahum* (ICC), 1912.
[2] *Micah, Obadiah, Joel, Jonah* (Westminster Commentaries), London, 1925.

literally 'a consecrated one', hence 'a leader'. We should notice that their task is to rule the Gentiles, not the Jews.

The chief significance of this passage for our purpose is negative: it is not quoted in the New Testament with reference to the Remnant or the apostles. The first line, 'this man shall be our peace', may possibly be quoted in Eph. 2.14, but see our discussion of this passage below. One reason for the passage not being quoted may be that the LXX mistranslated 'principal men' as δήγματα ἀνθρώπων, which means literally 'bites of men'.[1] This would either convey complete nonsense to one who read his Old Testament in Greek, or give a very fierce picture of these subordinate rulers. But it is rather surprising that no modern theologian of the advanced typological school has as yet claimed this passage as one which inspired the appointment of the Twelve. If seven and eight are put together we have fifteen subordinate rulers under the Messiah, and this could easily be made up by adding, say, Paul, Barnabas, and Silas to the Twelve. More ingenious and less convincing conjectures have been put forward as evidence for our Lord's appointment of an 'essential' ministry.

It seems that in the Book of Daniel both rule and judgement are put into the hands of the faithful Remnant. We find this described in Dan. 7.13 f.:

> Behold there came with the clouds of heaven
> one like unto a son of man,
> and he came even to the ancient of days,
> and they brought him near before him.
> And there was given him dominion,
> and glory and a kingdom,
> that all the peoples, nations, and languages should serve him:
> his dominion is an everlasting dominion,
> which shall not pass away,
> and his kingdom that which shall not be destroyed.

The promise is repeated in 7.18, and in 7.22 we read: 'and judgement was given to the saints of the Most High'. There can be no doubt that the author of Daniel meant by this figure 'like unto a son of man' the faithful Remnant who should stand firm in time of persecution. The RSV translates v. 22 as 'and judgement was given for the saints of the Most High'. Both S. R. Driver[2] and J. A. Montgomery[3] consider that this is the right

---

[1] The LXX translator took the Hebrew נְסִיךְ as derived from נשׁךְ='bite'. NB: 'entrances thereof' in v. 6 is also wrong; RSV's 'with the drawn sword' is a good conjecture.

[2] *Daniel* (Cambridge Bible), 1900.　　　　[3] *Daniel* (ICC), 1927.

interpretation, and R. H. Charles agrees.[1] The Aramaic could be translated 'to the saints', but 'for the saints' is more natural.[2] The Greek is
quite ambiguous, whether one takes the LXX or Theodotion's version.[3]
Either version could just as well be understood as 'to the saints of the
Most High'.

Montgomery points out that the New Testament writers certainly took
it that the judgement was here given to the saints, or faithful Remnant,
and he cites Matt. 19.28; I Cor. 6.2; Rev. 20.4. In each case the persons
addressed seem to represent the faithful Remnant rather than the officers
of the Church. We meet also in the case of the figure of the Son of Man
what we met in the passages about the Servant of the Lord, and that is
that our Lord seems to have left it ambiguous: the Son of Man was an
individual, but he could also indicate a group. Matt. 19.28 associates
with the Messiah his faithful disciples as judges and echoes a passage in
Daniel where the individual actually represents a group. T. W. Manson
says: 'This at once suggests that what was in the mind of Jesus was that
he and his disciples *together* should be the Son of Man, the Remnant that
saves by service and self-sacrifice, the organ of God's redemptive purpose
in the world.'[4] At any rate we may be clear about two things: the faithful
Remnant in the Old Testament are thought of as ruling, and perhaps
judging, the Gentiles. And secondly, this is applied in the New Testament
to the faithful disciples of the Lord, who judge unfaithful Jews, and (in
Revelation perhaps) unfaithful Christians. There is no suggestion at all
that leading individuals among the Remnant are given ruling powers over
the rest.

In the intertestamental period the thought of the faithful Remnant
as judges is occasionally found, especially in the Book of Enoch, e.g.
Enoch 38.5:

> Then shall the kings and the mighty perish
> And be given into the hands of the righteous and holy.

Charles' comment here is, 'This seems to shew that the judgement is not
catastrophic',[5] and he thinks that it is unfaithful Jews that are judged and
not Gentiles. Here are two more passages to the same purport; the first
is 48.9:

---

[1] *The Book of Daniel*, Oxford, 1929.
[2] וְדִינָא יְהִב לְקַדִּישֵׁי עֶלְיוֹנִין
[3] LXX: καὶ τὴν κρίσιν ἔδωκε τοῖς ἁγίοις. Theod.: καὶ τὸ κρίμα ἔδωκεν ἁγίοις.
[4] *The Teaching of Jesus*, Cambridge, 1931, p. 231.
[5] *Apocrypha and Pseudepigrapha of the Old Testament*, Oxford, 1913, Vol. II, p. 210.

And I will give them over into the hands of mine elect:
as straw in the fire, so shall they burn before the face of the holy:
as lead in the water, shall they sink before the face of the righteous,
and no trace of them shall any more be found.

The second passage is 91.12:

And after that there shall be another, the eighth week, that of
righteousness,
and a sword shall be given to it, that righteous judgement may be
executed on the oppressors,
and sinners shall be delivered into the hands of the righteous.

Compare also 95.3; 96.1; 98.12. There is also the thought that the righteous shall bear witness against sinners at the judgement, e.g. 99.16,
addressed to sinners:

And all the holy and righteous shall remember your sins.

Cf. also 97.5. But this is very different from the witnessing Remnant of
Second Isaiah.

It is a little surprising to find something like eschatological judgement
put into the hands of the Remnant in the Book of Wisdom, but such seems
to be the case. Wisd. 3.7 f. in Greek runs:

καὶ ἐν καιρῷ ἐπισκοπῆς αὐτῶν ἀναλάμψουσιν
καὶ ὡς σπινθῆρες ἐν καλάμῃ διαδραμοῦνται·
κρινοῦσιν ἔθνη καὶ κρατήσουσιν λαῶν
καὶ βασιλεύσει αὐτῶν Κύριος εἰς τὰς αἰῶνας.

And in the time of their visitation they shall shine forth, and as sparks
among the stubble they shall run to and fro. They shall judge nations,
and have dominion over peoples; And the Lord shall reign over them
for evermore.

There seems to be a reference to Dan. 12.3 here, though there is very little
verbal similarity. Theodotion's version οἱ συνιέντες ἐκλάμψουσιν is the
nearest equivalent. The metaphor of sparks in the stubble is used in Isa.
5.24 and Obad. 18, but there is not such close verbal similarity as to suggest a quotation. W. J. Deane believes that Wisdom is echoing Daniel.[1]
J. A. F. Gregg is disinclined to accept any eschatological significance,
and even says, 'Kingship, not judgement, is the prospect held out by the
verse.'[2] This seems difficult to justify. S. Holmes believes that this passage
clearly indicates that the righteous are to be God's instrument in the
punishment of the ungodly.[3]

[1] *The Book of Wisdom*, Oxford, 1881.
[2] *The Wisdom of Solomon* (Cambridge Bible), 1909.
[3] In Charles, *op. cit.*, Vol. I, p. 539.

There are two interesting references in the Dead Sea Scrolls. In citing them we are not suggesting that our Lord or his disciples were influenced by them in their conception of the Remnant. It is rather that the Scrolls give us some idea of the theology of one section of the Jews round about the time when Christianity was born. In the *Habakkuk Commentary* the commentator notes *à propos* Hab. 1.12:

> God will not destroy his people by the hand of the nations, but into the hand of his elect will God deliver the judgement of all the nations and by their chastisement all the wicked among his people will be punished.[1]

Burrows points out that 'his elect' here is singular, but 'their chastisement' shows that the author intends a plural. One of the peculiarities of the Hebrew writing in the Scrolls is that singular and plural forms of the nouns cannot be distinguished when they have the possessive suffix of the third person masculine. Here the faithful Remnant is to judge the 'twelve tribes of Israel', i.e. the unfaithful among Israel. There is no suggestion of the Remnant itself being judged by its own leaders.

The War of the Sons of Light and the Sons of Darkness is a long and quite realistic account of what the righteous are going to do against the unrighteous. There is no doubt that the righteous are to be the instruments of God's judgement. For example XI 1–12:[2]

> By thy anointed ones, seers of testimonies, thou hast made known to us the orderings of the battles of thy hands to fight (or 'to get glory') against our enemies, to make the troops of Belial to fall.

Thus the thought that the Remnant are to be judges in the last days is a feature of the Old Testament, though not a very prominent one, and is more marked in the intertestamental literature. They are to judge both the Gentiles and the unfaithful among the Jews. There is no suggestion whatever that they are to judge themselves, or that leaders or princes are to be appointed to rule over the Remnant. In the light of this it seems very likely that Matt. 19.28 and Luke 22.30 refer not to the appointment of the Twelve as judges over the Church, but to the appointment of the faithful Remnant, the Church, to judge the rest of the world.

[1] Translation from M. Burrows, *The Dead Sea Scrolls*, London, 1956, p. 367.
[2] Burrows' enumeration, *op. cit.* p. 299.

3

The Remnant in Paul's Thought

THE STUDY of John 8 and I Peter 1 has led us to the conclusion that some at least of the writers of the New Testament identified the faithful Remnant in Second Isaiah with the Christian Church, and that the apostolic function of the Remnant was thought of as passing over to the Church. But these are relatively incidental references made by writers whose main preoccupation was with other aspects of Christian doctrine. It was Paul who was directly concerned with the question of the transition from Israel of old to the Christian Church, so we cannot avoid trying to discover what Paul has to say about the faithful Remnant. Does he, we must ask, think of the Remnant as having an apostolic mission?

The earliest letter in which Paul deals with the question of the Remnant is Galatians. In this Epistle he does not speak of the Remnant's mission, but he does tell us something about those whom he believed to be the true successors of Abraham. His teaching is largely presented through the allegory of Sarah and Hagar in ch. 4, and is therefore not very easy to follow. But, if we press the analogy which Paul offers us here, we can find out something about Paul's view on succession. Since Paul specifically tells us that he is using an allegory (4.24), we are justified in drawing logical conclusions from it, as we could not, for instance, from a parable or story. We can arrange Paul's figures in two columns of corresponding opposites, according to whether they belong to the free woman or the slave:

The Free Woman	The Slave	Ref. in ch. 4
'the free woman'	Hagar	vv. 22, 24
[heavenly Sion[1]]	Mount Sinai in Arabia	v. 25
'the Jerusalem that is above'	'the Jerusalem that now is'	vv. 25 f.
'thou barren that bearest not'	'her which hath the husband'	v. 27
'he that was born after the spirit'	'he that was born after the flesh'	v. 29 f.
'son of the freewoman'	'son of the handmaid'	
'children of the freewoman'	'children of a handmaid'	v. 31
[the new covenant]	[the old covenant]	v. 24

[1] Cf. Heb. 12.22.

It is important to notice that in v. 23 the contrast is between 'the son born after the flesh' and 'the son born through promise'. And in v. 28 Christians are identified with 'children of promise, as Isaac was'. At first sight the contrast would seem quite a simple one: Paul would seem to be contrasting 'the children after the flesh', the Jews, physical descendants of Abraham, with 'the children after the spirit', the Gentile Christians, who are Abraham's spiritual heirs. By this interpretation all in the left-hand column of our list would seem to refer to Christians, and all in the right-hand column to Jews. But in fact this cannot be the sense in which Paul uses 'after the flesh' in this passage; for in v. 23 he distinguishes Isaac as a son born, not after the flesh, but 'through promise'. But Isaac was just as much a physical descendant of Abraham as Ishmael was. So Paul is actually employing the flesh-spirit contrast here in the same way as he applies it throughout his Epistles (cf. especially Phil. 3.3). It means relying on works and external qualifications as contrasted with relying on God through faith in Christ. Isaac was born, St Paul suggests, because Abraham believed God's promise in faith. Ishmael was not born in such circumstances. Hence it is perfectly possible for Jews also to be 'children of promise'. After all Isaac, a Jew by birth, is called 'a son born through promise'.

If one were to ask, 'When did the Jews become children of Hagar rather than of Sarah?' the answer would probably be: 'When they accepted the law on Mount Sinai.' This is shown by the reference in v. 24 to the covenant of Sinai 'bearing children unto bondage'. What then happened to the lineage of Isaac at that time? It seems to have been suspended until the coming of the Messiah, though Paul would certainly hold that there were frequent hints or prophecies of it scattered throughout the Scriptures, especially in the prophets. When the Messiah came proclaiming God's free grace to all, the line of Sarah-Isaac was resumed by those (Jews) who accepted Him and became the first Christian Church. The line was then continued in the Church and extended to the Gentiles also. Hence we may claim that Paul is here tracing the lineage of the Remnant from believing Abraham through Isaac to Christ, and from him through the believing Remnant of Jews to the Jewish-Gentile Church of his day. He acknowledges that from Moses to Christ this line was suspended, and he describes the time of suspension in 3.17–4.5. Notice how Paul defines the end of the Law period in 4.4 f.:

> But when the fulness of the time came, God sent forth his Son, born of a woman, born under the law, that he might redeem them which were under the law, that we might receive the adoption of sons.

Paul, by saying here that Christ was 'born under the law' means simply that he was born a Jew. He came to redeem those who were under the law, the Jews; so it seems likely that the pronoun in 'we should receive the adoption of sons' means 'we Jews'. Of course the Jews were bound to pass on this sonship to the Gentiles, and they actually did so. In v. 8, recollecting that he is writing to Gentiles, even though Judaizing Gentiles, Paul describes what roughly corresponds to the Jews' slavery to the law: the Galatians have been slaves to 'them which are by nature no gods'. So the argument of this difficult passage about the allegory runs thus: 'From Abraham to Moses was the period of promise, when the dynasty of promise began in Abraham and his successors. From Moses to Christ the dynasty was interrupted. But it was resumed in Christ, who was sent to the Jews. A faithful Remnant among the Jews accepted him and passed the dynasty of promise on to the Gentiles.' Thus in Galatians we do find a faithful Remnant of Jews playing its essential part in handing on the mission, though it is not brought as much into the open as it is in Romans.

We must now turn to Paul's classic exposition of his doctrine of the Remnant in Rom. 9–11. In 9.6–9 we find clear confirmation of the interpretation of Gal. 4 suggested above. In Rom. 9.8 Paul repeats a principle which he has already expressed in Gal. 4.28; he says:

> It is not the children of the flesh that are counted children of God; but the children of the promise are reckoned for a seed.

In the previous two verses he has explained the sense in which he means this to be taken:

> For they are not all Israel, which are of Israel: neither because they are Abraham's seed, are they all children: but, in Isaac shall thy seed be called.

That is to say, 'the children of the promise' are Jews. The contrast is not between physical descent and spiritual adoption, but between the true Israel consisting of Jews who receive the promise by faith, and the old Israel consisting of Jews who do not.

In Rom. 9.24 Paul further explains his meaning. He is referring to those upon whom God's mercy has been shown, and he describes them as 'us, whom he also called, not from the Jews only, but also from the Gentiles'. This cannot mean that the Gentiles were called at exactly the same time as the Jews, for, as we have seen, the true Israel is first and foremost a part of the old, the faithful part. He must mean that the faithful Jews were called first and then through them the Gentiles: cf. Rom. 2.9–10. Paul does not apply the world 'remnant' or 'seed' to the Jewish-Gentile

Church, but to the Messiah (e.g. Gal. 3.16), or to the small number of Jews who accepted the Messiah and thus became the first Church. The two quotations (Rom. 9.27–29) from Isa. 10.22 f. and 1.9, must both refer to a Remnant of the Jews. In vew of Gal. 3.16, it is quite possible that Isa. 1.9 ('Except the Lord of Sabaoth had left us a seed') is interpreted by Paul as referring to the Messiah. Paul's peculiar rendering of Isa. 10.23 in Greek gives the quotation an idea of fulfilment which is absent from the Hebrew. The Hebrew literally translated is: 'Complete destruction and a decision will the Lord God perform in the midst of the earth.'[1] The LXX is: ὅτι λόγον συντετμημένον ποιήσει Κύριος κτλ. Paul does not exactly reproduce this. His version runs: λόγον γὰρ συντελῶν καὶ συντέμνων ποιήσει Κύριος ἐπὶ τῆς γῆς. The nearest equivalent in contemporary Greek to this use of συντελῶν occurs in a magical tablet addressed to a god: συντέλεσον τὰ ἐγγεγραμμένα ἐν πεδάλῳ τουτῷ ('Fulfil what is written in this tablet').[2] συντέμνων must mean 'cutting short'. Compare Moulton and Milligan s.v.: τὰ ἐν με[σ]ῷ [κεφ]άλαια συντέμνων ὑπέταξ[ά] σοι, which is presumably to be translated, 'Hastening on the business I had in hand, I obeyed thee.' Thus Paul has extracted from Isa. 10.23 the sense: 'Fulfilling and hastening on his work will the Lord do on earth.' It is possible that Paul is translating from the Hebrew here, as he does offer two words corresponding to the two words in Hebrew. At any rate he has imported into the Isaianic prophecy a suggestion of fulfilment in the Messianic era which it does not possess in the Hebrew. He takes it as a confirmation of the reference to the Remnant: God will fulfil this word and shorten the time. Then follows the reference to the 'seed' which, as we have seen, may very well mean Christ. It is very interesting to notice that in Rom. 9.31 he uses Israel of *disobedient* Israel; so far was he from applying the name to the Gentiles. This is strictly incompatible with 9.6, but he seems to be able to use the name for the faithful Remnant of Jews, for the disobedient majority of Jews, and even (11.26) for all Israel, including those now disobedient, who will ultimately be obedient. He does not seem to use the name for the Christian Church inclusive of Gentiles.

So far Paul has established that a faithful Remnant of Jews who should believe in and accept the Messiah was prophesied in Scripture. Then in ch. 10 he goes on to show that the task of this faithful Remnant of Jews has been to preach the word, and that this also was prophesied in Scripture. Once again, as in Gal. 4, Paul's argument is not very clearly expressed,

[1] כִּי כָלָה וְנֶחֱרָצָה אֲדֹנָי יְהוִה צְבָאוֹת עֹשֶׂה בְּקֶרֶב כָּל־הָאָרֶץ

[2] J. H. Moulton and G. Milligan, *Vocabulary of the Greek Testament* (one vol. ed.), London, 1930, p. 614.

as he is expounding a passage from Deuteronomy which, on the surface at least, would seem to contain a meaning just the opposite of what Paul finds in it. In 10.3–8 he tries to show that Deuteronomy speaks of a righteousness which is by faith in Christ and is available to all. This righteousness is not gained by doing, as is the legal righteousness, but, as Deut. 30.12 f. says, the word concerning this righteousness is near in our mouths and hearts. The word referred to there is the message about Christ which we apostles preach to you. Verse 9 makes it plain that this passage from Deuteronomy did not refer to a word contemporary with Moses, but that it foretells a time when the message about Christ would be preached to both Jews and Gentiles. Verse 10 is meant to show that both believing and open acceptance (probably including baptism) were prophesied. Verses 14 f. ('How then shall they call on him on whom they have not believed?' etc.) show that not only was believing foretold, but also preaching and being sent to preach. Verse 15 must be quoted:

And how shall they preach, except they be sent (ἐὰν μὴ ἀποσταλῶσιν)? even as it is written, How beautiful are the feet of them that bring glad tidings of good things!

The reference to Isa. 52.7 is significant here: Paul is thinking of the apostolic mission of the faithful Remnant proclaimed in Isaiah, and he is claiming its fulfilment in the work of the apostles, the true faithful Remnant in the days of the Messiah. He uses the verb ἀποσταλῶσιν here to make his reference clear. The very next verse confirms this, where Isaiah is quoted as saying: 'Lord, who hath believed our report?' (Isa. 53.1). This *must* be the apostles speaking: they are referring to the unbelief of the Jews; and only Jews could evangelize Jews.

Paul reverts to the faithful Remnant of Jews early on in the next chapter. He has to face the question: has God entirely rejected the Jews, and replaced them by the Gentiles? Paul answers (11.2–4): No, there is a Remnant of faithful Jews left. He quotes I Kings 19.10 as an example in Israel's past history, where of course the Remnant consisted entirely of Jews, and he draws the conclusion:

Even so then at this present time also there is a remnant according to the election of grace (11.5).

The Greek phrase is λεῖμμα κατ' ἐκλογήν, and two verses later he actually refers to the Remnant as ἡ ἐκλογή. It is interesting that in later times apparently ἡ ἐκλογή could mean simply 'the Christians'. Moulton and Milligan (s.v.) quote the phrase ἡ ἐκλογὴ τοῦ γένους μου as meaning 'the

C

Christian members of my family' from the epitaph of a bishop of Laodi-
caea c. AD 340. But in Rom. 11.7 it certainly means 'the faithful Remnant
of Jews', for in the same verse Paul says, 'the rest were hardened', where
he must mean 'the rest of the Jews'. So now Paul has sufficiently proved
his point: what was prophesied in Scripture has come to pass. The
majority of the Jews have rejected the Messiah, but there has been left a
faithful Remnant who have accepted him and have carried out their
apostolic function of proclaiming him to the Gentiles throughout the
world (Rom. 10.18).

It seems therefore that Paul, although he believed that all the promises
made to Israel of old were fulfilled in the Christian Church, yet refrains
from applying the name of Israel to that Church as a whole, and reserves
it either for the old Israel, or for the Remnant of faithful Jews who
acknowledged the Messiah when he came. As we frequently hear it
claimed that in the New Testament the Church is the New Israel, it may
be as well to examine two other passages in Paul's Epistles where he
seems at first sight to be identifying Israel with the Jewish-Gentile Church
of his day. The first is Gal. 6.16:

> And as many as shall walk by this rule, peace be upon them, and mercy,
> and upon the Israel of God.

It is not surprising that most editors understand the phrase 'and upon the
Israel of God' as referring to the whole Christian Church, Jewish and
Gentile alike. This is the interpretation of Luther and Calvin,[1] and among
moderns of Lightfoot, Ramsay, Emmet and H. H. Rowley.[2] The first to
question it was apparently Burton,[3] who points out that nowhere else
does Paul use Israel of the whole Church. He therefore claims that
Paul means by this phrase 'those Jews who have accepted Christianity
but not my version of it', and even suggests that Paul is invoking peace
on those who agree with him (as many as shall walk by this rule) and mercy
on those who do not (the Israel of God). The 'and' after 'mercy' however
makes this difficult to accept. Duncan[4] modifies this and suggests that it
merely means 'the faithful Remnant in Israel'. This seems the most satisfactory interpretation and agrees best with what Paul has said earlier in

---

[1] Luther, St Paul's Epistle to the Galatians, ET, ed. P. S. Watson, London, 1953.
Calvin, On Paul's Epistles to the Galatians and Ephesians, ET, Edinburgh, 1954.
[2] J. B. Lightfoot, Galatians, 10th ed., London, 1890. W. M. Ramsay, Historical Commentary on . . . Galatians, London, 1899. C. W. Emmet, St Paul's Epistle to the Galatians,
London, 1912. H. H. Rowley, The Biblical Doctrine of Election, pp. 145-8.
[3] E. de Witt Burton, Galatians (ICC), 1921.
[4] G. S. Duncan, Galatians (Moffatt New Testament Commentary, hereafter cited as
MNTC), London, 1934.

this Epistle and with what he says later in Romans. No doubt Duncan is right in seeing in this division between Gentile and Jewish believers a sign of the early date of Galatians. Perhaps when Paul wrote it there were as many numerically in the Church of believing Jews in Palestine as there were in the Church of believing Gentiles in Palestine and beyond.

The other passage that might suggest an identity in Paul's mind between Israel and the whole Jewish-Gentile Church is Phil. 3.2 f.:

> Beware of the dogs, beware of the evil workers, beware of the concision: for we are the circumcision, who worship by the Spirit of God, and glory in Christ Jesus, and have no confidence in the flesh.

All commentators appear to take—'we' in v. 3. as 'you and I'. Ellicott[1] refers to Rom. 2.29, which we must presently examine. The only qualification to this unanimity is found in Moule[2] and Michael,[3] both of whom introduce a category of 'true Christians'; e.g. Moule paraphrasing Paul's thought here says: 'I speak with a general reference, of all true disciples.' Michael similarly explains it as 'you and I and all true Christians'. This importation of the concept of 'all true Christians' seems quite foreign to Paul's thought and means actually reading into Philippians ideas which seem to have originated at the time of the Reformation. Michael does however realize the difficulty of interpreting 'we' here as 'you and I'. The Philippians, being Gentiles, would have no reason to boast in the flesh anyway. Paul goes on to describe what he means by this phrase in the ensuing verses: it is plain that he means boasting of the national and spiritual privileges peculiar to the Jews. This the Philippians could not do. But Michael's way of removing the difficulty will not commend itself to many: 'If, however, these verses were not originally part of our Epistle, they may for aught we know have been addressed to some Jewish Christians.' It is simpler to take 'we' here as 'we believing Jews', or even 'we, Paul and Timothy', in whose name the letter is written. We know that Timothy was circumcised. So there is no good reason for maintaining that the use of 'the circumcision' here suggests that Paul could apply the name Israel to Gentiles.

In Col. 2.11 Paul says of all Christians:

> Ye were also circumcised with a circumcision not made with hands, in the putting off of the body of the flesh, in the circumcision of Christ.

He then goes on to refer to baptism. But Paul does not actually call Christians 'the circumcision' here, and in the Philippians passage just

---

[1] C. J. Ellicott, *Philippians, Colossians and Philemon*, 3rd ed., London, 1865.
[2] H. C. G. Moule, *Philippian Studies*, London, 1897.
[3] J. H. Michael, *Philippians* (MNTC), 1928.

quoted the circumcision of which Paul speaks does not seem to be associated with baptism at all. So it seems reasonable to conclude that in
Colossians Paul is simply saying that the Christian's circumcision is
baptism. The evidence for Colossians having been written late in Paul's
life is much stronger than is the evidence for a late date for Philippians,
and a comparison of baptism with circumcision in one of his last writings
is not at all incompatible with the use of 'the circumcision' for Jewish
Christians in an earlier one.

We must next examine Rom. 2.28 f. referred to above.

> For he is not a Jew, which is one outwardly; neither is that circumcision,
> which is outward in the flesh: but he is a Jew, which is one inwardly;
> and circumcision is that of the heart, in the spirit, and not in the letter;
> whose praise is not of men, but of God.

The question here is: what does ὁ ἐν τῷ κρυπτῷ Ἰουδαῖος ('a Jew which
is one inwardly') refer to? Does it mean any man, Jew or Gentile, who
obeys God from the heart? It is not very easy to decide, as Paul goes on to
make it clear that he does not believe such an individual exists among
either Jews or Gentiles. Similarly the 'righteous' whom our Lord did
not come to call are a non-existent class of people. In the first few verses
of ch. 3 Paul shows plainly that he does not regard circumcision as an
empty and meaningless rite. It has its significance for those (Jews) who
adopt the way of faith. We may put with this the fact that in many places
in the Old Testament we find the theme of inward circumcision, or circumcision of the heart. In all these circumcision of the heart is, of course,
applied only to Jews. Hence it seems probable that Paul means by
ὁ ἐν τῷ κρυπτῷ Ἰουδαῖος 'the Jew who obeys from the heart'.

There is in fact an illuminating parallel to Paul's thought in Jeremiah;
it may even be that the Jeremiah passage to some extent inspired Rom.
2.28 f. The passage is Jer. 9.23–26 (vv. 22–25 in Hebrew). The most relevant verses are 25 f.:

> Behold, the days come, saith the Lord, that I will punish all them which
> are circumcised in their uncircumcision; Egypt, and Judah, and Edom,
> and the children of Ammon, and Moab, and all that have the corners
> of their hair polled, that dwell in the wilderness: for all the nations are
> uncircumcised, and all the house of Israel are uncircumcised in heart.

What Jeremiah is apparently saying is that bodily circumcision will not
avail in itself: it is shared by Gentile nations, and is no more efficacious
in itself than the clipping of the hair forbidden to Jews. What avails is
circumcision of the heart, which is possessed by neither Gentiles nor

Jews. This fits in very well with Paul's thought. Unfortunately the Hebrew text here is obscure. The phrase 'circumcised in their uncircumcision' is strange. Driver calls it an oxymoron.[1] Most editors agree that what Jeremiah is saying is that 'Judah cannot rely on a rite which she shares with the heathen'.[2] But it is difficult to get this sense from 'circumcised in their uncircumcision'. As a matter of fact 'uncircumcised in their circumcision' would suit the sense better. W. Rudolph in Kittel's *Biblia Hebraica* suggests that the LXX of v. 24 (περιτετμημένους ἀκροβυστίας αὐτῶν) presupposes a Hebrew text meaning 'circumcised in their foreskins'.[3] This would give the required sense. So Jeremiah seems to be saying that circumcision in itself is of no avail; it is only effective if it goes with circumcision of the heart. He no more than Paul imagines that the Gentiles could become Israel if only they were circumcised in heart, but like Paul he maintains that circumcision is only valuable as a sign of inward purity.

One more small point about Paul's doctrine of the Remnant is worth recording. In I Cor. 10.1–13 Paul draws a moral from the experience of Israel in the wilderness. The lesson drawn seems to be that not all Israel was saved. The crucial passage is v. 11:

ταῦτα δὲ τυπικῶς συνέβαινεν ἐκείνοις,
ἐγράφη δὲ πρὸς νουθεσίαν ἡμῶν.

Now these things happened unto them by way of example; and they were written for our admonition.

The word τυπικῶς has rather tended to confuse interpreters, who have sometimes suggested that the events in the Old Testament happened primarily in order to be types of the New Testament.[4] But this really makes the second clause unnecessary: 'This happened to them as an example to us'; in that case why add that it was written for our admonition? A much more satisfactory sense is gained by taking τυπικῶς with ἐκείνοις and translating: 'This happened as a warning example to them, and was recorded for our admonition.' This avoids the awkwardness of suggesting that an Old Testament event did not happen, so to speak, in its own right, but only took place for the sake of people living centuries later. It happened for the sake of the Old Testament contemporaries; it was *recorded* as a warning to us. Paul is therefore actually suggesting that in Old

---

[1] S. R. Driver, *The Book of the Prophet Jeremiah*, London, 1906.

[2] E.g. A. S. Peake, *Jeremiah and Lamentations* I (Century Bible), London, 1910.

[3] The MT is מוּל בְּעָרְלָה. Rudolph suggests that it originally read מוּלֵי עָרְלָתָם. He also suggests that in the next verse for עֲרֵלִים one should read הָאֵלֶּה.

[4] E.g. H. L. Goudge, *I Corinthians* (Westminster Comentaries), 5th ed. rev., London, 1926.

Testament times only a Remnant survived God's judgements, and that the same thing may happen to the faithful Remnant (here thought of as having grown to the dimensions of the Jewish-Gentile Church) in the days of the Messiah. In fact there might be only a Remnant of the Remnant. This fact has its significance in connection with Paul's doctrine of the ministry which we shall be considering in a later chapter.

Our final passages illustrating Paul's doctrine of the Remnant come from the Epistle to the Ephesians. At this stage in the development of scholarship it is impossible to be dogmatic about the authorship of Ephesians. One cannot assume that it is direct from Paul's pen, but nor can one be as certain that Paul did not write it as one can be about Hebrews, for example. However, the thought about the Remnant is, as we hope to show, entirely consistent with Paul's thought. If the Epistle is not by Paul himself, it is by a disciple who thoroughly understood his master's mind.

The main passage is Eph. 2.11–22;

> Wherefore remember, that aforetime ye, the Gentiles in the flesh, who are called Uncircumcision by that which is called Circumcision, in the flesh, made by hands; that ye were at that time separate from Christ, alienated from the commonwealth of Israel, and strangers from the covenant of promise, having no hope and without God in the world. But now in Christ Jesus ye that once were far off are made nigh in the blood of Christ. For he is our peace, who made both one, and brake down the middle wall of partition, having abolished in his flesh the enmity, even the law of commandments contained in ordinances; that he might create in himself of the twain one new man, so making peace; and might reconcile them both in one body unto God through the cross, having slain the enmity thereby: and he came and preached peace to you that were far off, and peace to them that were nigh: for through him we both have access in one Spirit unto the Father. So then ye are no more strangers and sojourners, but ye are fellow-citizens with the saints, and of the household of God, being built upon the foundation of the apostles and prophets, Christ Jesus himself being the chief corner stone; in whom each several building, fitly framed together, groweth into a holy temple in the Lord; in whom ye also are builded together for a habitation of God in the Spirit.

In this passage Paul (we will dispense with the invariable qualification 'or his disciple') is describing exactly the process which we have been studying throughout this chapter, the change-over from old Israel to new Christian Church. We notice first that according to him, before the coming of the Messiah the Jews were near as compared with the Gentiles; the use of 'near' and 'far' in 2.13, 17 seems to imply this. The Jews had a circumcision whose main significance was as a symbol of a spiritual condition, not of something outward (2.11). This is the view of Abbot[1] and Scott.[2] The latter writes: 'The rite to which they (the Jews) attached so much significance had at best a symbolic value.' With the coming of Christ the 'covenants' and 'commonwealth' became open to all, both 'near' and 'far'. The Jews may now receive that peace with God which they never fully enjoyed under the old dispensation, and the Gentiles may receive everything which the Jews receive (2.14–18). In v. 17 Paul speaks of Christ coming and preaching peace both to those who are near and to those who are far; literally it is 'he evangelized peace' (εὐηγγελίσατο εἰρήνην), he preached the gospel of peace. This must surely be a reference to the ministry of the apostles, not to our Lord's own ministry in the days of his flesh, since he did not preach directly to the Gentiles himself. Moreover, the peace he preached was a peace secured by his own blood (v. 16). It is very interesting that the activity of the apostles here is described as the activity of Christ himself, and it is significant in the light of Paul's own doctrine of the ministry as we find it in the Corinthian Epistles.[3] He does not seem to think of the time interval between the Messiah's coming and the preaching of the apostles as being of very great significance, for he goes straight from 'having slain the enmity' to 'and he came and preached peace' (vv. 16 f.). This is very like Rom. 10, where the coming of Christ, his rejection by the Jews, and the preaching of the apostles all seem to belong to the same moment or period, the ultimate Messianic age that has now dawned. There can be little doubt that 'he came and preached peace' refers to the apostles rather than to their successors, for they are the only group who could be described as preaching to both Jews and Gentiles.

Verse 17 contains in fact an echo of Isa. 57.19. We must quote the whole context in the LXX, for it is full of signficance for Paul's thought. We begin at v. 18:

τὰς ὁδοὺς αὐτοῦ ἑώρακα καὶ ἰασάμην αὐτὸν
καὶ παρεκάλεσα αὐτὸν καὶ ἔδωκα αὐτῷ παράκλησιν ἀληθινήν,
εἰρήνην ἐπ᾿ εἰρήνην τοῖς μακρὰν καὶ τοῖς ἐγγὺς οὖσιν·

I have observed his ways and I have healed him and I have comforted him and I have given true comfort: peace upon peace to those far off and to those near.[4]

---

[1] T. K. Abbott, *Ephesians and Colossians* (ICC), 1897.
[2] E. F. Scott, *Colossians, Philemon and Ephesians* (MNTC), 1930.
[3] J. Macpherson, *Ephesians*, London, 1892, seems to be the only commentator who takes this as referring to the direct activity of Christ during his ministry.
[4] The LXX is a very free tr. of the Heb.: וְאֲשַׁלֵּם נִחֻמִים לוֹ.

Above in v. 14 Paul has defined this peace as Christ himself: 'for he is our peace'. This actual phrase may be a quotation from Micah 5.5;[1] but in any case the peace which Christ proclaimed cannot be separated from the peace which Christ was. The thought then seems to be that God has given Christ to the Gentiles as well as to the Jews. We notice how appropriate the LXX phrase in Isa. 57.18 would be to this thought: Christ is not only peace but also παράκλησις ἀληθινή ('true comfort'). It is impossible that a New Testament writer who took εἰρήνη in Isa. 57.19 as a prophecy of Christ should not take παράκλησις ἀληθινή occurring just before it in the same sense.

So far then we have the thought of Christ being given to the Church as its true peace and comfort. Then follows in v. 20 the famous figure of the building:

Being built upon the foundation of the apostles and prophets, Christ Jesus himself being the chief corner stone.

There has been much dispute both about the meaning of the word 'foundation' here and also as to the precise nature of the stone with which our Lord is identified. Earlier editors have hesitated to say that the apostles and prophets themselves are the foundation, in view of the fact that Jesus Christ ought to be the foundation according to I Cor. 3.11. For example Alford takes it as 'the foundation belonging to the apostles and prophets, the same one as they laid, i.e. Christ'.[2] Ellicott follows this interpretation also.[3] But there is no need to be so literal. If St John the Divine could speak of the names of the apostles as written on the foundations of the holy city (Rev. 21.12), there is no reason why St Paul should not speak of the apostles as foundations. Nor would anyone but a pedant claim that this is inconsistent with the assertion that Christ is the only foundation. Another difficulty has been with the prophets. We would like to think that they are the Old Testament prophets; with our modern historical approach to the Bible we naturally see the prophets as standing behind the apostles in the line of God's self-revelation. But Eph. 3.5 and 4.11 seem absolutely decisive against taking the prophets here as the Old Testament prophets. In both these places the context makes it clear beyond a doubt that the prophets are prophets belonging to the new dispensation. In both these latter places also they are associated with the apostles. Hence it is not surprising that all commentators without exception seem to take the prophets in 2.20 as the New Testament prophets. It is indeed true that,

---

[1] Though hardly from the LXX as we have it, which is καὶ ἔσται αὕτη εἰρήνη.
[2] H. Alford, *The Greek Testament*, rev. ed., London, 1894, Vol. II.
[3] *Ephesians*, London, 1864.

as long as we insist on drawing a sharp line of distinction between the old dispensation and the new, we must understand the prophets in 2.20 as the New Testament prophets. But we must first inquire whether any such sharp distinction is in Paul's mind here.

The metaphor of the foundations and the corner stone is drawn from Isa. 28.16, a favourite proof text among New Testament writers. The LXX runs as follows:

Ἰδοὺ ἐγὼ ἐμβαλῶ εἰς τὰ θεμέλια Σιὼν λίθον πολυτελῆ
ἐκλεκτὸν ἀκρογωνιαῖον εἰς τὰ θεμέλια αὐτῆς, καὶ
ὁ πιστεύων ἐπ' αὐτῷ οὐ μὴ καταισχυνθῇ.

Behold I am laying into the foundations of Sion a precious stone, elect, a corner stone, valuable into her foundations; and he that believeth on it shall never be put to shame.[1]

Now it is remarkable that in this figure the corner stone, far from being a foundation stone, is actually placed on (or more exactly 'into') the foundations. Some scholars have tried to combine both ideas by envisaging a sort of corner foundation stone that joins together two foundation stones meeting at right angles. E. Best has examined the word ἀκρογωνιαῖος very carefully, and comes to the conclusion that it must mean not a foundation stone at all, but the 'final stone', probably the keystone of the arch above the entrance.[2] This conclusion is confirmed by the language of the LXX of Isa. 28.16 quoted above. It is twice stated that the ἀκρογωνιαῖος is to be placed εἰς τὰ θεμέλια. It is plainly something which comes after the foundations have been laid. The thought, then, is of Christ as the *completion* of the apostolic and prophetic building. This is remarkably appropriate to Paul's theme here: he is speaking of the transition from old Israel to new Church. That transition was effected by means of the faithful Remnant to whom the Messiah came, and who accepted him and proclaimed him, first to Jews and then to Gentiles also. The Remnant was apostolic and prophetic before the Messiah came; the Messiah was himself Apostle and Prophet *par excellence*, as well as Redeemer and Lord. After his death, resurrection, and ascension the Remnant was still apostolic and prophetic, indeed their apostolic and prophetic ministry was only now truly fulfilled.

[1] The Heb. is אֶבֶן בֹּחַן פִּנַּת יִקְרַת מוּסָד מוּסָּד. Presumably ἐκλεκτόν corresponds to בֹּחַן and ἔντιμον to יִקְרַת. Actually the first word apparently means 'grey-green' and the second 'meeting', from קרה. LXX, RV and RSV have all derived יִקְרַת from יקר and tr. 'precious'. See Koehler-Baumgartner on these two words. Obviously Paul is following the LXX, not the Heb.

[2] *One Body in Christ*, London, 1955, pp. 162 f.

This may help us to approach anew the question: Who are the apostles and prophets in Eph. 2.20? They are the faithful Remnant, both before and after the time of Christ. We must beware of emphasizing too much our modern historical approach to the Bible. We think of prophecy as having come to an end with Malachi,[1] and then of a long pause of four hundred years or so till the appearance of John the Baptist. But St Paul and the other writers of the New Testament were not so acutely conscious of the perspective of time. For them, there were the prophets of the old dispensation who by their divine insight projected themselves forward into the time when their prophecies were to be fulfilled. There was also the faithful Remnant, itself, according to the greatest of all the prophets, called to be apostolic, and called also to be the witnesses to prophecy fulfilled. Then came to this body the Messiah as the crown and fulfilment of their hopes and ministry, and his coming resulted in a new and eschatological activity on the part of the Remnant, who could now be called both apostles and prophets. So we do not need to ask with great exactness: Are the apostles and prophets of Eph. 2.20 figures of the Old Testament or of the New? They belong to both: there is a continuous line of apostolic and prophetic activity passing from the prophets of old through the faithful Remnant and the Messiah to the apostles and prophets of Paul's own day. This view seems to be taken also by Leuba in his recent book, *New Testament Pattern*.[2] He thinks that the prophets in Eph. 2.20 are the Old Testament prophets, and he thinks of Christ as the keystone that holds together the two pillars of the old dispensation (the prophets) and the new (the apostles). Whatever we may say of Leuba's architecture (for keystones do not hold pillars together), he does seem to have grasped the essential continuity of the Church from the old age to the new. But we would go further and claim that the apostles also may be said to belong to the old dispensation as well as to the new. The Remnant always had an apostolic task.[3]

The only other thing to be noted about this important passage is that, if we follow out Paul's argument, we must conclude that the 'commonwealth' now belongs to the Christian Church, and that Jews who refuse to accept the Messiah are themselves alienated from the covenants and 'without Christ' (v. 12) in a way they were not before. They are the 'sons of disobedience' referred to in 5.6.

[1] Though even here we would probably be wrong, as there are several parts of OT prophecy which must be later than Malachi, e.g. Joel and Zechariah 9–14.
[2] J. L. Leuba, *New Testament Pattern*, ET, London, 1953, p. 64.
[3] Cf. also Polycarp, *Philippians* VI 3: οἱ εὐαγγελισάμενοι ἡμᾶς ἀπόστολοι καὶ οἱ προφῆται οἱ προκηρύξαντες τὴν ἔλευσιν τον Κυρίου. Note the order.

One more passage in Ephesians tells us something about the Remnant, Eph. 5. 25–27:

> Husbands, love your wives, even as Christ also loved the church, and gave himself up for it; that he might sanctify it, having cleansed it by the washing of water with the word, that he might present the church to himself a glorious church, not having spot or wrinkle or any such thing; but that it should be holy and without blemish.

Naturally there has been much discussion as to the precise meaning of τὸ λουτρόν ('the washing'), and ῥῆμα ('the word'). There can be little doubt that baptism is referred to here. Some scholars insist that 'the word' is the baptismal formula,[1] or the creed recited by the candidate.[2] But in view of Rom. 10.8 it seems more likely that the word is the gospel. The figure seems to be taken from the ceremonial bath given to the bride before marriage, though it must not be pressed, as it is not the bridegroom who normally gives it! Christ is thought of as himself administering baptism to the Church through his own death and resurrection and through the gospel which proclaims these things. In that case the pre-existence of the Church is certainly implied. The Church existed before Christ's coming as the commonwealth of Israel, kept from complete apostasy by the faithful Remnant. But it was not holy, it needed cleansing; even the disciples ran away at Gethsemane. By his death and resurrection Christ cleansed the Church and made it holy. This is also true proleptically of the Gentiles who were to enter the Church, and who needed cleansing quite as much as the faithful Remnant of Jews.

As we study what is implied about the Remnant in Ephesians, we cannot help noticing how closely it corresponds to what St Paul says about the Remnant in his other Epistles. Perhaps it should make us pause before assuming too hastily that there really was an 'Ephesian Continuator'. Despite the problems raised by the theory of Pauline authorship, the theory that it was entirely composed by a disciple has also many remarkable similarities to account for.

If what has been said above about Paul's doctrine of the Remnant is true, he may surely be acquitted of a charge which has recently been brought against him by a number of distinguished scholars. C. H. Dodd in his commentary on Romans accuses Paul of nursing a conviction that in some way the Jews did have an advantage over the Gentiles even under the new dispensation: 'His [Paul's] Pharisaism—or shall we say his patriotism?—was too deeply engrained for him to put right out of his

---

[1] E.g. Charles Gore, *Ephesians*, London, 1898.
[2] W. Lock, *Ephesians* (Westminster Commentaries), London, 1929.

mind the idea that somehow the divine covenant with mankind had a "most favoured nation clause".[1] W. D. Davies strongly supports this view: 'The logic of his (Paul's) conception of the Church demanded that Paul should not think of Israel after the flesh as having any special office, but this is somehow what he could not conceive.'[2] On the contrary, they did have a special office: theirs was the essential task of constituting the faithful Remnant in the Messianic Age, and of passing on to the Gentiles their witness to God's acts in the Messiah. Paul's heart did not prove stronger than his head when he said that the Jew had much advantage every way (Rom. 3.1). The Jew, and he meant the true Jew, the Jew who had recognized and accepted the Messiah, had the advantage which the apostle has over those to whom he is sent. But of course that advantage was not one of status or achievement, what Paul would call 'of the flesh'. How could it be in the thought of one at the centre of whose gospel was the free grace of God? It was an advantage that was only given to be used in God's service and to be passed on to others. We must not fail to note that in the previous verse (2.29) Paul has defined what he means by 'Jew' in this context. It is the believing Jew, the Christian Jew, who possesses the advantage, not the unbelieving Jew, to whom the 'oracles of God' mentioned in Rom. 3.2 have proved to be of no avail.

We must now turn to St Paul's doctrine of the ministry, and the circumstances which produced it. But before we do so it may be as well to review the ground we have covered so far, so that we may see the relevance of our next step. In the Old Testament, especially in the prophecy of Second Isaiah, the Remnant with which the Servant is associated and to some extent identified is to be a witnessing Remnant. It has a mission to declare God's nature to Israel and to the Gentiles, and to witness to the fulfilment of the predictions of God's prophet. But this ministry is evidently conceived of as being exercised in the eschatological future. Then in St Paul's writings the Remnant has carried out its function. The Messiah came and was rejected by most of Israel, but was recognized and accepted by a faithful Remnant of Jews. Despite the disciples' failure at Gethsemane and Golgotha, they did carry out their essential function after the resurrection of the Messiah. They proclaimed him as God's agent in redemption and they witnessed to prophecy fulfilled in him. Then, largely (though not entirely) through the ministry of Paul, the last of the apostles, the message was handed on to the Gentiles, who thereby became heirs to God's promises to faithful Israel. We can even

[1] *Romans* (MNTC), London, 1932, pp. 43 f.
[2] *Paul and Rabbinic Judaism*, London, 1948, p. 75.

trace a suggestion that the apostolic and prophetic function of the Remnant was in some sense continuous from before the Messiah's coming till the time of the evangelization of the Gentiles. It seems therefore a clear deduction from Paul's teaching that the first disciples *were* the faithful Remnant and that their apostolate sprang from this fact. In other words, the apostles were apostles because they were the first Church.

4

Paul and His Fellow-Workers

BEFORE WE begin to examine Paul's doctrine of the ministry in detail we must spend some time in establishing that Paul has a doctrine of the ministry at all. This we do, not by asking whether there are any passages in his writings where he gives us a carefully considered exposition of the doctrine of the ministry (for we shall not find any), but by looking at Paul's actual situation and examining how his ministry was carried out in actual fact. When we do so, we find that his ministry was intimately connected with that of his fellow-workers, so we shall not be going astray if we try to define the place of his fellow-workers in his thought.

Though the notion, popular fifty years ago, that Paul invented orthodox Christianity is no longer widely accepted, there is still a tendency, especially apparent perhaps in the Moffatt Commentaries, to treat him as an individualist, a lone pioneer preaching a form of Christianity based entirely on his own conversion experience. For example both Plummer[1] and Strachan[2] interpret II Cor. 4.6, 'Seeing it is God . . . who shined in our hearts, to give the light of the knowledge of the glory of God in the face of Jesus Christ', as referring primarily, and perhaps exclusively, to Paul's own experience on the Damascus Road. Such a method of exegesis means taking 'we' in the Pauline Epistles as normally referring to Paul and Paul alone.

It is time that this interpretation was challenged. In fact, when we study Paul's movements as reflected in his Epistles and in Acts, we do not find a lone pioneer; we find him surrounded by a host of assistants and colleagues, Barnabas, Silvanus, Apollos, Timothy, Titus, Epaphras, and many others, some of them anonymous. Indeed the only letter to a church in which Paul does not associate his colleagues with himself in the initial salutation is Romans.[3] Moreover a certain part of every letter is taken up with information about the movements of his colleagues. We

---

[1] A. Plummer, *II Corinthians* (ICC), 1915 (also Cambridge Bible, 1903).
[2] R. H. Strachan, *II Corinthians* (MNTC), 1935.
[3] In Gal. 1.2 he has 'and all the brethren which are with me', and I assume that Ephesians is written as a pastoral, not directed exclusively to one church.

might also add that experience in the modern mission field shows that no missionary can hope to evangelize and build up churches entirely on his own. The foreign missionary in particular (and Paul must have seemed a foreigner to Gentile converts) is absolutely dependent on the help of assistants, either indigenous Christians or others. Hence it would seem likely that when Paul uses 'we' in his letters, we should normally expect him to mean 'I and my colleagues'. The investigation that follows is based on the conviction that Paul was much less of an individualist in both theory and practice than he is commonly represented as being, and that he very often speaks on behalf of his colleagues when we imagine him to be speaking of himself alone.

In an investigation like this statistics are very little use: the majority of places where Paul uses 'we' are not clear; we have to decide from the context whether Paul means 'I' or 'I and my colleagues'. There is of course a third possibility: he may mean 'I and you', indeed this is obviously his meaning far more often than not. In some of the Dravidian languages of South India there are two forms of the first person plural pronoun, one inclusive ('I and you') and one exclusive ('we but not you'). Greek, for all its subtlety, never reached this distinction; if it had, our task would be easier. I have examined every case of the first person plural in Paul's letters, but of course we may put aside at once the vast majority of places where it occurs, for in them the meaning is plain: 'we' means 'you and I' and 'ours' means 'yours and mine'. For example there would obviously by no significance in listing the number of times '*our* Lord Jesus Christ' occurs. We will confine ourselves therefore to those places where it is a question of deciding between 'we'='I' and 'we'=either 'you and I' or 'I and my colleagues'.

We begin with Gal. 1.8 f.:

But though we, or an angel from heaven, should preach unto you any gospel other than that which we preached unto you, let him be anathema. As we have said before, so say I now again. . . .

Paul has begun the letter by associating the brethren that were with him in his salutation, and we know from Acts that when he evangelized South Galatia he had Barnabas at least with him (Acts 13.13 refers to 'his company').[1] Then in v. 6 he drops into the first person singular. Hence we may safely assume that the first person plural in vv. 8 f. refers to Paul and his companions who preached the gospel with him. Verse 9 in particular, with its transition from the plural referring to the past to the singular referring to the present, seems to confirm this.

---

[1] See Acts 13 and 14. I am assuming that the South Galatian theory is correct.

Similarly in I Thess. 1.2-9 Paul seems to be speaking on behalf of his companions Silvanus and Timothy throughout the passage; they had shared in preaching the gospel to the Thessalonians. I think this applies also to 2.1-12. The plural τὰς καρδίας ('our hearts') in 2.4 suggests this, and ὡς Χριστοῦ ἀπόστολοι ('as apostles of Christ') in v. 7 seems to make it certain. Paul might say of himself 'we preached the gospel to you', but could he say 'we are Christ's apostles' unless he meant more than himself only? The same conclusion is indicated by τὰς ἑαυτῶν ψυχάς ('our own souls') in v. 8. Paul might use the epistolary plural of himself, but he had only one life. This interpretation involves the inference that Silvanus also worked with his hands to support himself, but there is nothing unreasonable in that. In I Cor. 4.12 Paul says, 'we toil, working with our own hands,' in a passage where he is certainly thinking of Apollos as well as himself. Compare also I Cor. 9.6, which suggests that perhaps Barnabas also supported himself by his own work.

In I Thess. 2.17-3.2 we have the first place where 'we' must refer to Paul only, i.e. the epistolary 'we'. Paul had been separated from his companions (in Athens or Corinth) and could not visit the Thessalonians. But notice that he makes it clear that this 'we' refers to himself only: 'Because we would fain have come to you, I Paul once and again.' Then in 3.3 'hereunto we are appointed' must refer to all Christians, and v. 4 to Paul and his fellow missionaries. Verse 5 with its reversion to the first person singular recalls us to Paul's own experiences again, and in 3.6-12 he uses the epistolary 'we' of himself only for the second time. The only doubtful passage in II Thessalonians is 3.7-14; but here we may safely take the first person plural as referring to the group of missionaries on the analogy of I Thess. 1.2-9. II Thessalonians, like the first Epistle, is written in the name of Silvanus and Timothy as well as of Paul. This conclusion is confirmed by II Thess. 3.17, where Paul distinguishes himself as an individual included in the 'we' of 3.7-14.

In I Corinthians Paul associates Sosthenes with himself in the salutation. Then in 2.1-5 he gives his own personal experience at Corinth, using the first person singular. At v. 6 he drops into the first person plural, which continues until v. 13; this is because he is explaining the missionary policy of his group, and it applies to all his fellow-workers. In 2.16, 'we have the mind of Christ', he is surely speaking of all Christians. It would be too presumptuous a claim to make for himself alone or even for his group of missionaries alone. In 3.1 he reverts to his personal experience with the words: 'And *I*, brethren . . .' Again, in 9.4 f., 'Have we no right to eat and drink . . . ?' comes after a passage in which the first person singular has been used, and must therefore refer to Paul and his companions. This is made clear by the reference to Barnabas in v. 6. In that case 'the rest of the apostles' in v. 5 would refer to the other apostles in Judaea, the rest of the Twelve, and perhaps others as well. We must also take I Cor. 15.14 f. as applying to Paul and his fellow-missionaries: ' . . . then is our preaching vain. . . . Yea, and we are found false witnesses of God.' The plural ψευδομάρτυρες surely rules out the possibility of this applying to Paul only. I Cor. 15.30 must also be taken of Paul's companions as well: 'Why do we also stand in jeopardy every hour?' We know from Acts that Paul was not the only missionary to endure dangers for the gospel, cf. I Cor. 4.9 and II Cor. 6.4, both passages where Paul must be speaking of his companions as well. In the next verse (I Cor. 15.31) Paul applies what he has said of all the missionaries to his own case.

It is in II Corinthians that we find most difficulty in deciding where Paul is using epistolary 'we' and where he is not. So many of the details connected with the circumstances in which this Epistle was written are unknown to us that it sometimes seems almost impossible to decide whether Paul is referring to himself only or to his colleagues as well. II Cor. 1.3 f. is a case in point: he writes the Epistle in the name of Timothy as well as of himself. Then he plunges into a magnificent account of the way in which God has turned 'our' sufferings into victory. We do not know what these sufferings were. Some have conjectured a serious illness others have suggested imprisonment and the expectation of a death sentence.[1] This might apply to Timothy also. Verse 13 suggests a transition from 'our group of missionaries' to 'myself': 'For we write none other things . . . than what . . . I hope ye will acknowledge unto the end.' But 'I hope' may be a conventional phrase. We must leave it doubtful whether this passage contains an epistolary 'we' or not. At any rate in v. 18 Paul is speaking on behalf of his colleagues when he says 'our word'. This is made absolutely certain by the next verse, 'who was preached among you by us, even by me and Silvanus and Timothy'. This sense certainly carries on until 1.24, as the plural in 'our hearts' of v. 22 testifies. Verse 24 is interesting: 'Not that we have lordship over your faith, but are helpers of your joy.' See I Cor. 3.9, where Paul describes Apollos and himself as Θεοῦ συνεργοί, 'God's fellow-workers'; here he describes himself and his companions as συνεργοὶ τῆς χαρᾶς ὑμῶν, which seems to mean 'fellow-workers with the Corinthians'.[2] In the same way II Cor. 2.14–17 should be taken as applying to Paul's companions as well as to himself.

---

[1] E.g. G. S. Duncan, *St Paul's Ephesian Ministry*, London, 1929, pp. 131 f.
[2] See pp. 51, 83 below.

D

In the previous verses he has been relating how he waited (probably in Philippi) till Titus arrived with news of the Corinthians' repentance. In this account he uses the first person singular throughout (2.1–13). Then he bursts into a splendid ascription of praise: 'But thanks be unto God, which always leadeth us in triumph in Christ.' He is not thinking selfishly of himself alone but of all his helpers also. If we compare vv. 15 f. with with I Cor. 1.23 this conclusion is confirmed.

We must continue this interpretation right through 3.1–13. In 3.1–3 Paul speaks about the credentials of himself and his helpers and says in v. 2, 'Ye are our epistle'. The sense is that the Corinthians can witness to the sincerity of their founding missionaries, primarily Paul but also his assistants. In any case the phrase in v. 2, ἐν ταῖς καρδίαις ἡμῶν ('in our hearts'), cannot refer to one individual.[1] Then in v. 4 onwards Paul begins to speak of the nature of the Christian ministry; the plural διακόνους ('ministers') in v. 6 makes it certain that he has others in mind besides himself, cf. I Cor. 4.1; there also Paul is speaking of the ministry, and there can be no doubt at all that in the whole of I Cor. 4, wherever Paul writes 'we' or 'our', he is thinking of Apollos and himself, and indeed of all who have undertaken the Christian ministry. A similar passage occurs in II Cor. 6.3–10.

II Cor. 5.1–10 poses a different problem: is it 'we' inclusive or 'we' exclusive? In v. 2 Paul writes, 'In this [earthly tabernacle] we groan.' This reminds us of Rom. 8.23; 'We groan within ourselves, waiting for our adoption.' It suggests therefore that in II Cor. 5.2 Paul is speaking of all Christians. Similarly Paul certainly believed that all Christians had received 'the earnest of the Spirit' (v. 5). Hence we may confidently suggest that vv. 1–5 describe the experience of all Christians. On the other hand vv. 6–9 seem to apply better to the ministry, though Paul may have wished his words to be true of all Christians. In v. 10 he writes, 'We must all be made manifest before the judgement seat of Christ', which suggests that in vv. 6–10 he may have been thinking of less than all.

We now pass on to an extraordinarily involved and obscure section, 5.11–6.10. Verse 11 at least is fairly clear: 'We persuade men, but are made manifest unto God.' Paul must be speaking of the ministry, and this would also seem to apply to v. 12 (see the note above on 3.1.). Verse 13 seems to apply to Paul alone: 'Whether we are beside ourselves, it is unto God.' Would the opposition faction in Corinth have accused anyone but Paul of madness? It is possible that Paul may be unconsciously identifying his helpers with himself in the same accusation. Verses 16–19 when care-

---

[1] See next page on II Cor. 7.2–4.

fully considered must be classified as applying to the ministry where they do not apply to all Christians. We must not accuse Paul of claiming that he was the only example of the 'new creation' (v. 17) or the only one who was 'in Christ'. In v. 18 he continues: 'All things are of God, who reconciled us unto himself through Christ, and gave unto us the ministry of reconciliation.' The first 'us' must apply to all Christians (Paul is no strict Calvinist!), and the second probably does also (but this point is discussed in greater detail in the next chapter). In v. 19 the phrase θέμενος ἐν ἡμῖν τὸν λόγον τῆς καταλλαγῆς is translated in the RV, 'having committed unto us the word of reconciliation', but the RV margin literally translates 'having placed in us', which is more accurate. One thing is certain, θέμενος ἐν ἡμῖν cannot refer to one individual. It must refer to the ministry at least; whether it does not also refer to the whole church will be considered later. Verse 20, 'We are ambassadors therefore on behalf of Christ', must refer to the ministry. Of course v. 21 refers to all Christians: 'Him who knew no sin he made to be sin on our behalf' etc. In 6.1 we revert to the ministry, 'Working together with him'. See I Cor. 3.9; II Cor. 1.24. Then follows one of those great descriptions of the ministry in 6.3–10 to which we have already made allusion.

In 6.11 f., on the other hand, we may admit an example of the epistolary 'we': 'Our mouth is opened unto you, O Corinthians, our heart is enlarged.' Notice that 'heart' is singular. We omit 6.14–7.1 as belonging to an earlier letter, and come on to 7.2–4:

> Open your hearts to us: we wronged no man, we corrupted no man, we took advantage of no man. I say it not to condemn you: for I have said before that ye are in our hearts to die together and live together. Great is my boldness of speech towards you. . . .

Here is a strange passage: he begins with the first person plural. The second sentence begins with 'I' but refers to 'our hearts'. The third sentence (v. 4) begins with 'my boldness' and keeps the singular up all through till the very end, when he speaks of 'our affliction'. Must we therefore conclude that Paul uses singular and plural of the first person absolutely indiscriminately without any significance needing to be attached to the difference? This is not the impression we gain by his usage so far, so we are left with the assumption that his use of 'I' and 'we' has significance. When he uses both in the same sentence, we may assume that the singular indicates himself, and the plural includes his fellow-workers. There is nothing in 7.2–4 to conflict with this conclusion. Indeed Plummer insists that ἐν ταῖς καρδίαις ἡμῶν in v. 3 must refer to Paul's fellow-workers as well. He cites I Thess. 2.4, 'But God which proveth our hearts', and he quotes Lightfoot's opinion that this must refer to more than Paul alone.[1] As for 'our affliction' in II Cor. 7.4, both Titus and Timothy cannot have failed to share in Paul's distress at a church situation in which they were themselves implicated. Of this Epistle we may in general say that Paul's primary intention is to speak on behalf of his fellow-workers as well as of himself, but sometimes he attributes to all of them sentiments which would strictly speaking apply to himself alone, e.g. 5.13 and possibly 6.11 f. We may also suggest that the reference of προείρηκα ('I have said before') in 7.3 is to 4.12, 'So then death worketh in us, but life in you.' In 4.12 Paul is certainly speaking on behalf of his fellow-workers; a cross-reference to I Cor. 4.6–13 makes this clear.

There follows a passage, 7.5–16, in which we are perplexed by Paul's rapid transition from singular to plural. Most of it is in the first person plural, but three times he passes from plural to singular and singular to plural in the course of one sentence (7.4 also gives us an example of this). See v. 7, 'while he told us your longing . . . your zeal for me', v. 12, 'I wrote . . . that your earnest care for us might be made manifest,' and v. 14, 'If in anything I have gloried . . . I was not put to shame; but as we spake all things to you in truth, so our glorying also, which I made before Titus, was found to be truth.' Here we cannot avoid the impression that Paul is thinking mainly of his own feelings while he was waiting in Macedonia for Titus and when Titus arrived with the happy news of the Corinthians' repentance. At the same time however we must not forget that Paul was not alone as he waited in Macedonia; he probably had Timothy with him (Timothy was certainly with him when he wrote II Cor. 1–9); and we learn in ch. 8 of this Epistle of two other brethren whom Paul is sending to the Corinthians with the letter. A common conjecture is that the first of these was Luke (see Plummer and also Strachan on II Cor. 8. 18–23); at least it was someone of 'influence and standing' (Strachan's phrase) who was certainly to be reckoned in the number of Paul's fellow-missionaries. Hence we may claim that, though Paul sometimes uses 'we' and 'our' of sentiments and actions which can only properly be attributed to himself alone, the background of his thought is not made up of his own reactions as an individual, but of the sentiments of the group of missionaries of which he was the leader.

We may therefore conclude that in II Cor. 8.18–24, where Paul uses the plural, 'We have sent together with him (i.e. with Titus) the brother',

---

[1] I am aware that both II Cor. 6.11 and I Thess. 2.4 are echoes from the Old Testament. The former therefore could be taken as a reference to Paul's companions as well; but I cannot believe that Paul could use 'our hearts' in I Thess. 2.4. of himself alone.

he is indicating the group of missionaries who were in Macedonia (probably Philippi), including at least Timothy. It is difficult to believe that in v. 23, where he describes Timothy as 'my partner' and the two others whom he is sending as 'our brethren', he means exactly the same thing by the two phrases. The words 'our brethren' were meant to remind the Corinthian Christians that they belonged, not to an individual, Paul, but to a group, the Church. At the same time in 9.3 precisely the same event is described thus: 'I have sent the brethren, that our glorying on your behalf may not be made void.' We conclude, not that Paul uses singular and plural indifferently to indicate himself alone, but that in his relations with the Corinthian church he did not always make a clear distinction in his own mind between himself and his fellow-workers. Had he never had his fellow-workers in mind, we might expect a consistent use either of the singular or of the plural. The vacillation indicates that the fellow-workers cannot be left out of account.

Obscure as are the circumstances in which the first nine chapters of II Corinthians were written, those surrounding the 'painful letter' are even more obscure.[1] It seems fairly certain that it was Paul himself who was insulted by some member of the Corinthian church, and not his fellow-workers. Hence we should naturally expect that most of the painful letter would be concerned with Paul as an individual. This is certainly the main impression conveyed by II Cor. 10.1–18; but from v. 2 onwards the tendency is to use the first person plural rather than the singular. The singular however does occur in vv. 1, 2, 8, and 9. The description of Paul's warfare in vv. 3–6 applies certainly to all who are in the ministry, and it is possible that the alternation between singular and plural in v. 8 is deliberate:

> For though I should glory somewhat abundantly concerning our authority (which the Lord gave for building you up and not for casting you down), I shall not be put to shame.

Paul may have wished to remind them that he claimed authority not as an individual, but as an apostle along with other apostles. In 13.10 he uses exactly the same phrase for this authority and says 'which the Lord gave me'. But the fact that Paul possessed apostolic authority over the Corinthians does not preclude others possessing it also.

In II Cor. 11.6 we meet an exceptionally obscure verse:

> εἰ δὲ καὶ ἰδιώτης τῷ λόγῳ, ἀλλ' οὐ τῇ γνώσει, ἀλλ' ἐν παντὶ φανερώσαντες ἐν πᾶσιν εἰς ὑμᾶς.

---

[1] I assume that II Cor. 10.1–13.10 is part of a separate letter written before II Cor.1–9.

But though I be rude in speech, yet am I not in knowledge; nay, in everything we have made it manifest among all men to you-ward.

The RV has faithfully reproduced the unintelligibility of the Greek. The difficulty is of course φανερώσαντες, introduced quite ungrammatically into the sentence. The Textus Receptus reads φανερωθέντες and D* φανερωθείς, both no doubt attempts to ease the sense. Strachan seems to give it up, for he writes: 'The last clause of the verse is grammatically very obscure, and the text seems uncertain.' James Joyce has persuaded many people that the ungrammatical sentence reveals the true intention of the heart. Perhaps therefore Paul is referring to his fellow-workers: 'We have all shewn our possession of the gospel; I am no individualist but a member of the apostolic band.' Otherwise the plural is very difficult to understand. The same sense may lie behind the change to the plural in 11.12: 'that wherein they glory they may be found even as we'. This would contrast the true apostles with the false apostles very appropriately. We are on firmer ground in 13.7-9, where the first person plural is used throughout: 'We rejoice, when we are weak, and ye are strong.' This recalls I Cor. 4.10, where Paul is certainly speaking of his fellow-workers as well.

Outside the Thessalonian and Corinthian Epistles, there is only one clear instance of the epistolary 'we', Rom. 1.5. Paul writes, 'through whom we received grace and apostleship'. Colossians in particular shows a very clear alternation between 'I' meaning 'Paul' and 'we' meaning 'Timothy and my fellow-workers as well'. Col. 1.1-12 refers to the missionaries who greet the Colossians; then in 1.23 Paul emphasizes his own ministry: 'whereof I Paul was made a minister'. In 1.28 he reverts to his fellow-workers, 'whom we proclaim', and in the next verse distinguishes himself again in the words 'whereunto I labour also'. We find just the same sequence in 4.3 f., 'withal praying for us also', then he speaks of 'the mystery of Christ, for which I am also in bonds'. We may assume that Timothy was not in prison. The only other place in the Pauline writings where there could be any doubt is II Tim. 4.15, which we take to be a Pauline fragment. The phrase 'for he greatly withstood our words' occurs in the middle of an 'I' passage. We may assume that Paul and his companions were preaching. In Philippians, Philemon, and Ephesians there are either no 'we' passages or they plainly signify 'we' inclusive.

In the rest of the New Testament it is the author of the Epistle to the Hebrews who uses the epistolary 'we' most frequently, e.g. 5.11; 6.9; 6.11; 13.18. In the Johannine Epistles the question is more difficult to decide; in the splendid opening passage in I John 1.1-4 the 'we' probably refers to the apostolic witness rather than to the witness of the author alone;

so also in I John 4.14; III John 12. In III John 9 he writes, 'Diotrephes
. . . receiveth us not', but the context makes it plain that it is the brethren
whom Diotrephes refuses to receive. I Peter gives no example at all of the
epistolary 'we', but the author of II Peter uses it in 1.1, 16, 18. In 1.16 he
actually uses a plural noun of himself: ἐπόπται γενηθέντες τῆς ἐκείνου
μεγαλειότητος, 'We were eyewitnesses of his majesty.' This is quite
unparalleled elsewhere, for in the Pauline writings we can use the presence of a plural noun with the first person plural as a sign that he is not
using the epistolary 'we'. However we must remember that the author of
II Peter is deliberately imitating an 'apostolic' style. If we could believe
that the author really had been an eyewitness of his majesty, his use of
the plural would have greater significance.

In the sub-apostolic writings there is no certain example of the epistolary 'we'. Neither Clement, nor Ignatius, nor Polycarp, *Philippians*,[1]
gives us an example of 'we' that is not better understood as 'you and I'
or 'I and my companions'. There are three doubtful places in the *Epistle
of Barnabas*. In IV 9 the author writes:

πολλὰ θέλων γράφειν, οὐχ ὡς διδάσκαλος, ἀλλ' ὡς πρέπει ἀγαπῶντι ἀφ'
ὧν ἔχομεν μὴ ἐλλείπειν, γράφειν ἐσπούδασα.[2]

But Lake is no doubt right in suggesting that ἀφ' ὧν ἔχομεν μὴ ἐλλείπειν
is probably a maxim or proverb.[3] In VI 18 the author uses the phrase
προειρήκαμεν δὲ ἐπάνω ('we have stated above'), but the reading is very
doubtful.[4] Finally in IX 8, after his ridiculous exposition of the 318 men
whom Abraham circumcised, he complacently adds: οἶδεν ὁ τὴν ἔμφυτον
δωρεάν τῆς διδαχῆς αὐτοῦ θέμενος ἐν ἡμῖν.[5] But he may be echoing II
Cor. 5.19; and in any case ἐν ἡμῖν must surely refer to a group and not to
an individual.

The general effect of the evidence given here may well be to make us
ask whether there really is such a thing as a consciously used epistolary
'we' in Paul's writings at all. He does, it is true, use the first person plural
in sentences which can only really apply to himself; but the way in which
he can so easily pass over in the same passage, and sometimes in the same

---

[1] Nor is there any example in the *Epistle to Diognetus*. But it is doubtful if this work
should be treated as an epistle at all; see H. G. Meecham, *The Epistle to Diognetus*, Man-
chester, 1949.
[2] 'Since I wish to write . . . to you, not as a teacher, but as befits one who loves not to
neglect the store which we have, I have been diligent to write' (my translation).
[3] Kirsopp Lake, *The Apostolic Fathers* I (Loeb Classical Library), London, 1912.
[4] προειρήκαμεν is the reading of ℵ. C (Codex Constantinopolitanus) and G (archetype
of eight defective mss.) read προείρηκε. L (a Latin ms. in Leningrad) omits the whole
sentence.
[5] 'He knows this who placed among us the innate gift of teaching.'

sentence, to using 'we' of himself and his fellow-workers suggests that he may not consciously use 'we' in his letters of himself alone. He wrote to the churches always in the name of, and on behalf of, what we may call the mission, that is the group of workers of whom Paul himself was leader and centre, but not by any means the only member.

A remarkable parallel for this usage can be found in the letters of Ziegenbalg, the pioneer Lutheran missionary who began work in Tranquebar, South India, in 1706. His letters home show a constant variation between the first person singular and plural, according to whether he is writing on behalf of himself alone or of his fellow missionaries.[1]

This has considerable significance for our interpretation of Paul's thought about the ministry. It means that what Paul says about his work and that of his colleagues is not the incidental comment on one man's activity, but provides in fact at least the foundation for a doctrine of the ministry. In several places, especially in the Corinthian Epistles, Paul brings the work of himself and his colleagues into close connection with the work of Christ on the one hand, and the vocation of the Church on the other. Paul, as we know, often refers to his apostolic office, but the language he uses about his fellow-workers shows that he included them also as partakers in this apostolic work; and we can learn from what he says about his work and theirs something of what he believed about the apostolate. So our study of Paul's use of 'we' has been necessary in order to establish that he is writing about the ministry, and not merely offering *obiter dicta* about his own personal experience.

[1] See A. Lehmann, *Alte Briefe aus Indien*, Stuttgart, 1957, p. 255. (I owe this reference to my wife.)

5

Paul's Doctrine of the Ministry:
I Corinthians

THOSE WHO are looking for Paul's doctrine of the ministry would naturally turn to I Cor. 12 and Eph. 4. It is not surprising that the debate about the ministry in the New Testament has tended during the past seventy years to concentrate on these two passages as far as the Pauline evidence is concerned, for it was the Reformers, and especially Calvin, who took their doctrine of the ministry from these passages. Calvin, anxious to find texts from which he could construct a biblical doctrine of the ministry, eagerly seized on these. Subsequent discussion has not on the whole removed them from the centre of interest. This is no doubt because, largely for historical reasons, the debate about the ministry has been a debate about the orders within the ministry, and these two passages say, or seem to say, something about the orders within the ministry. But in fact they do not tell us very much about the ministry itself. They certainly do not supply us with anything like an adequate theology of the ministry.

Some recent scholars seem to have realized this: indeed, there seems to be general agreement today that in these two passages Paul is not recounting the various orders or degrees within the ministry, but is mentioning some of the chief functions of the ministry. But this has not meant that attention has been turned to any other part of Paul's writings in the hope of finding a doctrine of the ministry in them. On the contrary, the impression left on one by reading many commentators today is that Paul did not actually have a doctrine of the ministry, that it was a subject in which he was not much interested. Now this conclusion I believe to be mistaken: Paul did have a doctrine of the ministry; it is to be found in the two Corinthian Epistles, and especially in II Corinthians. But it seems so far to have escaped the notice of theologians because it is not expressed in the terms which we are accustomed to use when discussing the theology of the ministry, terms such as validity, regularity, and authority.

Nor do the passages where Paul expounds his doctrine of the ministry
answer the questions which modern theologians want answered, such as:
How is the authority of the ministry transmitted? How many orders are
there in the ministry? and so forth. The consequence is that such passages
as I Cor. 4 and II Cor. 3–6 have been largely neglected by those who have
written about the New Testament doctrine of the ministry. Moberly, for
example, in his exposition of the Scriptural doctrine of the ministry, does
not devote more than two pages to these five chapters.[1] Yet Paul probably
says more about the theology of the ministry in these five chapters than
in the whole of the rest of his writings. Similarly, in Gore's book on the
ministry, except for a reference to οἰκονόμος in I Cor. 4.1, I doubt if
there is any treatment of these passages at all.[2] But in fact it is in the two
Corinthian Epistles that we must look for Paul's doctrine of the ministry
if we are to find it anywhere. Above all it is in these two Epistles that Paul
deals with what should have been the first consideration for those who
expound the Christian doctrine of the ministry, namely the relation of the
ministry to the Church. This is a subject which has been strangely neglected
by theologians, and when anything has been said about it, too often
they have contented themselves with making general statements without
trying to find a biblical basis for them.[3] It will be our aim therefore in this
chapter to expound Paul's doctrine of the ministry and to show how it
fits in with what we have already observed about the mission of the Remnant in the Old Testament and the doctrine of the Remnant in Paul's
thought.

We begin with I Cor. 3.18–4.7. Paul seems to be warning the Corinthians against pride. They have no need, he says, to make bold claims for
themselves, for God has already given them all things in Christ. He sums
it up in 3.21–23 by saying:

> For all things are yours; whether Paul, or Apollos, or Cephas, or the
> world, or life, or death, or things present, or things to come; all are
> yours; and ye are Christ's; and Christ is God's.

In 3.5 Paul has already described himself and Apollos as 'ministers
through whom ye believed', so we may be sure that he is here suggesting
that the ministry belongs to the Church, it is not independent of it. Several
commentators (e.g. Parry[4]) draw comparisons between this passage and
the Stoic doctrine of πάντα τοῦ σοφοῦ ἐστιν ('All things belong to the

---

[1] B. C. Moberly, *Ministerial Priesthood*, pp. 284 f.
[2] Charles Gore, *The Church and the Ministry*, p. 203.
[3] E.g. the great Archbishop William Temple, see pp. 143 f. below.
[4] R. St J. Parry, *I Corinthians* (Cambridge Greek Testament), 1916.

wise man'). But this is hardly to the point: Paul is not thinking of the Corinthians as isolated individuals, but of the Corinthian church as representing the universal Church. The ministry belongs to the Church as a whole, not to the individual Christian only.

Then Paul drives home his lesson of humility by taking the example of the ministry. We too, he says in 4.1 f., are not autonomous agents, but men with a trust. We are 'ministers of Christ and stewards of the mysteries of God' (4.1—the word for 'ministers' is ὑπηρέται, not the διάκονοι of 3.5). In fact he says that the ministry is responsible to Christ, though its task is to serve the Church. When he has made this clear, he makes the transition to the Church with the difficult words (4.6 f.):

Now these things, brethren, I have in a figure transferred to myself and Apollos for your sakes; that in us you might learn not to go beyond the things which are written; that no one of you be puffed up for the one against the other. For who maketh thee to differ? and what hast thou that thou didst not receive? But if thou didst receive it, why dost thou glory, as if thou hadst not received it?

The difficult part is: μετεσχημάτισα εἰς ἐμαυτὸν καὶ Ἀπολλῶν δι᾽ ὑμᾶς, ἵνα ἐν ἡμῖν μάθητε τὸ Μὴ ὑπὲρ ἃ γέγραπται. Commentators on the whole tend to see in this passage subtle rebukes of the false teachers; e.g. Edwards says Paul is indirectly referring to teachers who have been troubling the Corinthians,[1] and Plummer suggests that Paul is really referring to others who were more to blame.[2] But there is no evidence that Paul is *blaming* anyone here. In 4.1–5 we do not meet words of censure tactfully applied to himself and his colleagues but really aimed at others. In these verses Paul is simply pointing out that the ministry is responsible to Christ. Then in the next two verses he goes on to show that therefore the Church is responsible to Christ. It is as if he is saying: 'I am showing you the strictly subordinate relationship of the ministry to Christ in order that you may grasp the subordinate relationship of the Church as a whole to Christ.' In effect the ministry shows us in little what the Church as a whole should be. The Church also must be a ὑπηρέτης and an οἰκονόμος.

This means that we must take μετεσχημάτισα in v. 6 in the sense which it bears in Phil. 3.21 rather than in that which it bears in II Cor. 11.13 f. This is to say, as Massie well remarks, 'there is no thought here of fiction'.[3] Such a sense is also found outside the New Testament. See

---

[1] T. C. Edwards, *I Corinthians*, London, 1885.
[2] In A. Robertson and A. Plummer, *I Corinthians* (ICC), 1911.
[3] J. Massie, *I and II Corinthians* (Century Bible), London, 1902.

Moulton and Milligan (*s.v.*), who give an instance of it being used of altering the appearance of a hermitage, in the sense of 'changing the outward appearance of that which remains in itself the same'. There is no reason therefore why Paul should not be saying that he has changed the application of the lesson of subordination to Christ so as to make it refer to the ministry, though he really wants it to refer to the Church as well (not 'instead'). The ambiguous phrase τίς σε διακρίνει must be taken to mean: 'Who has made you differ from the ministry?' If they are subordinate to Christ, so are you. Parry's explanation of the mysterious Μὴ ὑπὲρ ἃ γέγραπται seems to suit the context best. He takes it as 'Not to go beyond the terms of your commission'. Just as the ministry has a commission from Christ and does not consist of free agents, so is the Church as a whole. This would fit in well with Rom. 12.3: ' . . . not to think of himself more highly than he ought to think; but so to think as to think soberly, according as God hath dealt to each man a measure of faith.'

The ministry then shows in miniature what the Church should be. This principle is expounded in a still deeper sense in the passage that follows, 4.8–16. Paul draws his famous contrast between himself and his fellow apostles on the one hand, and the Corinthian Christians on the other. The apostles are 'men doomed to death, . . . a spectacle, . . . fools for Christ's sake, . . . the filth of the world, the offscouring of all things'. On the other hand the Corinthians are comfortable, they 'are filled', they have 'become rich', they 'reign', they 'are strong, . . . have glory'. There can be no doubt that the passage is ironical. Paul is not just describing their respective positions in an objective manner. Verse 8b surely makes this clear; RSV well translates it:

> Already you are filled! Already you have become rich! Without us you have become kings! And would that you did reign, so that we might share the rule with you!

Goudge has undoubtedly hit the right sense of the passage when he says: 'The Apostles are what God means the members of the Church to be, while the Corinthians are not.'[1] In fact when he draws a picture of the harassed, precarious life of the ministry in v. 9–13, Paul, far from appealing to the Corinthians for pity, is indirectly telling them that this is the sort of life they ought to be leading. It is therefore very significant indeed that the description of the apostles' life is remarkably like our Lord's own life. He too was an ἐπιθανάτιος, condemned to death; he too was a spectacle on the cross, he too was weak and dishonoured; he too blessed when

---

[1] H. L. Goudge, *I Corinthians* (Westminster Commentaries), 5th ed. rev., 1926.

he was insulted (cf. I Peter 2.23). The apostles 'entreat' here as they entreat on God's behalf in II Cor. 5.20 (the verb παρακαλεῖν is the same in both passages).

In these circumstances we should naturally expect that the two words Paul uses in v. 13, περικαθάρματα and περίψημα ('filth' and 'offscouring'), would have something of an atoning significance. Some commentators (e.g. Edwards, Massie) agree that there is some such meaning here, though they tend to go a little too far in speaking of a 'propitiatory' significance. But others, among them the more modern, incline to deny any suggestion of atonement in the words. For example Godet,[1] Plummer, Goudge, Parry and Moffatt[2] all argue that the words simply mean 'lowest scum' and do not suggest anything further. When however we look at the way in which these words are used in the LXX, we find that the evidence weighs definitely in favour of some sort of an atoning significance. The word περικάθαρμα occurs in Prov. 21.18: περικάθαρμα δὲ δικαίου ἄνομος. The RSV translates: 'The wicked is a ransom for the righteous.'[3] Toy's comment on this passage is:[4] 'When punishment is inflicted (by God) on a community, it is the bad man, and not the good, on whom it falls.' He does not think that the bad man is represented as accepting punishment voluntarily instead of the good, it is rather that the punishment of the wicked has an atoning value so that the good escapes unharmed. The same word in Hebrew (kōpher) is translated λύτρον in Prov. 6.35 and 13.8. This is significant in view of Mark 10.45. The word περίψημα occurs in Tobit 5.18. Anna says to Tobit: ἀργύριον τῷ ἀργυρίῳ μὴ φθάσαι, ἀλλὰ περίψημα τοῦ παιδίου ἡμῶν γένοιτο—'Be not greedy to add money to money; but let it be as refuse in respect of our child.' As a matter of fact a better translation might well be: 'Let it go in exchange for our child.' The idea is that they should forgo the chance of gaining extra money by sending Tobias to a distant country, and thus gain their son. It may therefore have the sense of λύτρον here. It is true that περίψημα came later to have a very conventional meaning, indicating not very much more than 'your humble servant'. Ignatius says of himself περίψημα τό ἐμον πνεῦμα τοῦ σταυροῦ,[5] 'my spirit is the scum of the cross', which might mean: 'I am carrying out the atoning work that Christ began on the cross'; but it may merely mean 'I am not worthy to be compared to the cross'. The author of the *Epistle of Barnabas* refers to

---

[1] F. Godet, *I Corinthians*, ET, Vol. I, Edinburgh, 1886.

[2] J. Moffatt, *I Corinthians* (MNTC), 1938.

[3] The Hebrew is כֹּפֶר לַצַּדִּיק רָשָׁע.

[4] C. H. Toy, *Proverbs* (ICC), 1899.   [5] *Ephesians* XVIII 1.

himself as περίψημα twice, in IV 9 and VI 5. And Moulton and Milligan (*s.v.*) quote an epitaph written by a wife on her dead husband, where she says of herself ἐγώ σου περίψημα τῆς καλῆς ψυχῆς. Here it might mean, 'May I be a ransom for thy noble soul.' We are thus thoroughly justified in understanding both περικαθάρματα and περίψημα in I Cor. 4.13 as having an atoning significance, though we need not say a propitiatory significance.

Consequently this whole passage I Cor. 3.18–4.16 has very great importance for Paul's doctrine of the ministry. From it we learn that the task of the ministry is to serve the Church, but to serve it by itself first living out the suffering, redeeming life of Christ in the world, in order that the Church as a whole may do likewise. We notice especially 4.16: 'I beseech you therefore, be imitators of me.' Thus the ministry has a double relationship: it is related to Christ as responsible to him and as being the primary means by which his life is reproduced in the world. And it is related to the Church as serving the Church, and as leading the Church as a whole into the same life which itself is exhibiting. There is no suggestion here of the ministry doing anything which the Church as a whole cannot do: it is rather that the ministry is the pioneer in Christian living for the Church, as Christ was the pioneer for all of us.[1]

In I Cor. 9.1 f. there is an interesting point that links up with a passage in Philippians. In 9.2 Paul says to his Corinthians: 'The seal of mine apostleship are ye in the Lord.' It is not absolutely clear what it is in the Corinthians that constitutes the seal of Paul's apostleship: the existence of the Corinthian church (Godet), or their remarkable gifts (Plummer and Goudge), or their union with Christ (Parry), or their fellowship (Moffatt). We need not necessarily choose between these; all may be implied. The important thing to notice is that the existence of the church is the object of the apostle's work, and also that Paul apparently regards himself as specially related as apostle to the churches he founded rather than to the whole Church (so Goudge). In view of the close connection between the founding apostle and the churches founded by him, we may question whether there really was such a clear division between the original

---

[1] Cf. T. W. Manson's essay, 'Realized Eschatology and the Messianic Secret', in *Studies in the Gospels*, ed. D. E. Nineham, 1955, pp. 215 f. He draws attention to the repeated parallels between what must befall the Son of Man and what must befall the disciples. I owe this reference to J. A. T. Robinson, *Jesus and His Coming*, London, 1957, p. 174. Compare also A. Ehrhardt, *The Apostolic Ministry* (Scottish Journal of Theology Occasional Papers 8), Edinburgh, 1958, p. 9: 'It is the imitation of Jesus Christ in this world which is incumbent upon the Church and its ministry.' And Stig Hanson, *The Unity of the Church in the New Testament* (Acta Seminarii Neotestamentici Upsaliensis 14), Uppsala, 1946, p. 92: 'Thus Paul continues the work of Christ, and his mission is the same as that of Christ.'

apostles on the one hand and the local apostles of churches on the other
as some modern scholars would have us believe. A similar passage occurs
in Phil. 2.15 f.:

> . . . that ye may be blameless and harmless, children of God without
> blemish in the midst of a crooked and perverse generation, among whom
> ye are seen as lights in the world, holding forth the word of life; that
> I may have whereof to glory in the day of Christ, that I did not run in
> vain neither labour in vain.

The thought here is that the proof of Paul's successful ministry lies in the
fact of his converts appearing as lamp-bearers and as holding forth the
word of life. This is very much the same as the thought of I Cor. 9.1 f.,
but here the apostolic function of the Church is added. The aim of Paul's
apostleship is that his converts should be apostles. Throughout this
passage in Philippians Paul is echoing Isa. 49. 1–6. The phrase κενῶς
ἐκοπίασα in v. 16 comes from Isa. 49.4 in the LXX ('I have laboured in
vain'); and in Isa. 49.6 the Servant is described as φῶς ἐθνῶν (' a light to
the Gentiles'). It is most interesting that Paul should apply to himself
language concerning the Servant here, for it supplies just that link which
we have found in I Cor. 3.18–4.16. The ordained ministry, carrying out
the Messiah's ministry, passes that ministry on to the Church which it
founds.

The famous passage I Cor. 12.24–30 can hardly pass unnoticed. It is
very remarkable that v. 28 coincides with the figure of Eph. 2.20. Christ
is not here called the foundation; it is apostles and prophets who are the
foundation; God placed them first in the Church. In view of what has
gone before, the language about the more unseemly members having
greater honour, it is exceedingly unlikely that Paul means here a primacy
of honour or prestige as belonging to the apostles. It is much simpler
to take his meaning as 'first in time': the apostles were the Remnant
and therefore were the first Church. The prophets come next, because
the Remnant also bore a prophetic function. The teachers are perhaps the
local ministry appointed by the founding apostle. But Paul is certainly
not here speaking about orders within the ministry; in his view the apostles
are the ministry because they are the first Church. He asks, 'Are all
apostles?' but he can hardly mean by this that the apostolic work of
preaching the gospel and founding churches is for ever to be restricted
to the original apostles, for as we have seen, he exhorts the Philippians
to be lights in the world and to hold forth the word of life. But not all
are called to undertake the specifically apostolic task of being the first
church in some hitherto unevangelized area. In this connection, Goudge's

attempt to explain why 'evangelists' are not mentioned here as they are in Eph. 4.11 is most unconvincing: 'Evangelists are not mentioned here because St Paul is speaking of the inner life of the Church and not of her outward activity.' It is difficult to see how being lights in the world and holding forth the word of life can be excluded from the sphere of the Church's inner life, and yet these are undoubtedly evangelistic activities. It is far more likely that 'apostles' in I Cor. 12 refers to the first apostles, and 'evangelists' in Eph. 4.11 to their successors in the apostolic task of spreading the gospel and founding churches.

In so far, then, as there was any ministry when Paul wrote I Corinthians, it is referred to in the word 'apostles' in the list given in I Cor. 12. But Paul regards their ministry as consisting primarily in the fact that they were first, the first Church. As he wrote they were engaged in the task of passing on their ministry to the churches they were founding, as described in I Cor. 3.18–4.16. It is very significant that Paul here discusses the nature of the whole Church in the context of the local church, the church in Corinth. This is because he always treats the local church as the representative of the whole Church. It is the whole Church in little. It will be plain to those who have followed the argument of this chapter that our exposition of Paul's doctrine of the ministry is based on two assumptions. The first assumption is that when Paul speaks about the relation of himself and his colleagues to the Corinthians, his arguments are valid for the whole Church and not for the Corinthians only. The second assumption is that in Paul's mind the relation of himself and his colleagues to the Corinthians adequately represents the relation of the ministry as a whole to the Church as a whole. Both these assumptions seem fairly securely founded, and they lead us on to the formulation of a definite and theologically significant doctrine of the ministry in Paul's writings.

6

Paul's Doctrine of the Ministry: II Corinthians

IN THE very first paragraph of II Corinthians, after the opening salutation, we find exactly that pattern of Christ—ministry—Church which
we have noted in I Corinthians, and which is so fundamental to Paul's
doctrine of the ministry. In 1.3–7 we learn that God has comforted Paul
(v. 3); then in v. 4 Paul says that the purpose of this is to enable him to
comfort the Corinthians. In v. 5 that comfort is connected with the sufferings of Christ, so that the life of Christ is seen to be involved in this
experience. In v. 6 Paul shows that this double experience of suffering
and comfort is undertaken for the benefit of the Corinthians. And in v. 7
the movement is completed by his statement that the Corinthians are
partakers both of the sufferings and of the comfort.

Two passages follow in which Paul tells us something more of his
apostolic relationship to the Corinthian church. The first is 1.24:

> Not that we have lordship over your faith, but are helpers of your joy:
> for by faith ye stand.

All commentators seem to agree that συνεργοί ('helpers') here means
'fellow-workers with the Corinthians' not with God. Many editors however try to interpret 'your faith' as if it meant 'the doctrine you accept'.
Thus Hodge,[1] following Erasmus, thinks it means that Paul claimed
authority in matters of discipline but not of faith. Massie,[2] Menzies,[3] and
Plummer[4] all seem to follow this interpretation, but in view of the last
clause in the verse it seems most unlikely. This is the only place in the
New Testament where κυριεύω is used of a thing; elsewhere it is always
of persons, e.g. Luke 22.25 (of the Gentiles), Romans four times, always
of lordship over persons. Moulton and Milligan do not give any instance of
it being used with an abstract object as here. Faith was for Paul primarily

---

[1] C. Hodge, *II Corinthians*, New York, 1860.
[2] J. Massie, *I and II Corinthians* (Century Bible).
[3] A. Menzies, *II Corinthians*, London, 1912.
[4] A. Plummer, *II Corinthians* (ICC).

E

a personal relationship with Christ: perhaps therefore he means that neither he nor his colleagues have any desire to come between the Corinthians and Christ. All he wants is to help them to experience the joy of that relationship. The second passage is 2.9:

> For to this end also did I write, that I might know the proof of you, whether ye are obedient in all things.

The last passage showed the limits which Paul set to his apostolic authority. This one shows that he nevertheless viewed that authority as a real and personal one. He expected the Corinthians to be obedient to him in a matter of church discipline, as this was. Some editors have made strenuous efforts to avoid interpreting ὑπήκοοι here as 'obedient to me personally'. For example Massie interprets it as 'obedient to right principles', and Plummer paraphrases 'whether to every call of duty you lend an ear'. We may perhaps legitimately suspect that a fear of excessive authoritarianism in Church government has unduly influenced these commentators. The word is used only twice elsewhere in the New Testament: Acts 7.39 of obedience to an angel, and Phil. 2.8 of our Lord's obedience to death, which hardly means obedience to a principle, though it could be construed as obedience to duty. Of the five instances of the word in the LXX, four certainly indicate obedience to persons. The fifth (Prov. 21.28) is ambiguous, but does not suggest obedience to a person. All examples quoted in Moulton and Milligan are of obedience to persons. There can be little doubt therefore that Paul, as the founding apostle of the Corinthian church, is claiming obedience to his authority.

In ch. 3 begins the great, sustained exposition of the nature of the Christian ministry which lasts until well into ch. 6. It is entirely appropriate that near the beginning should occur a sentence which reiterates what Paul has already said in I Cor. 9.1 f. about the existence of the Corinthian church being an attestation of his apostleship. We quote 3.3 in the RSV, which brings out the sense more clearly than does the RV: 'You shew that you are a letter from Christ delivered by us.' The meaning in the context is not completely clear: is it a letter to others from Christ? It is difficult to see to whom it could be delivered if not to others, that is to the outside world generally. What does the letter contain? Judging by the reference to 'epistles of commendation' in v. 1, it would seem to be first and foremost a letter authenticating Paul's status as an apostle and that of his fellow-workers. If so, this exactly reproduces the thought of I Cor. 9.1 f. and Phil. 2.16. But no doubt Menzies is right in saying, 'The letter is . . . a living testimony the church bears to the Apostle and to

Christ who sent him.' This means that this letter has an evangelistic purpose, as in Phil. 2.15 f. In that case, the Corinthian church is by its very existence carrying out an apostolic function: it is witnessing to Christ.

Then in 3.4 f. comes the comparison between the old dispensation and the Christian ministry. It is important to establish at the outset that when Paul speaks of διάκονοι and uses the first person plural, as he does in vv. 5 f. here, he is not thinking only of himself. He has already in I Cor. 4.1 referred to himself and Apollos and Cephas as 'stewards' and 'ministers' (ὑπηρέτας), and as διάκονοι in I Cor. 3.5, and has then gone on in I Cor. 4.9 to refer to the same group as 'apostles'. In the opening chapters of II Corinthians he is speaking possibly of himself only but possibly also of Timothy, e.g. 1.8 ff. Then in 1.19 he explicitly defines the phrase 'preached among you by us' as meaning 'by me and Silvanus and Timothy'. In 1.23–2.13, where he is dealing with the very personal matter of the insult which he received in Corinth and the action which he took as a result, he slips into the first person singular again (except of course where he means 'you Corinthians and I' as in 2.11). In 2.14–17 he resumes the first person plural, but we have already suggested that he is thinking of Silvanus, Timothy, and Titus as well, who were after all helping Paul in his ministry of preaching the word in sincerity (2.17). In 3.1–3 it looks at first as if Paul is using the plural to refer to himself only. But when he first visited Corinth, as we know from Acts, he was not alone but had the help of Timothy and Silas. There has been a tendency in recent times to represent Paul as very much of an individualist; we are shown a picture of a man who founded churches by himself, directed and disciplined them by himself, and expected obedience to himself as an individual. Similarly commentators have been quick to see references in Paul's theology to his own conversion experience, and, as we shall see in our discussion of II Cor. 5, they have tended to interpret much of what he says in terms of his own conversion experience. It is not perhaps fanciful to suggest that this mode of interpretation is sometimes a hangover from the excessive individualism of the last century, and even that the emphasis on Paul's own experience as normative for his theology derives more from that reliance on Christian experience as the main source for doctrine which was so popular in the last century also. We should rather begin from the fact that Paul in this section of II Corinthians is setting forth a theology of the Christian ministry, and not merely defining his own personal position. Naturally his exposition is deeply coloured by his own experiences, both in his conversion and in his subsequent ministry all over the Graeco-oriental world of his day. But nowhere does he specifically exclude his fellow-workers, unless he is actually discussing definite exchanges that took place between himself and the Corinthians; and in several places he explicitly includes them, e.g. I Cor. 3.5; 4.1; 4.9; II Cor. 1.19. Thus when Paul writes in II Cor. 3.6 that God 'made us sufficient as ministers of a new covenant' (he uses διακόνους here), he is referring to all the ministers of the new covenant, not to himself only.

In 3.4–11 we learn something about this ministry: it is in some sense 'spiritual' (v. 6), it is a ministry 'of righteousness' (v. 9). 'Spiritual' does not here mean 'not external', and 'of righteousness' does not mean exactly 'morally righteous'. The contrast is between spiritual and that which is written on tablets of stone. Just above Paul has hinted at this contrast when he says that the Corinthians are a letter written 'not in tables of stone, but in tables that are hearts of flesh' (3.3). He means that the faith of the Corinthians is the commendatory letter of those who founded the Corinthian church. So here the ministry of the spirit means a ministry that depends on faith, comes in faith, and preaches faith, rather than one (like Moses') that provided and commended a written law. So also the ministry of righteousness is contrasted with the ministry of death (v. 7) and condemnation (v. 9). The written law brought moral frustration and spiritual death; the strange righteousness of God manifested in Jesus Christ brings justification and life. We note also that Moses' ministry, according to St Paul, seems to consist primarily in his giving the tablets of the law; by analogy the Christian ministry seems to consist primarily in proclaiming the righteousness of God in Jesus Christ. What else it consists in, we shall see later; it will prove to be living and suffering rather than celebrating the Sacraments. Perhaps the ministry of the Sacraments (which may indeed be referred to in I Cor. 4.1 under 'mysteries') was thought of as being primarily the task of the local church. But this ministry in its turn cannot be separated from the apostolic ministry, as we shall see. Verse 10 in this passage is extraordinarily obscure; in the AV it is very nearly meaningless, and is little clearer in the RV. The RSV offers much better sense:

> Indeed, in this case, what once had splendour has come to have no splendour at all, because of the splendour that surpasses it.

We thus find here the suggestion, already encountered in our study of the Remnant, that there was some validity in the old dispensation, though of course it has been done away with by the coming of the new.

One of the most obscure pieces of Old Testament exegesis that Paul ever wrote is found in 3.12–18, but it also contains further description of the Christian ministry, so we must try to find Paul's real meaning. In vv. 12 f. we come on another contrast between the old and the new: the ministers of the new covenant use great boldness of speech, unlike Moses, who deliberately obscured the true state of affairs. We must presume that this freedom of speech concerns proclaiming the gospel, for Paul is here discussing the activities of the two respective ministries, and not his own personal difficulties with the Corinthians. But we are bound to ask: why did Moses put a veil on his face? In the passage in Exodus to which Paul refers the motive seems to have been to obscure the exceeding brightness of his face which resulted from his speaking with the Lord, as otherwise the Israelites would be too much alarmed. But Alford rightly points out that according to the Exodus narrative Moses only put the veil on after he had finished uttering the words of the Lord to Aaron and the rest.[1] Presumably while the words were being uttered the Israelites were expected to bear the brightness, but not, we are given to understand, a moment longer than was necessary. Paul however suggests that Moses had another motive in putting a veil over his face: he did it so that the Israelites should not look on 'the end of that which was passing away'. The word 'end' here ($\tau\epsilon\lambda\sigma$) may simply mean 'termination'. In that case Moses is represented as deliberately hiding the fact that the glory which so much impressed the Israelities was destined to pass away, or was actually passing away at the time. But if $\tau\epsilon\lambda\sigma$ means 'fulfilment' here, then Paul suggests that Moses, knowing Christ to be the destined fulfilment of the law, deliberately hid that fact from the Israelites. This is the interpretation of R. P. C. Hanson, who quotes Rom. 10.4 in confirmation of it.[2] Whichever interpretation be true, Paul's suggestion about Moses' motive has tended to disturb commentators: is Paul accusing Moses of duplicity? Menzies and Strachan both suggest that Moses is being treated merely as a lay figure. If we remember however that Moses here stands for several things at once, we may fairly acquit Moses of duplicity and Paul of slandering dignities. Moses represents first and foremost the law: as such he manifested a glory that was destined to pass away. But according to Paul the law itself in some sense and in some parts pointed to the new dispensation. It was prophetic of Christ and of the righteousness of God; when properly understood the law could be seen to preach the gospel. All this, we must presume, Moses knew, according to Paul's interpretation. Hence when Moses put on the veil so that the fading of the glory should not be seen, it was not merely with a view to 'saving his

---

[1] H. Alford, *The Greek Testament*, rev. ed., 1894, Vol. II.

[2] *II Corinthians* (Torch Bible Commentaries), London, 1954.

face', so that the Israelites should not witness the fading of his glory; it was in a sense a prophetic action. The act foretold the πώρωσις, the 'hardness in part' that was to befall the Jews when the Messiah came (see Rom. 11.25 and v. 14 here, ἐπωρώθη). Thus Moses' action is akin to the happenings referred to in I Cor. 10.1–13; they took place in their own right, but were also indicative of what was to come in the Messianic era.[1]

Then in v. 14 follows the much disputed sentence:

ἄχρι γὰρ τῆς σήμερον ἡμέρας τὸ αὐτὸ κάλυμμα ἐπὶ τῇ ἀναγνώσει τῆς παλαιᾶς διαθήκης μένει, μὴ ἀνακαλυπτόμενον ὅτι ἐν Χριστῷ καταργεῖται.

This is translated in the RV:

For until this very day at the reading of the old covenant the same veil remaineth unlifted; which veil is done away in Christ.

This translation assumes that ὅτι is a relative pronoun agreeing with κάλυμμα, that ἀνακαλυπτόμενον is a participle agreeing with κάλυμμα (μὴ ἀνακαλυπτόμενον='remaineth unlifted'), and that καταργεῖται governs κάλυμμα. The RSV gives much the same translation, but offers 'because' for ὅτι instead of 'which', and renders 'because only through Christ is it taken away'. But both these translations fail to take account of an objection which was made originally, I believe, by Alford. The verb which in these versions is translated 'taken away' and applied to the veil is καταργεῖται. But this does not mean 'taken away'; it means 'done away' or 'rendered void'. The word for 'taken away' is περιαιρεῖται, as found in v. 16, which quotes the LXX of Ex. 34.34. Hence Alford does not apply the word καταργεῖται to the veil at all, but to the glory, or, more generally, the Old Testament dispensation. He therefore renders ἀνακαλυπτόμενον as an accusative absolute and translates:

A veil remains on the reading of the Old Covenant, it not having been revealed that that Covenant is done away.

This fits in admirably with v. 13, where, as we saw, according to Paul Moses put a veil on his face in order that the Israelites should not perceive that the glory was fading.

We then take v. 16 in the sense of the RSV and RV margin: 'But when a man turns to the Lord the veil is removed.' Paul is thinking of the Jew of his own day: when he allows himself to receive the Spirit in baptism, the veil is removed and he understands the Scriptures in their true sense. It follows therefore that we must take the first clause of v. 17 as 'Now "the Lord" here is the Spirit.' Paul has quoted a sentence from Ex. 34.34

[1] I am indebted to my brother's exegesis of this passage for most of this paragraph.

where the divine Name occurs,[1] and he interprets the divine Name there as referring to the Lord the Spirit. This is not a conclusion which has been accepted by modern commentators. They maintain that, since Paul uses Κύριος once in the same verse and once in the next verse to refer undoubtedly to Christ, he cannot use it of the Spirit here. They are consequently driven to various expedients to explain how Paul can so explicitly identify two Persons of the Trinity. But it does not seem inevitable that Paul should use Κύριος only of Christ, even in the same verse. He uses Κύριος of the Spirit at the end of v. 18, and indeed why should he not be specifically indicating in v. 17 that he understands Κύριος in Ex. 34.34 as applying to the Spirit, and not, as is Paul's usual interpretation of the Old Testament, to Christ? He has been emphasizing that the New Testament ministry is a ministry of the Spirit, and now he actually quotes Scripture to prove that the Spirit is needed in order rightly to understand Scripture.[2]

In v. 18 the only difficulty lies in the interpretation of κατοπτριζόμενοι The RV 'reflecting' is tempting, as it has an obvious homiletic value, but the linguistic evidence is decidedly against it: in fact no one can produce any example of the middle voice of meaning 'to reflect'. The normal usage is that the active means 'reflect', the middle means 'contemplate in a mirror', and the passive means 'be reflected'. Neither Moulton and Milligan, nor Grimm-Thayer,[3] nor the 1940 edition of Liddell and Scott can produce a clear example of the middle mood of the verb being used to mean 'reflect'. The last named quotes this passage and suggests that it may mean 'reflect' here, but produces no additional evidence.[4]

After this attempt to discern Paul's meaning in this difficult passage, we must try to sum up what it actually has to tell us about the Christian ministry. The Christian minister, unlike Moses, gazes boldly on the glory of God now fully revealed in Christ, and as boldly proclaims that glory. He is able to see the Scriptures as the place where that glory is foretold, because he has the gift of the Spirit who enables Christians to understand the Scriptures. Then, in v. 18, at the end of this passage, we find that transition from the work of the ministry to the work of the

---

[1] Very loosely, it must be confessed, judging by our texts of the LXX. Alford thinks that Paul borrowed ἐπιστρέψῃ from ἐπεστράφησαν in Ex. 34.31.

[2] A. M. Ramsey, *The Glory of God and the Transfiguration of Christ*, London, 1949, p. 52, insists that the phrase must be translated, 'The Lord [in this context means] the Spirit'.

[3] *A Greek-English Lexicon of the New Testament . . .*, tr. and rev. by J. H. Thayer, 4th ed., Edinburgh, 1901.

[4] Ramsey, *op. cit.*, p. 53, agrees that the linguistic evidence is decisive for 'beholding', but gives several instances of valuable comments on the interpretation 'reflecting'.

Church which we have already seen implied in I Cor. 4. The ministry uses great boldness (v. 12), but we *all* behold the glory of the Lord and are transfigured according to the same image from glory unto glory. Now this process of being transformed from glory to glory surely cannot be separated from the thought that those who are thus transformed do thereby show forth the glory which they increasingly receive. In v. 4 the Christian minister uses great boldness, and he is contrasted with Moses, who hid the glory. It follows that the Christian minister's task is to uncover the glory, to show it forth. The effect of this is that bit by bit we *all* become centres of radiating glory, and thus all partake in the apostolic function of the Church. This is no mere pious conclusion on Paul's part; it is the logical outcome of his doctrine of the ministry. The pattern is Christ—the ministry—the Church, and the task of the ministry is, not to undertake some specialist activity from which the rest of the faithful are excluded, but to pioneer in doing that which the whole Church must do. And the ministry itself is no originator, but receives its task from Christ. The ordained ministers only exercise the ministry which Christ himself has first exercised, and which he continues to exercise through them, and through their activity in the whole Church also.

In 4.1–6 Paul enlarges on the theme of the new ministry, showing that it does indeed show forth the glory of God in Christ, despite the fact that there are some who fail to perceive this glory. We must insist that in these verses Paul is still speaking of the ministry as a whole; he is not simply thinking of himself.[1] We must never forget his fellow-ministers in the background, who served with him so faithfully and in whose name Paul so often writes his Epistles and speaks to the churches. We notice that the task of the ministry is 'the open statement of the truth' (RSV of v. 2). In the same verse Paul refers to those who refuse to accept this truth. Commentators have unnecessarily complicated this passage by assuming that Paul is here referring to Judaizing Christians; this is a view adopted by Menzies, Plummer,[2] and Strachan. But this is to misunderstand what Paul is doing in this passage: he is contrasting Judaism and Christianity in order thereby to refute Judaizing Christians. It is no part of his policy to suggest that Judaizing Christians are themselves perishing. The parallel with I Cor. 1.18 is all in favour of οἱ ἀπολλύμενοι here being not Christians (not even Judaizing ones) but non-Christians, both pagans and Jews. In I Cor. 1.18 Paul refers to τοῖς ἀπολλυμένοις ('they that are

[1] Cf. Ramsey, *op. cit.*, p. 47: this passage is 'a description of the work of the apostles in the preaching of the Gospel'; cf. also p. 99.
[2] *II Corinthians* (ICC).

perishing'), and then in 1.22 defines them as 'Jews and Greeks'. These cannot be Judaizing Christians, who did accept a crucified Messiah. Besides, it is very doubtful if the word which Paul applies to 'those who are perishing' in II Cor. 4.3 could be applied to Jewish Christians. The word is ἄπιστος, 'unbelieving'. The word occurs twelve times in Paul's writings (but only six separate contexts). In none of the other places can it refer to anyone except non-Christians.[1] In the other three places in the New Testament where it occurs, it is, to say the least, most unlikely that it refers to Judaizing Christians.[2] This means that in this passage Paul is not thinking in terms of a sort of private conflict between himself and his opponents, as is so often represented by commentators. The choice is not between two brands of Christianity, but between Christianity and Judaism. What makes the difference is not the party you belong to, but baptism.

Verse 5 reminds us of I Cor. 4.1; there the ministry was described as 'ministers and stewards' (ὑπηρέτας καὶ οἰκονόμους), and also of I Cor. 3.5, where Paul uses διάκονοι. In this verse (II Cor. 4.5) a still more striking word is used, δούλους, 'slaves'. We cannot help thinking of Jesus Christ, who 'took the form of a servant' (Phil. 2.7, δούλου), and who came 'not to be ministered unto, but to minister' (Mark 10.45, the verb is διακονεῖν); and indeed Paul makes the connection explicit, for he says 'ourselves as your servants for Jesus' sake'. In v. 6 we have that transition to the Church which we have seen to be part of Paul's conception of the Christian ministry:

> Seeing it is God, that said, Light shall shine out of darkness, who shined in our hearts, to give the light of the knowledge of the glory of God in the face of Jesus Christ.

But does this in fact refer to the Church? Most modern commentators would say, No. They would maintain that Paul is here referring explicitly to himself, and in particular to his experience on the Damascus road. God shined in his heart then, and that is why he preaches the gospel. Here indeed we meet that definite tendency towards interpreting Paul's theology in terms of his subjective experience to which we have already referred. It is surely not a coincidence that every English commentator on II Corinthians between Hodge and R. P. C. Hanson assumes that Paul is thinking of his own conversion exclusively in this verse. Hodge and R. P. C. Hanson do not. Hodge is one of the last representatives of the old-fashioned, pre-critical school of commentators. But he stands in the high Calvinist tradition which looked on Christianity as the proclamation of a

---

[1] Besides this passage: I Cor. 6.6; 7.12–15 (four times); 10.27; 14.22–24 (three times); II Cor. 6.14 f. (twice). [2] I Tim. 5.8; Titus 1.15; Rev. 21.8.

series of events, and thought of the gospel as witnessing primarily to objective facts, not to subjective experiences. R. P. C. Hanson belongs to the modern school of biblical theology. Despite the profound difference that the rise of biblical criticism has made, he is one with Hodge in his approach to Christianity as the proclamation of objective events. All in between, whatever their church tradition, appear to have been influenced by the liberal attempt to interpret Christianity primarily in terms of religious experience: Menzies, Plummer, Strachan, even Thornton,[1] assume almost without argument that Paul in v. 6 is speaking of his own special religious experience. This interpretation depends upon two assumptions: the first is that ἐν ταῖς καρδίαις ἡμῶν means 'in my heart'. We have already examined Paul's use of this phrase,[2] and have come to the conclusion that it must refer to others as well as Paul.[3]

The second assumption on which the 'subjective' interpretation of 4.6 rests is that φωτισμός in that verse means 'illumination', not merely 'light'. (RV and RSV both translate 'to give the light of the knowledge'.) The linguistic evidence is on the whole against this, as Hodge points out. In the LXX the word is only used to translate 'or or ma'or, Hebrew words which can only mean 'luminary' and not 'illumination'. In 4.4 above the word must mean 'light (consisting of) the gospel', not 'illumination (provided by) the gospel'. Grimm-Thayer indeed do translate the word in 4.6 as 'enlightening', but they give no other examples of its being used in this sense, and in 4.4 they translate it as 'light'.[4] Hence we are by no means compelled to take φωτισμός as 'illumination' in v. 6. There is no reason why we should not translate it:

> God ... has shined in the hearts of all of us so as to be the light which consists in the knowledge of the glory of God in the face of Jesus Christ.

We assume therefore that in 4.6 Paul is referring, not exclusively to his own experience on the Damascus road, nor even exclusively to the vision of God's glory in Christ which the New Testament ministry has been granted, but simply to the fact of the incorporation into Christ of those who have been made members of the Christian Church. This surely is in line with what he says in v. 5:

[1] See L. S. Thornton, *The Common Life in the Body of Christ*, London, 1942, p. 305 n.2.
[2] See pp. 50 f., above.
[3] Archbishop Ramsey, *op. cit.*, p. 48, inclines to the interpretation defended here: 'God, who said, "Let there be light" ... has by a new creation set in the hearts of men the illumination brought by the glory of God in the face of Jesus ... St Paul may have in mind not an experience peculiar to himself but the illumination which the Gospel has brought to all the apostles and their converts.'
[4] Liddell and Scott give the primary meaning of the word as 'illumination, light', and quote in illustration of this Diocles ap. Galen (Kuhn 19, p. 530); Plutarch 2. 292e, 931b (Teubner); Sextus Empiricus, *adv, Mathematicos* 10.244.

We preach not ourselves, but Christ Jesus as Lord, and ourselves your servants for Jesus' sake.

To preach one's own experience is in a sense to preach oneself; there is certainly a place for one's testimony to what Christ has done in one's own life, but it is not the gospel. The gospel concerns the lordship of Jesus Christ and how that lordship was manifested in history. God shining in the hearts of Christians is the counterpart in the life of the Church to the lordship of Christ as proclaimed in the gospel.

So we find here that same pattern which runs all through Paul's exposition of the Christian doctrine of the ministry. The ministers are servants for Christ's sake; they accept the same lowly service which Christ came to do. They preach Christ because in him God has revealed his glory, a glory that can be known by all Christians. And the aim of their ministry is, not only that all men should see his glory in Christ, but that all who see it should themselves show it forth.

In 4.7–16 we continue the description of the ministry in words very reminiscent of I Cor. 4.8–14. The language makes it plain that 'we' here means 'we ministers', so the 'treasure' of v. 7 must mean the gospel. This is not quite the same as Strachan's interpretation, which is that it means 'Paul's apostolic ministry'. The ministry consists in making the treasure available to others; it is not the treasure itself. The ministry is a ministry, i.e. it is not an end in itself. Verses 10–12 treat of that profound mystery already touched on in I Cor. 4.7–16, whereby we die in Christ that we may live; more than that, the ministers must live out Christ's dying life in the world in order that those to whom they minister may live. Thus we revert to that great pattern in its most profound form: Christ has died and lived again that we may live. Christ's ministers must therefore likewise die daily and live out the life of suffering and dying in this world, that life may work in the Corinthians (the RSV translation is good here: 'death is at work in us, but life in you'). But this is no substitutionary activity on the part of the ministry, it is rather vicarious. They die that the Corinthians may live, but also that the Corinthians may in their turn die. Verse 14 hints of this death, with its implication that the Corinthians also will be raised from death by God. The ministry then leads the way in dying; but they do not obviate the necessity for the Corinthians' death. Verse 14 gives us the sequence of events with exceptional clarity:

Knowing that he which raised up the Lord Jesus shall raise up us also with Jesus, and shall present us with you.

It is impossible to say whether Paul is thinking of this life, in which we are raised from spiritual death, or of the life to come, when we are raised from physical death. Probably he did not distinguish, and nor should we. The movement goes from Christ to the ministry to the Church, and v. 15 (like I Cor. 3.21) shows that the ultimate end is the salvation of the Church. We observe how the same thought is implicit here as elsewhere in this magnificent exposition of the work of the ministry: the ministry does not really do anything that the rest of the Church cannot do or must not do. But it is a pioneer as Christ was a pioneer (see Heb. 6.20, πρόδρομος). It does not carry out Christ's work instead of the Church; it rather enables the Church to carry out that work in its (the Church's) own life. The last clause of v. 15 reminds us that even the salvation of the Church is not the final objective: greater than all is the glory of God. The RSV translation is much clearer:

> . . . so that as grace extends to more and more people it may increase thanksgiving, to the glory of God.

There is no specific mention here of the Eucharist, but here surely is where we may find the materials for a true theology of the Eucharist. Verse 14 tells us that God will present us (presumably to himself) to-together with Christ. Here is the thought of the divine love coming down in Christ and laying hold of us so that we are led up to his presence, an action reproduced and represented in the Church's central act of worship, the Eucharist (see εὐχαριστίαν in v. 15). What we offer is our thanksgiving, and the end is the true end of all worship, the glory of God.

The quotation in v. 13 is full of significance. Paul quotes Ps. 116.10 (115.1 in LXX). The LXX is: ᾿Επίστευσα διὸ ἐλάλησα. Paul must be quoting from the LXX, because the Hebrew version is different.[1] The RSV renders it correctly:

> I kept my faith, even when I said,
> 'I am greatly afflicted.'

The relevance of the quotation is not immediately obvious. Is Paul simply applying to himself the predicament of the Psalmist? This is not very like his usual practice, which is to find references to Christ or to the Church in the Psalms, not to himself individually. Besides he is here speaking on behalf of the ministry as a whole. It is therefore well worth considering R. P. C. Hanson's suggestion that Paul imagines Christ as speaking

---

[1] MT: אמן הֶאֱמַנְתִּי כִּי אֲדַבֵּר אֲנִי עָנִיתִי מְאֹד׃ in Hiph'il has the sense of 'stand firm'. The LXX has missed the special sense of the Hiph'il, and has taken כִּי as 'therefore' instead of 'even though'.

here. When we look at the psalm as a whole we find it to be extraordinarily appropriate to Christ; and we must remember how ready all New Testament writers were, especially Paul and the writer to the Hebrews, to see utterances of the Messiah in the Psalms. Below we reproduce the Psalm as it is in the LXX with a translation of the LXX version following. We must remember that in the LXX (and probably this means in Paul's LXX) Ps. 115. 10–19 in the Hebrew is written as a separate Psalm, 115 in the Greek. This would tend to concentrate its significance in Paul's mind.

'Επίστευσα διὸ ἐλάλησα·
ἐγὼ δὲ ἐταπεινώθην σφόδρα.
ἐγὼ εἶπα ἐν τῇ ἐκστάσει μου,
πᾶς ἄνθρωπος ψεύστης.
τί ἀνταποδώσω τῷ Κυρίῳ
περὶ πάντων ὧν ἀνταπέδωκέν μοι;
ποτήριον σωτηρίου λήμψομαι
καὶ τὸ ὄνομα Κυρίου ἐπικαλέσομαι.
τίμιος ἐναντιόν Κυρίου
ὁ θάνατος τῶν ὁσίων αὐτοῦ.
ὦ Κύριε, ἐγὼ δοῦλος σός,
ἐγὼ δοῦλος σὸς καὶ υἱὸς τῆς παιδίσκης σου.
διέρρηξας τοὺς δεσμούς μου,
σοὶ θύσω θυσίαν αἰνέσεως·
τὰς εὐχάς μου τῷ Κυρίῳ ἀνταποδώσω
ἐναντίον παντὸς τοῦ λαοῦ αὐτοῦ
ἐν αὐλαῖς οἴκου Κυρίου,
ἐν μέσῳ σου, 'Ιερουσαλήμ.

I believed, therefore did I speak:
  but I was greatly humbled.
I said in my excitement:
  'Every man is a liar.'
What shall I repay unto the Lord
  in return for all he has rewarded me?
I will take the cup of salvation
  and I will call upon the name of the Lord.
Valuable before the Lord
  is the death of his holy ones.
O Lord, I am thy servant,
  thy servant and the son of thy handmaid.
Thou hast broken my bonds asunder.
  I will sacrifice to thee the sacrifice of thanksgiving.
I will repay my vows to the Lord
  before all his people,
In the courts of the house of the Lord,
  in the midst of thee, Jerusalem.

Paul says about this quotation, 'Having the same spirit of faith . . . we also believe.' The same spirit as who? It is not likely that Paul meant 'the same spirit as David', to whom the details of the psalm do not apply. It is far more probable that he meant 'the same spirit of faith as Christ, who is speaking in this psalm'. Indeed the phraseology of the psalm fits remarkably well the circumstances of our Lord's life, death, and resurrection. 'I was greatly humbled' reminds us of Phil. 2.8 ἐταπείνωσεν ἑαυτόν. The 'cup of salvation' brings to mind the cup which he had to drink: Mark 10.38; 14.36. It was the cup of death, but it proved to be the cup of salvation. The words 'Valuable before the Lord is the death of his holy ones' suggest the atoning efficacy of our Lord's death, or would to Paul. In Acts 2.27 τὸν Ὅσιόν is quoted from Ps. 16 as referring to Christ. The word δοῦλος in 'I am thy servant' reminds us of Mark 10.45, and behind that lies the thought of the Servant of the Lord in Second Isaiah. In 'the son of thy handmaid' we have perhaps a reminder of Luke 1.38 and Gal. 4.4. Again the words 'Thou hast broken my bonds asunder' could well be taken as referring to the resurrection of Christ, cf. Acts 2.24. The final verses about praising God in the midst of his people can be paralleled in Rom. 15.9, where Christ is represented as praising God from the midst of the Gentile church in the words of Ps. 18.49. It is quite true, of course, that the words of Ps. 116 would also to some extent fit Paul's case, especially the recent deliverance from death (cf. II Cor. 1.10), but there is no reason why both meanings should not apply. At the same time, we need another term to the comparison: Paul has the same spirit of faith—as who? Indeed the psalm illustrates well that pattern which we find to be part of the very texture of this great series of chapters in II Corinthians. The psalm illustrates first and foremost the sufferings and triumphant resurrection of the Messiah. This pattern is reproduced in the life of Paul and of his fellow-ministers. It is the pattern for the ministry. But it must also be reproduced in the life of the Church. It is significant that the psalm ends with the redeemed giving thanks to God in the midst of God's people, and in II Cor. 4.15 Paul gives a picture of the growing Church giving thanks to God.

What they give thanks for is their redemption in Christ. If the argument of the last few pages is valid, Paul is here speaking of God's act of redemption in Christ and its perpetuation in the Church. Hence we must be on our guard against that subjectivity which modern scholars so often import into Paul's theology in II Corinthians. Menzies, for instance, finds a difficulty in v. 15: Paul in v. 11 has been imagining his death taking place; in v. 15 he is expecting the Corinthians to give thanks for his deliverance.

How is this? In fact, Paul was not so much of an egoist: his death in v. 11 is the dying life of the ministry first outlined in I Cor. 4.8–14. And the deliverance for which they give thanks in v. 15 is the deliverance from the dominion of death and sin for which all Christians are always bound to give thanks. In the same way Strachan suggests that what the Corinthians give thanks for in v. 15 is Paul's own experience of grace abounding. But Paul does not ask his readers to accept his own experience at second hand. He points them not to any subjective experience, but to the objective fact of their redemption in Christ.

The next section, 4.16–5.10, has no direct relevance to the doctrine of the ministry, but it does to some extent reproduce the pattern which we have observed. In vv. 16 f. Paul begins by speaking of the ministry: 'we faint not' and 'our light affliction' must refer to the labours and perils of the Christian ministry. But by 5.5 he is using language applicable to all Christians, since all Christians have 'the earnest of the Spirit'; and 5.10, with its reference to 'we all must be made manifest' explicitly concerns all the members of the Church.[1] The section that follows, which we may conveniently distinguish as 5.11–15, brings out the pattern even more clearly. We have already suggested that vv. 11 f. apply to Paul and his fellow-workers.[2] Verse 13 refers to the charge of mental derangement that his opponents had apparently made against Paul:

> For whether we are beside ourselves, it is unto God; or whether we are of sober mind, it is unto you.

We must however remember that the reputation and success of Paul's assistants, such as Timothy, Silas and Titus, was bound up with that of Paul. A charge of mental derangement, or of not possessing true apostleship, would damage the ministry of the others as much as it would Paul's. At least in 5.14 f. Paul goes on to set forth a principle which is absolutely fundamental for the relation of the ministry to the Church:

> For the love of Christ constraineth us; because we thus judge, that one died for all, therefore all died; and he died for all, that they which live should no longer live unto themselves, but unto him who for their sakes died and rose again.

Paul says this in order to explain why he is 'of sober mind unto' the Corinthians. The RSV translates the last phrase in v. 13 'for you', and the sense must be 'for your sakes'. Paul exercises his ministry among the Corinthians because Christ died for all. It would be absurd to treat this as an idiosyncrasy of Paul's. He is giving the *raison d'être* of the ministry.

---

[1] See p. 50, above.   [2] See p. 50. above,

The ministry is founded on the redeeming act of Christ, and its task is to carry out in the Church that task of mutual caring and redemption which its very being involves. We cannot fail to notice how important here is the objective fact of Christ's death. Here is no falling back on personal experience alone, but a going forward from the act of God in Christ in order to expound its implications for the work of the ministry.

As far as the doctrine of the ministry is concerned, 5.16–6.2 is the last important passage in this Epistle. In it Paul connects the work of the ministry with the work of God in Christ perhaps more explicitly than anywhere else. The passage may be divided into two parts: in the first part, 5.16–19, ἡμεῖς, 'we', should be taken throughout as referring to all Christians, not only to the ministry, still less to Paul alone. Paul is describing the difference which being ἐν Χριστῷ makes; this cannot be limited to the ministry. Such an interpretation needs perhaps some defence, especially in vv. 18 f. In v. 19 'the world' is the object of καταλλάσσων, and we must take ἦν καταλλάσσων together: God was reconciling the world to himself in Christ. In v. 18, ἡμᾶς, 'us', is the object of καταλλάξαντος, the aorist active participle. Here the reconciling process is regarded as successfully accomplished. The question arises: is ἡμᾶς here Paul and his fellow-ministers only, or is it all Christians? If we accept the first alternative, then all other Christians are relegated to the same category as 'the world' and αὐτοῖς ('not reckoning unto *them*') in v. 19, the category of those whom God is seeking to reach in Christ and concerning whom the reconciliation on God's part is complete, but who have not yet accepted it themselves. (Verses 20 f. we shall be considering below.) This first alternative explanation is accepted by Menzies and Strachan, both of whom adopt the interpretation that Paul is thinking of himself exclusively here, not even of his fellow-ministers as well. Strachan says: 'Nowhere else than in this Reconciliation passage does Paul make it more evident that his own conversion experience is the real origin of his thinking.' This drawing of a line between himself and his Corinthian converts is more typical of the gospel-hall evangelist than of the apostle of the Gentiles. Another passage in Paul's writings, Rom. 5.8–11, tells strongly against this interpretation. There Paul, speaking of all Christians, not only of himself and his helpers, says:

> But God commendeth his own love towards us, in that, while we were yet sinners, Christ died for us. Much more then, being now justified by his blood, shall we be saved from the wrath *of God* through him. For if while we were enemies, we were reconciled to God through the death of his Son, much more, being reconciled, shall we be saved by his life.

PAUL'S DOCTRINE OF THE MINISTRY: II CORINTHIANS 81

The Greek word for 'reconcile' in this passage is καταλλάσσω, the same as Paul uses in II Cor. 5.18 f. In the Romans passage he distinguishes between all mankind, who have been reconciled as far as God is concerned but who are not yet on the road to salvation, and Christians, who have accepted that salvation and are now in process of growth in the life of Christ.

We must therefore fall back on the second alternative interpretation of vv. 18 f., i.e. that in these two verses Paul is referring to all Christians. In that case δόντος ἡμῖν τὴν διακονίαν τῆς καταλλαγῆς ('gave unto us the ministry of reconciliation') and θέμενος ἐν ἡμῖν τὸν λόγον τῆς καταλλαγῆς ('having committed unto us the word of reconciliation') will also apply to all Christians. This is by no means a startling conclusion: the ministry of reconciliation is the Church's ministry and the world of reconciliation also belongs to the Church. This does not imply that there is no place for the ministry of apostles, presbyters etc.; on the contrary, as we have seen, it is the prime task of the ordained ministry to help the Church to carry out its own ministry, a task which the Church could not carry out without the mediation of the ordained ministry. It seems to follow from this that the giving of the ministry of reconciliation and the committing of the word of reconciliation took place at the same time as the act of reconciliation in Christ. In v. 18 the words καταλλάξαντος καὶ δόντος do not suggest any time interval between the action of the two verbs. In v. 19 the time sequence is slightly different: καταλλάσσων ... μὴ λογιζόμενος ... θέμενος. The first two are present tenses and the third is aorist middle.[1] But it is difficult to see what the significance of the aorist can be: God was reconciling, not reckoning sins, and having committed the word of reconciliation. To what event in the past can the aorist refer? Only, it seems, to the same event as δόντος ἡμῖν in v. 18. After all, the giving of the ministry of reconciliation and the committing of the word of reconciliation must be two descriptions of the same event. So we are led to the conclusion that God has reconciled all men to himself in the life, death and resurrection of Jesus Christ, as far as his own side of the matter is concerned, and whenever any man becomes a Christian, to him is committed the ministry of the word of reconciliation.

In the second part of this section, 5.20–6.2, the first person plural is

[1] It is doubtful whether the present participle τιθέμενος was in use in the Koine. There is no instance of it in the New Testament, and I have been unable to find any in Moulton and Milligan or Grimm-Thayer. J. H. Moulton in his Grammar of New Testament Greek, Vol. II, Edinburgh, 1929, p. 213, gives θέμενος as the only middle participle. On the other hand, A. T. Robertson and W. H. Davies, A New Short Grammar of the Greek Testament, New York and London, p. 124, 1931, give τιθέμενος as the present middle participle, but give no examples.

F

sometimes used for the ministry and sometimes for all Christians. 'We are ambassadors on behalf of Christ' must refer primarily to the ministry, since the words 'We beseech you on behalf of Christ, Be reconciled with God' define their ministry towards the Church. But in the next verse we find that the first person plural has extended its meaning:

> Him who knew no sin he made to be sin on our behalf; that we might become the righteousness of God in him.

This must refer to all Christians. The truth is that this rapid shifting of meaning of that word 'we' is indicative of that great principle of representation or identification which is at the root of Paul's thought here. God in Christ identified himself with mankind that he might win mankind to himself. Christ's ministers in the same way identify themselves with Christ's life, taking on themselves his suffering and sin-bearing, becoming in a sense *alteri Christi*. But this is not done in an exclusive sense: they only do so in order to induce the Church as a whole to do likewise, and thus reach out to the whole world and extend to it that salvation which God has already wrought for them in Christ.

We can now understand how it is that in v. 18 Paul can say that God has reconciled us all, and yet in v. 20 can say: 'Be reconciled to God.' It is the great principle of Christian ethics: be what you are. God has reconciled the world to himself; in a still more effective sense he has reconciled Christians to himself. Christians must live up to this and show their reconciliation in their lives. The words in 6.1 agree with this: 'We intreat also that ye receive not the grace of God in vain.' Paul is not saying: 'You have not been reconciled and therefore have not received the grace of God.' It is rather that by becoming Christians they have received the free gift (grace) of God. Paul is now exhorting them that they should not, by living unreconciled lives, prove to have received the grace of God in vain.

Paul drives home his point by a quotation from Isa. 49.8. The quotation in its context is as follows (49.7-9a):

> Thus saith the Lord,
>> the redeemer of Israel and his Holy One,
> to him whom man despiseth,
> to him whom the nation abhorreth,
> to a servant of rulers:
> Kings shall see and arise,
>> princes, and they shall worship;
> because of the Lord that is faithful,
>> even the Holy One of Israel, who hath chosen thee.

Thus saith the Lord,
In an acceptable time have I answered thee,
    and in a day of salvation have I helped thee;
and I will preserve thee,
    and give thee for a covenant of the people,
to raise up the land,
    to make them inherit the desolate heritages;
saying to them that are bound, Go forth;
    to them that are in darkness, Shew yourselves.

It is extremely likely that Hodge and R. P. C. Hanson are right in think-ing that Paul looked on this as a passage addressed by God to the Messiah. We note the phrase 'servant of rulers'.[1] The words 'him whom man des-piseth' would also fit the incarnate Messiah well. So would the reference to 'a covenant of the people' and to the function of the Servant as a bringer of light. If this is how Paul takes this passage, then he imagines God as addressing Christ at the time of his resurrection and ascension. This is the divine promise of salvation now fulfilled in Christ. But Paul unhesitatingly applies it to the Church also: God has in Christ offered the world his salvation. That offer is now available. How long it will be before the Parousia we do not know, so now is the time to take advantage of it.[2]

This quotation therefore serves further to link together the time of salvation and the time of the appointment of the ministry of reconciliation. It seems very likely that RV and RSV are right in translating συνερ-γοῦντες in 6.1 as 'working together with him', i.e. with God. Compare I Cor. 3.9: 'For we are God's fellow-workers' (συνεργοί). We might para-phrase the whole passage 5.16–6.2 thus: 'God has reconciled us all in Christ and given to us all a ministry of reconciliation. So we, who are aware of this, entreat you (who are not sufficiently aware of it) to accept this reconciliation. God has identified himself with us in Christ, not standing on his dignity, and this has identified us with Christ: we are his righteousness. So we ministers, carrying on God's work, entreat you not to ignore what you are. Christ has been made the redeeming agency

---

[1] The Hebrew is עֶבֶד, though the best texts of the LXX give ὑπὸ τῶν ἐθνῶν τῶν δούλων τῶν ἀρχόντων. But this may very well be a deliberate alteration on the part of the LXX translators.

[2] We have argued (pp. 76 f., above) that Paul thought of Ps. 116.10 as addressed by Christ to God; cf. Rom. 15.3–9, It is just possible that Paul thought of Ps. 44.22 as addressed by Christ to God in Rom. 8.36. This (II Cor. 6.2) would be the only example of an Old Testament quotation interpreted by Paul as addressed by God to Christ, but there does not seem to be any reason why he should not so interpret it. There are several examples in Hebrews; see Heb. 1.5 (Ps. 2.7); 1.8 (Ps. 45.6 f.); 1.10 (Ps. 102. 25–27); 1.13 (Ps. 110.1); 5.5 f. (Ps. 2.7 and 110.4). The latter is also quoted in Heb. 7.17, 21.

through his own death and resurrection. You are such a redeemed and redeeming agency in him.'

So we conclude that there is no distinction in this passage between the acceptance by Christians of God's reconciliation and the committing of the ministry of reconciliation to them by God. It is the Church that has this reconciling function, but that function comes to the Church from Christ through the ministry. Here if anywhere is the pioneer nature of the ministry made clear. Because God reconciled the world in Christ, Paul and his fellow-ministers entreat all men to accept that reconciliation. Their aim is to see that the ministry of reconciliation which has been entrusted to the Church takes its full effect. It is most impressive to see how in 6.2 Paul can take an Old Testament quotation which he believes was addressed by God to Christ and apply it to the Church directly. It shows that the transition from Christ to the Church is at the very heart of the doctrine of the ministry in Paul's thought, and that doctrine is bound up with the self-identification of God with mankind through the Incarnation. Thus Paul's doctrine of the ministry leads us into the very centre of the Christian faith.

II Cor. 6.3–10 contain another of these vivid descriptions of the Christian ministry which remind us so much of what the Christian life should be. It can hardly be doubted that Paul is referring to all his fellow-workers here, not solely to himself. He might refer to himself as 'we' but he would hardly describe himself as 'ministers of Christ'. Were he referring solely to himself he would have to use the singular here. Once more we observe the theme of life and death; he says in v. 9:

> As dying, and behold we live;
> as chastened, and not killed.

This does not merely mean that the ministers of Christ look as if they were going to die but somehow manage to survive. It means that they die daily and thereby receive the life of Christ. In this verse Paul is quoting Ps. 118.17 f. In the LXX (where it is Ps. 117.17 f.) it runs thus:

> οὐκ ἀποθανοῦμαι, ἀλλὰ ζήσομαι
> καὶ ἐκδιηγήσομαι τὰ ἔργα Κυρίου.
> παιδεύων ἐπαίδευσέν με ὁ Κύριος
> καὶ τῷ θανάτῳ οὐ παρέδωκέν με.[1]

This is a psalm of triumph over enemies; the writer has been rescued from death. It was certainly regarded as a Messianic psalm in the early Church,

---

[1] I shall not die, but live,
And declare the works of the Lord.
The Lord hath chastened me sore;
But he hath not given me over unto death.

for two other passages from it are directly applied to Christ in the New Testament. Verses 22 f. run thus:

> The stone which the builders rejected
> is become the head of the corner.
> This is the Lord's doing;
> it is marvellous in our eyes.

This is cited in Matt. 21.42; Mark 12.10–11; Luke 20.17; Acts 4.11; Eph. 2.20; I Peter 2.4–7. The other passage cited in the New Testament is v. 26:

> Blessed is he that cometh in the name of the Lord.

This is the crowd's greeting to our Lord in Mark 11.9, and the parallels in Matt. 21.9, cf. Luke 13.35, and is used by our Lord of himself in Matt. 23.39. Besides this, v. 24 seems very appropriate to II Cor. 6.2:

> This is the day which the Lord hath made;
> We will rejoice and be glad in it.

We may therefore suggest that in II Cor. 6.9 Paul is applying to the life of the ministry words which he believed were originally uttered by the Messiah to God the Father at or after (or at least concerning) the resurrection and the exaltation of the Messiah. Once again Paul is applying to the life of the ministry words which were first used of the Messiah. We cannot doubt that he desires these words to be proved true also in the experience of the Church as a whole.

After this study of the Corinthian Epistles we should be in a position to state Paul's doctrine of the ministry fairly clearly and succinctly. The ministry is appointed by Christ in order to carry out Christ's work in the Church, and thereby to induce the Church also to carry out that same work. It is responsible to Christ and it has authority in the Church, but it cannot accurately be described as ruling over the Church, since its main aim is to serve the Church. If we ask, what are its specific tasks, we must answer: first and foremost, to preach the gospel. But this preaching the gospel is not limited to speaking alone; the ministry must preach the gospel by living the life of Christ in the world. We could almost say: the ministry must *be* the gospel. At least it must represent Christ to the world, but primarily to the Church, so that the Church may represent Christ to the world. The administration of the Sacraments nowhere comes within the orbit of Paul's thought when he is speaking of the ministry. He seems to leave that to the local church.[1] But we must remember that his aim was

[1] Cf. I Cor. 1.17.

that the local church should itself exercise the apostolic ministry of the
Church, so we cannot say that the administration of the Sacraments has
nothing to do with the ministry. It is part of the Church's own ministry,
and we must give it rather more attention in the next chapter.

If it be asked, how was the ministry appointed according to Paul, we can
only reply that the ministry is apostolic, and the apostle is one of the
Remnant called into being, or rather recreated, by the coming of the Messiah. The title deeds of Paul and his fellow-workers when they came to any
hitherto unevangelized area did not consist in the fact that they had been
appointed by Peter or James or John, but that they were the apostolic
Remnant come to preach the good news in that area and to found a
church, being themselves the nucleus of that new church. When Paul
and Silas and Timothy first found themselves in Corinth on their missionary tour, they were the church in Corinth. They were apostles because
they had come from the church in Palestine in order to preach the good
news of the Messiah. They were sent by the Messiah himself, and Paul
never suggests that he or his companions were sent by anyone else. But
they were not independent individuals operating without reference to the
rest of the Church. They had been sent from the church in Antioch to be
the apostolic Remnant in (among other places) Corinth. Hence apostles
are always apostles of Jesus Christ, for they are his faithful Remnant.
But even when the church is founded in the new area they still have a
mission: they have to be the faithful Remnant within the church itself.
Their task is only completed when the church has raised up its own
ministry, its own band of apostles to spread the good news in new areas
and to be the pioneers in living the life of Christ in their midst.

Now if this is a fair account of Paul's doctrine of the ministry, can we
not say that it fits in very well both with the Old Testament conception of
the Remnant and with Paul's own doctrine of the Remnant as we have
traced it in chapter three? In the Old Testament we find the conception
of the band of faithful Jews who will remain steadfast in the coming tri-
bulation and survive to recognize and witness to the fulfilment of God's
prophecies concerning what he would do in the last days. In the second
half of the Book of Isaiah, which proved so vitally important in the
thought of Jesus and therefore of the early Church also, that Remnant is
closely associated with, even in some sense identified with, the Servant
of the Lord who is to redeem Israel and the world by his voluntarily
accepted sufferings. The Remnant are to be God's witnesses because he
is God's witness. Then in the New Testament we find the group of
apostles, with at least a nucleus of Twelve, who, despite temporary lack

of faith, have proved faithful to the Messiah after his resurrection, and who look upon themselves primarily, it seems, as witnesses to what God has done in the Messiah—and their witness is invariably confirmed by appeal to the fulfilment of prophecy. In Paul's writings also we find implicit the assertion that God has now called the Gentiles into his Church by the witnessing ministry of the faithful Remnant of Jews, the apostles. Finally we find this same apostolic ministry as it is exhibited in Corinth profoundly expounded by Paul in his Corinthian Epistles. It is doing in Corinth precisely what the apostles were intended to do: it is being the faithful Remnant, it is witnessing to God's acts in the Messiah in fulfilment of Scripture. It is striving to live out the life of the Messiah and to identify itself with him.

The conclusion seems clear that, in Paul's thought at any rate, the ministry is the pioneer Church. The apostles had their apostolic mission not because they were to be rulers of a Church that did not yet exist, but because they were themselves the nucleus of that Church. And when their apostolic activity is exercised in any new area, their authority still stems from the same source. They are apostles because they are the Church, the nucleus of the Church in that area. This account of the origin and significance of the ministry in the New Testament does at least do what many accounts have failed to do in the past, it does give a theological basis for the ministry. So much attention has in the past been focused on the actual means by which the authority of the ministry originated and was transmitted, that surprisingly little attention has been given to the question; why did our Lord appoint a ministry? Scholars have been content to prove to their own satisfaction that the sort of ministry which they seek to defend can be traced back to our Lord's appointment, and to leave it at that. Or else they have been content to prove that our Lord never intended to appoint any ministry and that it was a later expedient invented by the Church. Neither solution answers the fundamental question: what is the theology of the ministry in relation to the life, death, and resurrection of the Messiah? Today, when we are increasingly discovering that doctrines and practices in the New Testament formerly suspected of being importations from Hellenistic thought and practice have in fact Hebraic roots, it is surely appropriate that the ministry also should prove to have its roots in the Old Testament.[1] But this is only because it is so closely connected with the Church.

---

[1] It is undoubtedly this connection with the Jewish concept of *shaliach* that forms part of the attraction of the *shaliach* theory for many today. But quite apart from its historical difficulties, the *shaliach* concept belongs to rabbinic Judaism only. I do not know that anyone claims to have traced it in the Old Testament.

This is in itself another advantage which the doctrine of the ministry outlined above possesses: it does connect the ministry with the very being of the Church. One of the greatest difficulties about the 'catholic' doctrine of the ministry is that it could apparently in theory continue functioning without any Church at all. This has been brought home to us in the Church of South India very clearly in the course of the exchanges between our Theological Commission and the various authorities of the Church of England. We have more than once been asked whether we accepted the Lambeth Quadrilateral. Our theologians certainly have no difficulty in accepting the Scriptures, the gospel Sacraments, the catholic Creeds, and the historic episcopate as the basis for the life of the Church, but they have made the criticism that this famous statement of fundamentals has apparently no reference at all to the laity and the actual life of the Church. Bible, Creeds, Sacraments, and Ministry could, as far as the Lambeth Quadrilateral is concerned, be preserved and perpetuated by clergy alone. Defenders of the 'catholic' theory of the ministry frequently protest that according to them the ministry is not to be separated from the Church, it must operate in the Church, it represents the Church. But it is difficult to see in what way the existence of the laity is essential to their theory: according to that theory the ministry is not subordinate to the Church in doctrine and discipline, it does not derive its authority from the Church, it is not responsible to the Church. The Church depends on it for its very being and continuance. The ministry on the other hand could perpetuate itself without any reference to the Church at all. This is not in the least like the picture of the ministry which St Paul gives us in his Corinthian Epistles. There the ministry begins by being the Church, goes on to pioneer the life of Christ in the Church, and ends by helping the Church to carry out its apostolic function by itself, though never by dispensing with the ministry. The relation between ministry and Church in Paul is absolutely fundamental: one passes over into the other.

7

Apostolate and Ministry

WE HAVE now traced the missionary function of the Remnant in the Old
Testament, and examined the place of the Remnant in the New Testament,
especially in Paul. We have tried to outline Paul's doctrine of the ministry,
and have seen that the ministry derives its authority from the fact that it is
the apostolic nucleus of the Church. We have identified the faithful Remnant in the time of the Messiah with the apostles, and we have claimed
that the task of the apostles passes over *via* the ministry to the Church.
But one question yet remains to be answered: what does Paul himself
believe about the apostolate? If our argument hitherto is right, Paul ought
to have a rather fluid or dynamic doctrine of the apostolate; we would
expect him, starting from the original apostles, to see the apostolic task
and the apostolic body as something that widens out in the course of its
passing over into the Church. I believe that this is in fact what we find;
but we must first meet the arguments of those who take a more static view
of the apostolate. We shall also find that what Paul, and others, say about
diakonia throws light upon our subject.

Naturally all those who believe that the twelve apostles handed on their
authority as rulers of the Church to the first bishops, and that this authority has descended by succession to the historic episcopate of today, will
tend to emphasize the uniqueness of the original Twelve, and will represent the number of the apostles as definitely limited.[1] Indeed the difficulty involved in limiting the title 'apostle' to any definite number of
persons known to us in the New Testament is apparent from *The Apostolic
Ministry*, as its critics have been quick to point out. Beyond the Twelve
(inclusive of Matthias), Paul must be allowed the title. It is extremely
difficult to deny it to Barnabas, and the authors of *The Apostolic Ministry*
to concede it to him.[2] But if Barnabas was an apostle, was not Silvanus

---

[1] I use the phrase 'historic episcopate' for those bishops who claim descent by laying
on of hands by bishops from the second century at least. This would (for example) include the episcopate of the Swedish Lutheran Church and the Church of South India, but
exclude that of the Danish Lutheran Church or the American Methodist Church. I do
not necessarily assume that this claim can be proved valid.   [2] *Op. cit.*, pp. 120, 127.

also one, and what of Timothy, Titus, and Paul's other fellow-workers?
Then there is the question of James the brother of the Lord: Paul nowhere unequivocally describes him as an apostle (Gal. 1.19 and I Cor.
15.7 are ambiguous), but considering the important position he held in
the Jerusalem church, we must admit, either that he was an apostle, or
that the apostles did not have the final word in the Church. But if he was
an apostle, was he one of the Twelve? There is no definite evidence that
he was, though the authors of *The Apostolic Ministry* seem to assume that
he was.[1] It can hardly be maintained that Barnabas was one of the Twelve,
but if he was not, and yet was an apostle, then the range of the word
'apostle' is wider than the Twelve. The question is: how wide? Another
problem for those who hold the 'apostolic succession' theory is posed by
Andronicus and Junias of Rom. 16.7; we know absolutely nothing of them
from any other source, but Paul describes them not only as 'apostles' but
as 'distinguished among the apostles'.

For those who wish to preserve the title 'apostle' for an original ruling
body, the only way out of this difficulty is to introduce a distinction in the
use of the word in the New Testament. It is said that the word originally
denoted the Twelve, but that it came also to be used for men of lesser
authority, 'apostles of the churches' such as are referred to in Phil. 2.25
and II Cor. 8.23.[2] We shall be examining these passages later; for the
moment it is enough to remark that such an assumption about the use of
the word apostle might not have been made if the theory it is used to
defend had not been evolved first.

Very recently however a new representative of the theory of the original
ruling authority of the apostolic body has arisen in Switzerland (though
he would not, I think, accept the 'apostolic succession' theory as set forth
by the authors of *The Apostolic Ministry*). J. L. Leuba's book *New Testament Pattern* was translated into English and published in London in
1953.[3] He does not refer to *The Apostolic Ministry*, though he would
have found some of his arguments anticipated in it. Leuba draws a sharp
distinction between the institutional apostolate of the Twelve and what
he calls the spiritual apostolate of Paul himself;[4] in order to emphasize
this, he tries to restrict the name 'apostle' to as few individuals as possible.
He is even doubtful whether anyone except the original Twelve (plus
Matthias) and Paul could really be called apostles; he suggests that

---

[1] *Op. cit.*, p. 267; see also W. Knox, *Paul and the Church of Jerusalem*, Cambridge,
1925, p. 363, where he suggests that James the brother of the Lord was brought in to fill
the vacancy caused by the martyrdom of James the son of Zebedee.
[2] E.g. *The Apostolic Ministry*, p. 127.   [3] French original, 1950.
[4] *Op. cit.*, pp. 51 f.

ἐπίσημοι ἐν τοῖς ἀποστόλοις in Rom. 16.7 means 'well-known to the apostles', and even favours the traditional but unlikely theory that James the Lord's brother is identical with James the son of Alphaeus.[1] Throughout his book he contrasts the direct calling of Paul to the apostolate, and his claim to have received his apostolate not from man, with the institutional character of the apostolate of the Twelve, as if they constituted the sole source of authority for the Jewish church. For example on p. 104 he makes a great point of the fact that the church in Judaea had Jerusalem as its centre and new converts in Samaria were thought of as belonging to the Jerusalem church, and not to a church of their own in Samaria. But Gentile converts, he maintains, were not thought of as added to the Jerusalem church; they rather formed churches of their own, the church in Corinth, the church in Ephesus, etc. This seems rather artificial: Jerusalem was the natural centre of the old Jewish country as Rome was of Italy. We know so little about Jewish-Christian missionary activity apart from St Paul's work that we have no means of judging what would have happened if there had been Jewish-Christian churches anywhere outside Palestine. W. Manson has recently suggested that the Epistle to the Hebrews was written to a Jewish-Christian congregation in Rome before AD 70.[2] There is no evidence that such a congregation thought of itself as belonging to the Jerusalem church. Again W. Knox apparently accepts the hypothesis that Peter, during the unknown part of his career between Acts 12.17 and his eventual arrival in Rome, did missionary work in Bithynia.[3] If so, his letter does not suggest that he had enrolled his converts in the church of Jerusalem. The truth seems to be rather that any church anywhere was founded by an apostle, not necessarily one of the Twelve, but one who was an apostle because he was carrying out the apostolic task of being the faithful Remnant and preaching the gospel. And any new church is simply added to the one apostolic Church. The reason why we hear more of the original Twelve is that they were the original Church, the faithful Remnant from whom the rest of the Church must ultimately have taken its origin.

In the same way, Leuba draws a marked contrast between Paul's conception, expressed in I Cor. 12 and other passages, of a charismatic ministry on the one hand, and on the other the 'institutional' ministry of the apostles in Jerusalem. But this is to contrast what is known with what is unknown or only half known. We do not know what the apostles in Jerusalem believed about their ministry and that of the 'elders' with them. For all we know, they may have entirely agreed with Paul's doctrine as

[1] *Ibid.*, p. 59. [2] *The Epistle to the Hebrews*, London, 1951. [3] *Op. cit.*, p. 296.

set forth in I Cor. 12. When Paul says, in 12.28, 'He called some to be apostles', we have no reason to think that he was excluding the apostles in Jerusalem, though we shall see presently that he was certainly including others as well. In effect too much emphasis on the separateness of the Twelve (plus whoever it may suit this or that theorist to add to their number) leads to a dangerous dichotomy between the Jewish church on the one hand and the Gentile church on the other. Leuba is almost reminiscent of the Tübingen school of a hundred years ago in his insistence on the complete difference between Paul and the Twelve.

This is surprisingly apparent when he deals with the ὑπερλίαν ἀπόστολοι of II Cor. 11.5 and 12.11, 'the very chiefest apostles', as the RV rather inadequately translates it. Leuba identifies these men with the Twelve in Jerusalem,[1] and proceeds to describe the ψευδαπόστολοι ('false apostles') of II Cor. 11.13 as emissaries of the Jerusalem apostles.[2] Austin Farrer goes even further, and identifies the ὑπερλίαν ἀπόστολοι with one individual, one of the Twelve who was opposing Paul's teaching.[3] It is a remarkable fact that those who emphasize most strongly the sole authority of the Twelve and Paul as apostles seem driven to posit the most unpleasant relationships within the apostolic body. It is true that in Galatians Paul does use slightly disparaging language about James and Peter and John: 'they were reputed to be somewhat . . . they were reputed to be pillars' (Gal. 2.6–9). But this is a very different thing from the contemptuous phrase ὑπερλίαν ἀπόστολοι, 'those wonderful apostles of yours'. If we accept the interpretation of Farrer and Leuba, we must believe that James and Peter and John deliberately sent emissaries to the Corinthian church to undermine Paul's authority and accuse him of the most varied faults, from embezzling church funds to downright lunacy! Moreover we must assume that Paul responded by openly sneering at the apostles and describing their emissaries as pseudo-apostles, treacherous workers, and agents of Satan. If emphasis upon the sole authority of the Twelve leads to such very unpleasant conclusions about the way in which the princes of the Church, trustees of all authority and tradition, behaved towards each other, surely we are justified in examining the evidence again.[4]

Before doing so, we should perhaps look at the evidence from the Gospels brought forward by those who think of the Twelve as invested by

---

[1] *Op. cit.*, p. 79.   [2] *Ibid.*, p. 114.   [3] *The Apostolic Ministry*, p. 130.
[4] A minor objection to Leuba's thesis is that it posits a very keen awareness of the existence and authority of the Twelve on Paul's part, even though he may have claimed equal authority with them. But in fact Paul only specifically refers to οἱ δώδεκα once, in I Cor. 15.5, where he cites them as witnesses to the Resurrection.

our Lord with ruling authority over the church. L. S. Thornton[1] cites Luke 22.29 f. as evidence that our Lord gave the Twelve ruling power over the Church:

> And I appoint unto you a kingdom, even as my Father appointed unto me, that ye may eat and drink at my table in my kingdom; and ye shall sit on thrones judging the twelve tribes of Israel.

Thornton especially emphasizes the phrase 'ye shall sit on thrones judging the twelve tribes of Israel'. His explanation of the words 'that ye may eat and drink at my table in my kingdom' is that all regenerate Israel comes to the banquet, but that the Twelve are to represent Christ to the rest of the regenerate. The thrones, he thinks, indicate that they represent Christ and share in his ruling power. But this seems to be pressing the symbolism unnecessarily: if all the regenerate are to come to the feast, why should they need to be judged? We have seen from our study of the Old Testament and of the intertestamental literature that we never find the conception of some members of the faithful Remnant judging other members of it, but rather we find the picture of the faithful Remnant judging the unfaithful. It is much more natural to think of these three promises as belonging simply to the faithful Remnant: all the Remnant will inherit the kingdom, all the Remnant will sit at his table, and all will judge the unfaithful, the old Israel. Alan Richardson takes a similar view to Thornton's. He suggests that in Luke 22 we have Luke's account of the solemn ordination of the apostles. It should be noted that the Fourth Gospel does not support this view: a close study of John 17 must surely show that Our Lord is praying for his disciples as representing the whole Church, not just as representing the ministry. Professor Richardson cites Dan. 7.14–27 as precedents for the appointment of the apostles here, but, as we have seen (pp. 25 f. above), the author of Daniel certainly means to teach that the whole faithful Remnant, and not a part of it only, is appointed to rule. He argues that the two clauses of Luke 22.29 f. show that the apostles are first admitted to table fellowship and then thereby appointed to rule over the Church.[2] It seems much more natural to take the clauses as two sides of the same thing, first the blessing and then the judgement which membership of the Messianic kingdom carries with it. The true interpretation of passages such as this is much better expressed by Stig Hanson: 'The number of the Disciples is twelve. The number twelve definitely indicates how the Messianic circle is to be considered. The number twelve corresponds to the twelve tribes of Israel, . . . the

---

[1] *The Apostolic Ministry*, p. 104.
[2] *Introduction to the Theology of the New Testament*, London, 1958, pp. 315 f.

People of God. The circle of Disciples might be called the kernel of the New People. They are a *populus designatus*.'[1] Thornton quotes Acts 10.40–42 by way of confirming his assertion that there is a distinction between the Twelve and the rest of the regenerate: 'God . . . gave him to be manifest, not to all the people (λαός), but unto witnesses that were chosen before of God, even to us, who did eat and drink with him after he rose from the dead.' But here 'all the people' means 'all the Jews', i.e. unregenerate Israel. In Acts λαός almost invariably means the Jews as a nation, and could mean nothing else in a speech addressed to non-Christians, as here. Similarly Farrer claims that our Lord's reply to James and John in Mark 10.39 shows that they are to rule, however humbly.[2] But the question is, over whom? Thornton quotes Dan. 7.13 f. But this passage suggests rule over the unregenerate, not over the regenerate.[3] Indeed the only passage in the Gospels that would seem to suggest that there are to be earthly rulers over the faithful Remnant is Luke 12.42:

> Who then is the faithful and wise steward, whom his Lord shall set over his household, to give them their portion of food in due season?

Farrer thinks that this definitely applies to the ministry.[4] We naturally think of Paul's 'stewards of the mysteries of God' in I Cor. 4.1, where the same word is used, οἰκονόμος, though, as we have seen, it applies to Apollos as well as Paul. The passage in Luke must be from Q, as it also occurs in Matt. 24.42–51. But it is not at all easy to decide to whom exactly this piece of teaching is addressed. It seems to belong to the type of parable that includes the Parable of the Talents and the Parable of the Wise and Foolish Virgins. The main point seems to be: make the best use of what you have while there is time. To suggest therefore that our Lord intended it as teaching for the future rulers of the Church, rather than for the faithful Remnant as a whole, is perhaps to interpret it in the context of the first generation Church rather than of our Lord's own time. The impression therefore remains that the Twelve are not the rulers over the New Israel, but are themselves the nucleus of the New Israel.

When we look at the positive evidence for Paul's conception of the apostolate, we find several places where he seems to associate his fellow-workers with himself under the title 'apostles'. The first of these places is I Thess. 2.7: ' . . . when we might have been burdensome as apostles of Christ.' We have already argued (p. 48 above) that this passage must refer to a group because of the plural ἀπόστολοι. In that case Paul is speaking

---

[1] *The Unity of the Church in the New Testament*, p. 28.   [2] *Op. cit.*, p. 121.
[3] For a very similar conclusion on this point see W. H. Vanstone in *The Historic Episcopate*, pp. 34 f.   [4] *Loc. cit.*

of himself, Silvanus, and Timothy, in whose names the letter is written. It is a perfectly just description, for we know in fact that they were the first evangelists of Thessalonica. Farrer admits that Silvanus must be included among the apostles, but would except Timothy. On the basis of the salutation in II Corinthians and also in Colossians he argues that Timothy was not an apostle.[1] We shall be examining this evidence presently, but for the moment it seems reasonable to assume that Timothy is here included among the apostles. Farrer's reason for including Silvanus and excluding Timothy is not unconnected with his own theory of the apostolate.

We pass on to I Cor. 4.9. Here Paul says: 'For I think that God has set forth us the apostles last of all . . .' Only three verses previously he has said: 'Now these things, brethren, I have in a figure transferred to myself and Apollos,' and the sense of the whole passage seems to demand that 'apostles' in v. 9 includes Apollos as well as himself. It may even include Sosthenes as well, whom Paul associates with himself in writing the Epistle.[2] We have suggested above (pp. 48 f.) that another passage in this same Epistle (9.4–6) implicitly includes Barnabas among the apostles. As a matter of fact, most of the defenders of the exclusive theory of the apostolate would concede Barnabas a place in the apostolic body. The difficulty however remains: when did Barnabas receive his commission? The more special cases are conceded, the more difficult it becomes to maintain that an apostle must have a special commission and be a member of a limited ruling body. With these two passages from I Corinthians we can also put I Cor. 15.14 f. See especially v. 15:

And we are found false witnesses of God; because we witnessed of God that he raised up Christ. . . .

We maintain that Paul is including in this first person plural here all who first preached the gospel to the Corinthians. Paul speaks of them as witnesses of the resurrection. But, as we have seen, witnessing to the resurrection is the outstanding mark of the apostle.

In II Corinthians we can point first to 1.24. If we look at vv. 18 f. we see at once that the 'we' there refers to the first preachers of the gospel in Corinth, specifically named as Paul, Silvanus, and Timothy. Verse 22 cannot possibly refer to Paul alone because of the plural 'our hearts'. In v. 23 Paul drops into the singular to refer to himself, and then in v. 24 the plural certainly seems to indicate his two fellow-workers again: 'Not that we

---

[1] *Op. cit.*, p. 128.
[2] It does not matter much whether this Sosthenes is identical with the individual mentioned in Acts 18.17 or not—at least from the point of view of the argument.

have lordship over your faith.' It is a reference to the apostolic authority, even though Paul only refers to it in order to show its limits. And his fellow-workers are associated with him in this authority. Compare also II Cor. 10.8 and see above p. 49.

In II Cor. 8.23 we meet the obscure question of 'the apostles of the churches'. There certain brethren are described as ἀπόστολοι ἐκκλησιῶν, δόξα Χριστοῦ, 'apostles of the churches, the glory of Christ'. Both RV and RSV here translate ἀπόστολοι as 'messengers', but put 'apostles' in the margin. Most scholars assume that these 'apostles of the churches' are not at all to be ranked with the full apostolate.[1] They are merely representatives of their local churches. With this passage we should compare Phil. 2.25, where Epaphroditus is described as ὑμῶν δὲ ἀπόστολον καὶ λειτουργὸν τῆς χρείας μου, 'your apostle and the minister of my need'. We shall be considering the significance of the second epithet later, but it is sufficient to point out here that apparently both the 'brethren' of II Cor. 8.23 and Epaphroditus helped Paul in his pastoral and evangelistic work. That is to say that they took part in the work of the apostolate. This reinforces the impression that the difference between the regular apostles and the 'apostles of the churches' may not be as great as has often been suggested.

There is one other passage in II Corinthians which throws light on Paul's conception of the apostolate: 11.13–15. He is describing his opponents in Corinth and he says of them:

> For such men are false apostles, deceitful workers, fashioning themselves into apostles of Christ. And no marvel; for even Satan fashioneth himself into an angel of light. It is no great thing therefore if his ministers also fashion themselves as ministers of righteousness.

Notice who corresponds to whom here: the false apostles imitate the true apostles of Christ. These false apostles are further described as ministers of Satan and they imitate the ministers of righteousness. But the ministers of righteousness are already identified for us:[2] in 3.9 what is undoubtedly the ministry of Paul *and of his helpers* is described as the 'ministration of righteousness'. The conclusion seems unavoidable that the true apostles of Christ are Paul and his fellow-workers.

It is in the light of the above passages that we must approach the evidence of the salutations in Paul's Epistles. Many scholars have pointed out, for example, that Paul nowhere describes Timothy as an apostle,

---

[1] Hodge, Plummer, and of course the authors of *The Apostolic Ministry*.
[2] Naturally if chs. 10–13 were written before chs. 1–9, the word 'already' does not apply; but the argument still holds.

and actually seems to exclude him from the title in II Cor. 1.1 and Col. 1.1, both of which Epistles begin: 'Paul an apostle of Jesus Christ through the will of God, and Timothy our brother.' In much the same way Sosthenes seems to be excluded from the apostolate in I Cor. 1.1: 'Paul, called to be an apostle of Jesus Christ through the will of God, and Sosthenes our brother.' The authors of *The Apostolic Ministry*, who wish to exclude Timothy from the apostolate, use this as an argument in favour of their theory,[1] and W. Knox takes the same view.[2] Knox adds that II Cor. 8.23 excludes Titus also. But this conclusion depends upon accepting ἀπόστολοι ἐκκλησιῶν in the same verse in the sense of full apostleship. In that case it is impossible to exclude Epaphroditus in Phil. 2.25 from the full apostolate. In Phil. 2.25, however, Epaphroditus is also called συνεργός and συνστρατιώτης; but in II Cor. 8.23 Paul uses almost identical language of Titus (κοινωνὸς καὶ συνεργός); hence it can hardly be maintained that the brethren in II Cor. 8.23 are called apostles to distinguish them from the non-apostolic Titus. The fact is that in his salutations Paul never calls anyone an apostle except himself, and it really seems precarious in the extreme to build theories about the apostolate on the fact that others are not called apostles by Paul in his salutations. In certain Epistles Paul wanted to emphasize his own authority as apostle to the church which he was addressing. It was his apostolic authority that had been challenged. After all, in the salutation to the Philippians Paul does not call himself an apostle at all, because presumably his apostolic authority did not need vindicating to the Philippians.

The general impression one gains from Paul's references or allusions to the apostolate is that he was not very particular in his use of the word 'apostle'. He does not really give the impression that in his view the apostolate was confined to a certain body of people, who alone had authority in the church. He claims the title of apostle for himself, but does not seem to want to deny it to his fellow-workers. Naturally the Twelve are thought of as the original apostles, but this does not mean that no one but they (with the addition perhaps of one or two specially excepted individuals such as Paul himself) can rightly be called apostles. Perhaps we might say of the apostolate in Paul's writings what the authors of *The Apostolic Ministry* say of the episcopate in the New Testament: it is a function, not an office. The function derives from Christ through the original apostles, who were the faithful Remnant, and is passed on to men like Paul, Silvanus, Timothy, and Titus, who carry out the essentially apostolic function of preaching the gospel about the Messiah and living out the life of the

---

[1] *Op. cit.*, p. 128.   [2] *Paul and the Church of Jerusalem*, p. 364.

G

Messiah in the world. But the function is not confined even to Paul and his helpers. It belongs to anyone who carries out the apostolic work of the Church, and can be just as easily predicated of quite obscure people like Junias and Andronicus in Rom. 16.7.[1]

We have therefore found reason to believe that Paul thought of the apostolate as something which was not confined to a body or college, but was passed on from the original apostles to men such as himself and his fellow-workers, who were carrying out the apostolic mission of the faithful Remnant. When we come to examine his use of the word *diakonia* and cognates, we find that the apostolic task is taken a stage further: it passes over into the hands of the Church, what we today would call the laity. The word *diakonia* is normally translated 'ministry', but we must carefully distinguish this usage from the other meaning of ministry in English, i.e. the actual ministers. Their task and origin we have already examined in chapters five and six. We are now to estimate what Paul meant by the act of ministering, the service of the Lord. We cannot avoid also examining the usage of the two cognate words to *diakonia*; these are *diakonos*, 'servant', and *diakonein*, 'to serve'.

All these words seem to have been largely recreated by Christianity, much as *agape* was. They have very little pedigree in the LXX (the verb does not occur there at all). The noun *diakonia* in Paul has a double use: it is frequently used of the official Christian ministry, often by Paul of his own ministry, e.g. Rom. 11.13. It can also be used of a particular service, especially of Paul's great project of bringing financial aid to the Christians of Judaea from his Gentile converts, e.g. Rom. 15.31. But of course this *diakonia* was not confined to official ministers; it was shared by all Gentile Christians. We shall be estimating its significance a little later on. The widest sense is found in Eph. 4.12, where 'the work of the ministry' is defined as the building up of the body of Christ and is a task performed by 'the saints'. Exactly the same impression, of a narrower meaning and a wider meaning, is given by the use of *diakonia* in the rest of the New Testament; e.g. in Acts 1.17 it is actually used of the work of the apostolate (the Twelve); in Acts 11.29 of relief work in time of famine, and in Rev. 2.19 of the ministry of the whole church in Thyateira.

The verb *diakonein* is used in what we might call a deeply theological

---

[1] Farrer (*op. cit.*, p. 127) describes these two as 'inferior apostles'. The main reason for their inferiority seems to be that they do not fit into his scheme. He admits on p. 129 that they probably founded the church in Rome, no inferior achievement, surely! Professor Richardson (*op. cit.*, p. 320) strongly supports Farrer's view on this point, and does not even allow them apparently the credit of founding the church in Rome. He encounters the usual difficulty in explaining away the use of the word 'apostle' for anyone except the Twelve and Paul.

sense in the Gospels for the service which the Son of God has come to perform, e.g. in the great key text Mark 10.45. Compare also Luke 22.27: 'I am amongst you as he that serveth.' This is of course the root of all Christian ministry. In Matt. 25.44 the verb is used of general Christian service, especially the service of the sick and suffering. It is used sometimes in Paul's Epistles for the regular service of the ministry, e.g. Rom. 15.25, which also refers to the financial aid sent by the Gentile churches. In Philem. 13 we read that Onesimus was to minister to Paul 'in the bonds of the gospel', which makes it plain that this is Christian ministry.[1] Then there is a technical use in the Pastoral Epistles, 'to serve as a deacon', e.g. I Tim. 3.10.[2]

The noun *diakonos* is surprisingly rare in the LXX, and is never used to render any words designating the old Levitical ministry. In the Gospels we find the same 'incarnational usage' as we noticed in the case of the verb: e.g. Mark 10.43: 'Whosoever would become great among you, shall be your minister.' The parallel in the next verse is δοῦλος, 'slave'. There is an interesting reference in John 12.26: 'Where I am, there shall my *diakonos* be.' Plainly this refers to all faithful Christians. Every Christian is called in some sense to be a *diakonos*. Paul uses the word of himself and also (as we have seen) of his fellow-workers; see I Cor. 3.5; II Cor. 3.6; 11.23. In Col. 1.23 he describes himself simply as a *diakonos* of the gospel and two verses later as a *diakonos* of the Church. Epaphras in Col. 1.7 is described as 'a faithful *diakonos* on our behalf'.[3] This may refer to the fact that he first brought the gospel to Colossae. It is difficult to see in what way Epaphras as a *diakonos* in Colossae differs from Paul as an *apostolos* in Corinth, or Ephesus, or Thessalonica. In the same Epistle (4.7) Tychicus is called a faithful *diakonos*, which means that he has been helping Paul in his evangelistic work. Phil. 1.1 sets an interesting problem: the letter is addressed to 'all the saints in Christ Jesus which are at Philippi, with the *episkopoi* and *diakonoi*'. The *episkopoi* must be the local ministry, and they could certainly be described as *diakonoi* also. So *diakonos* must be used here in a general sense meaning 'other church workers'. It can hardly designate an order of deacons. We might paraphrase it: 'to the ordained ministry and the other workers'. This view is supported by Professor Richardson.[4] As we would expect, in the Pastoral Epistles the word means 'deacon' (e.g. I Tim. 3.8–12). But the author of the Pastorals

---

[1] Cf. also I Peter 4.11.
[2] Not 'be a deacon', as the 1940 edition of Liddell and Scott inaccurately renders it.
[3] But ὑμῶν has very impressive ms. support and is read by the latest Bible Society edition of the Greek Testament (ed. E. Nestle and G. D. Kilpatrick, London, 1958).
[4] *Op. cit.*, p. 333.

can use the word also in a more general sense, e.g. I Tim. 4.6. In Rom. 16.1 Phoebe is described as 'the *diakonos* of the church in Cenchreae'. Liddell and Scott (1940 edition) are misleading in translating this as 'deaconess'. 'Patroness' would be nearer the meaning.[1] In Rom. 13.4 Paul applies the word to (heathen) rulers as God's agents.

We may sum up all this by saying that in the New Testament *diakonia* and cognates are used generally of the Christian ministry, and if there is one word in the New Testament for the Christian minister it is *diakonos* rather than *presbuteros*. It could apply to apostles as much as to anyone else. The three words (*diakonos* only once—in John) are also applied to all Christians and to the service they are called to render to God. The words are used for special tasks as well, more particularly for the collection on behalf of the indigent Christians in Judaea. The verb and the noun *diakonos* are used in the Gospels to describe our Lord's work on earth. We have called this an 'incarnational' usage. Only in the Pastorals are the words used in a technical sense of separate orders within the Christian ministry. There is no sign whatever of any connection between these words and the sacrificial worship of the Old Testament. Thus we can claim that it is possible to trace in the use of these words in the New Testament the same pattern that we found in Paul's doctrine of the ordained ministry: *diakonia* passes from Christ to the ordained ministers and from them to the Church at large. We must now turn to some special examples of this.

We take first a group of passages where Paul apparently uses the language of sacrifice in order to describe his work. In II Cor. 2.14–16 he writes:

> But thanks be to God, which always leadeth us in triumph in Christ, and maketh manifest through us the savour of his knowledge in every place. For we are a sweet savour of Christ unto God, in them that are being saved, and in them that are perishing; to the one a savour from death unto death; to the other a savour from life unto life.

We notice first how the apostolic work of Paul and his friends is described as 'a sweet savour of Christ unto God'. 'Sweet savour' here is εὐωδία and ὀσμή is the word used for 'savour' in v. 14. In view of this we can hardly follow Plummer[2] when he says that there is probably no reference to sacrifice on the grounds that the phrase ὀσμὴ εὐωδίας as such does not occur here. The meaning seems to be that the preaching of the apostolic band is in a sense Christ's offering of himself to God. This is confirmed

---

[1] They have also omitted to notice the unusual usage in Rom. 15.8, where Christ is described as διάκονος . . . περιτομῆς. The sense seems to be 'one who brings a thing into action', 'makes it effective'.

[2] *II Corinthians* (ICC).

2.0500

by Eph. 5.2, where it is said of Christ that he 'gave himself up for us, an offering and a sacrifice to God for an odour of a sweet smell (εἰς ὀσμὴν εὐωδίας)'. This last phrase is the stock LXX translation of the Hebrew phrase *rēach nīchōach*. The original idea behind this phrase was that God was placated by the pleasant smell of the sacrifice (cf. Gen. 8.21), but in post-exilic times no doubt it was thought of as symbolizing the intention of him who offered the sacrifice. In Eph. 5.2 it seems to describe the result of the sacrifice: 'In thee I am well pleased.' Thus these two passages together show us the work of the ministry as being identified with the work of Christ.

Two passages in Philippians develop this idea further. In Phil. 2.17 Paul writes:

> Yea, and if I am offered upon the service and sacrifice of your faith, I joy, and rejoice with you all.

'Sacrifice' and 'service' are θυσία and λειτουργία. The word 'offered up' is literally 'poured out as a libation' (so RV margin). There is much dispute among editors as to who is thought of as offering the sacrifice here. On the analogy of Rom. 15.16 (which we discuss below), it seems likely that it is Paul who makes the offering: what he offers is the faith of the Philippians, whom he brought to Christ.[1] On the other hand, the end of their faith is that they should offer themselves. This is just what we find in the second passage in Philippians, 4.18. Here Paul describes the contribution of the Philippians as 'an odour of a sweet smell (ὀσμὴ εὐωδίας), a sacrifice (θυσία) acceptable, well-pleasing to God'. Thus the full pattern of the pioneer ministry is reproduced in these four passages (II Cor. 2.14–16; Eph. 5.2; Phil. 2.17; 4.18). The sacrifice of Christ is identified with the work of the ministry, the work of the ministry is to present the faith of the converts as a sacrifice to God. That faith produces as its fruit Christian service among the converts which is itself a sacrifice.

These four passages should help us with the interpretation of Rom. 15.16:

> That I should be a minister (λειτουργόν) of Christ Jesus unto the Gentiles, ministering (ἱερουργοῦντα) the gospel of God, that the offering (προσφορά) of the Gentiles might be made acceptable.

Thornton says 'the victims of the sacrifice are the Gentile churches' and adds that Paul himself offers them.[2] But this leaves the gospel out of the

---

[1] So Ellicott; Moule and Michael would make the Philippians the sacrificers; so also Lightfoot. The late T. W. Manson, in a posthumously published book, *Ministry and Priesthood, Christ's and Ours*, London, 1958, p. 49, agrees with the interpretation adopted here.   [2] *The Common Life in the Body of Christ*, p. 23.

picture. It seems more in accordance with Paul's thought to take it that Paul offers the sacrifice of the gospel. This is also, as we have seen, Christ's work, not that Paul offers Christ, rather that Christ offers his sacrifice in Paul. The purpose of Paul's evangelistic activity is that the offering made by the Gentiles (of themselves, their souls and bodies as described in Rom. 12.1 f.) may be well and truly made. Professor Richardson supports Fr Thornton's interpretation, and effectively quotes Col. 1.28, where there can be no doubt that Paul is expressing his aim of offering every man as a sacrifice in Christ.[1] But the other two passages which he quotes in defence of this interpretation are by no means clear: I Cor. 16.15 describes Stephanas and his house as 'the firstfruits of Achaia', but it is not clear that Paul is thinking of himself as offering them; they might be thought of as offering themselves. The other passage cited, Rev. 14.4, is definitely against Professor Richardson's interpretation; nothing whatever is said of who offered the 144,000 to God and to the Lamb. It is much more likely that they are thought of as having offered themselves. In view therefore of the difficulty of fitting the gospel into the other explanation of Rom. 15.16, we are justified in adhering to the interpretation suggested above.[2] This passage also, we may claim, exhibits the pattern of the pioneer ministry.[3]

A small confirmation of our presentation of the pioneer ministry in Paul's letters occurs in I Cor. 16.15 f. Paul refers to the household of Stephanas and describes them as having 'set themselves to minister unto the saints' (εἰς διακονίαν τοῖς ἁγίοις), and he goes on to exhort the Corinthians to be in subjection to all who labour (the verb is κοπιᾶν). It looks very much as if Stephanas and some of his household had been appointed presbyters by Paul in Corinth. This is the opinion of Ritschl (quoted by Edwards) and Goudge.[4] The verb κοπιᾶν is used of people in an official position in the church in I Thess. 5.12 f.; Gal. 4. 11; I Cor.

---

[1] *Op. cit.*, pp. 299 f.

[2] Professor Richardson's exact phrase for Paul's description of himself in Rom. 15.16 is 'an evangelizing priest-apostle, bringing his converts and laying them as an offering on God's altar'. This slightly blurs the fact that the object of the verb ἱερουργεῖν is the gospel, not the offering of the Gentiles or the Gentiles themselves. I have failed to find any passage earlier than, or contemporary with, Paul's time in which ἱερουργεῖν has a sacrifice as its direct object. Liddell and Scott quote one such example from Plutarch and one from Ammonius. The nearest parallel to Paul's usage occurs in IV Macc. 7.8, where the verb is used with 'the law' as its object, giving the sense 'making the law into a holy sacrifice by their blood'. This would tell rather against Professor Richardson's interpretation. But Rahlfs reads δημιουργοῦντας, and does not even mention the other reading in his *apparatus criticus*.

[3] T. W. Manson (*op. cit.*, p. 49 n.) inclines to the view that Paul is offering the Gentiles, but he does not seem to have satisfactorily solved the problem of accounting for the gospel here.

[4] See also Farrer, *op. cit.*, p. 147.

16.16; Phil. 2.16; Col. 1.29; Acts 20.35. The other word used in I Cor. 16.15 f. is συνεργεῖν ('helpeth in the work'—RV). It is used of the work of the ministry in II Cor. 6.1. But the chief significance of this I Corinthians passage for our purpose is that in the previous verse (I Cor. 16.15) Paul has described Stephanas as 'the firstfruits of Achaia'. It is surely not without importance that from the first family to be converted in a new area the first members of the ministry should be chosen: we see the apostolic ministry being handed on. At one time perhaps Stephanas and his family were the church in Corinth; they became the apostolic ministry in Corinth.

We find in II Cor. 9.12 f. language used about the collection for the needy Christians in Judaea which is characteristic of the way Paul treats this subject throughout his Epistles. He says of the collection:

> For the ministration of this service (ἡ διακονία τῆς λειτουργίας ταύτης) not only filleth up the measure of the wants of the saints, but aboundeth also through many thanksgivings (διὰ πολλῶν εὐχαριστιῶν) unto God; seeing that through the proving of you by this ministration (διακονία) they glorify God for the obedience of your confession unto the gospel of Christ.

We cannot help being impressed by the liturgical language: διακονία, λειτουργία, εὐχαριστία.[1] Admittedly all three words only gained a specifically liturgical significance long after Paul's day, but, all the same, we cannot but feel the underlying connection here between worship and life. All editors agree that δοξάζοντες in v. 13 ('glorifying God') applies to the recipients of the collection. It is all the more surprising that the RSV by translating 'you will glorify God' takes it of the Corinthians. What is greatly significant here is that this exalted language connected with divine service and praise to God is used, not of the Eucharist or of any service of worship, but of the relief work organized for the most part by the Gentile laity. It should remind us that in Paul's mind all *diakonia* is ultimately one, whether done by Christ, by the apostolic ministry, or by the laity.[2]

Paul's conception of the ministry is remarkably well illustrated in the

---

[1] For λειτουργία compare Phil. 2.25 and see p. 96.

[2] Compare Hort's fine dictum in a sermon preached in Westminster Abbey in 1890 at Westcott's consecration as Bishop of Durham: 'For ministering is the one universal function of all "saints", all individual members of the Church, the common element in all functions' (F. J. A. Hort, *The Christian Ecclesia*, London, 1897, p. 285). The same point is well made by J. A. T. Robinson in *The Historic Episcopate*, p. 14. Compare also M. Mezger, *Die Amtshandlungen der Kirche*, Munich, 1957, p. 25: 'The New Testament ministry as regards content is the proclamation of the message of salvation; as regards its form, it is service.' This of course applies to all ministry.

great passage on the ministry in Eph. 4.1–16, round which so much discussion concerning the New Testament ministry has taken place. He begins the passage with a plea for unity, and he ends it by describing the ultimate eschatological unity in Christ. As we read the list of unities in vv. 4–6, we realize that we are reading of the things which constitute the unity of the Church: the Holy Trinity, the Christian faith (we can take it as both the act of faith and the content of faith),[1] baptism, the Church, the goal of the Christian life. Two things are most noticeable by their absence: Paul does not say 'one ministry and one Eucharist'. This is not because he is not interested in these two, but because they do not constitute the unity of the Church; they are rather the two primary means of expressing that unity.[2] In vv. 7–10 Paul refers to the saving act of God in Christ whereby the Church was recreated; perhaps the quotation from Ps. 68 reminds us that the Church was not an entirely new invention. After that, in vv. 11–13 Paul speaks of the gift of the ministry, and here ministry means not *diakonia*, but *diakonoi*, the ministers. All modern scholars agree that the list of apostles, prophets, evangelists, etc. does not represent a graded hierarchy; but it does undoubtedly represent the ministry as a whole, so that what is said here about the ministry may fairly be taken as Paul's doctrine of the ministry. We note that the ministry is given by God, not invented by man; that it is given to the Church, and is therefore not itself constitutive of the Church; and above all that we are told the purpose for which the ministry is given. It is given

[1] Stig Hanson (*op. cit.*, p. 151) thinks the phrase refers exclusively to the content of the faith. E. Kenneth Lee in *Studies in Ephesians*, ed. F. L. Cross, London, 1956, p. 50, suggests that it 'probably refers to the content of the faith and possibly to its formulation'.

[2] I cannot refrain here from quoting the words of a distinguished modern theologian, Professor G. W. H. Lampe, since they so strikingly confirm the conclusion reached here about the ministry: 'The fundamental mistake which vitiates both the Cyprianic and the Augustinian teaching is the implicit insistence on the ministry as the source of unity. It is in fact the *sacraments* which are the source of unity, the ministry is an *expression* of the Church's unity which flows from the grace of Christ in the sacraments and at the same time a means of maintaining and preserving that unity. The sacraments are means of grace, efficacious signs. They are not mere seals set upon grace which has already been bestowed in other ways. This applies to the Church's unity as a gift of grace, as much as it does to the holiness of its members. It would seem to follow that it is wrong to regard sacramental fellowship as a goal to be achieved only when the Church has been united by non-sacramental means, such as the general acceptance of a particular form of ministerial order. It is not a seal to be set upon a unity that has been attained by concordats or some other "political" means. It is rather the means of grace, the way by which the gracious activity of Christ may constitute his unified Church as his own Body. The ministry of the Church is properly an expression of this supernaturally given unity, not the means towards its attainment; the reverse is true of the sacraments.' Article in *World Council of Churches Division of Studies Bulletin*, Vol. III, No. 1 (Lausanne, March 1957), p. 20. Except for a distinction between baptism and the Eucharist which we have maintained in this chapter, this is exactly the view outlined here.

for the perfecting of the saints unto the work of the *diakonia*, and unto the work of building up the body of Christ.

This is neither the RV nor the RSV translation, but it seems to be demanded by the usage of the prepositions. The Greek is

πρὸς τὸν καταρτισμὸν τῶν ἁγίων εἰς ἔργον διακονίας, εἰς οἰκοδομὴν τοῦ σώματος τοῦ Χριστοῦ.

The RV and the RSV, by putting a comma after 'saints', imply that Paul has used two different prepositions paratactically in exactly the same sense. It seems more natural to take πρός as expressing the object of the giving of the ministry and εἰς in each clause as expressing the purpose for which the saints are perfected. This then fits in admirably with the conception of the pioneer ministry which we have traced in Paul's other letters. The purpose of the ministry (*diakonoi*) is to equip all Christians for ministry (*diakonia*). The RV and RSV punctuation is defended by Stig Hanson on the grounds that the other punctuation would suggest that the individual Christian helps to build up the body of Christ, which he considers to be against New Testament usage.[1] But, as we have seen,[2] *diakonia* is very much the work of the whole body, and not of the ordained ministry only, and the individual Christian must play his part in the work of the whole body. With οἰκοδομή in v. 12 compare ἐποικοδομηθέντες in 2.20 (the first word means 'building up' and the second 'being built up upon'). We are both served by the apostolic ministry and must ourselves join in that service. The ministry then is not something given to the Church from outside to create it and hold it together: it is rather something given in the Church by Christ to be the Church, to be and do that which the Church, following it, must be and do.

Gore in his commentary on Ephesians *à propos* this passage quotes from a Roman Catholic writer, who says that the Church must have 'unity of faith, unity of worship, and unity of government'. On the basis of this passage in Ephesians, Gore repudiates this view. If by 'must' is meant 'Is not the Church if it does not possess these three unities', then we may agree with Gore. There is nothing about worship or government in Paul's list of unities. But if by 'must' is meant 'ought to have', then we may agree with the Roman Catholic writer. If the Church is to exhibit clearly the oneness which it possesses sacramentally in Christ, it must have one Eucharist and one ministry. In other words, the Eucharist and the ministry express the Church's unity; they do not constitute it.[3]

---

[1] *Op. cit.*, p. 156.   [2] E.g. p. 103 above.

[3] It may be worth while to observe that the alteration of the quotation from Ps. 68.18 from 'received gifts from men' to 'gave gifts to men' can hardly fail to strengthen the

We may briefly note that this conclusion about the Eucharist is confirmed by I Cor. 10.16 f.:

> The bread which we break, is it not a communion of the body of Christ? seeing that we, who are many, are one bread, one body: for we all partake of the one bread.

The argument, it seems, is: we could not all partake of the one bread if we were not already members of the one body. Edwards is surely right in his comment: 'The apostle's object is to prove, not the unity of the Church, but communion with Christ.'[1]

Finally, it is very appropriate to refer at the end of this chapter to two passages from the First Epistle of Peter, where we find very much the same conception of *diakonia* as we found in Paul. In I Peter 4.10 f. we read:

> According as each hath received a gift, ministering ($\delta\iota\alpha\kappa\nu\nu\tilde{\upsilon}\nu\tau\epsilon\varsigma$) it among yourselves, as good stewards ($o\dot{\iota}\kappa\nu\acute{o}\mu\upsilon\iota$) of the manifold grace of God; . . . if any man ministereth ($\delta\iota\alpha\kappa\nu\epsilon\hat{\iota}$), *ministering* as of the strength which God supplieth.

Plainly the author is here speaking of the sort of Christian service which any Christian might be expected to undertake. In v. 9 he has referred to hospitality, so perhaps in vv. 10 f. he is thinking of poor relief, prayer for those in distress, pastoral visiting, etc. The significant point is that the two words *diakonein* and *oikonomos* which are so frequently used of the official ministry by St Paul are here used quite freely of the non-ordained ministry. This does not imply that there was no official ministry at the time, but that one could quite naturally pass over into the other. All ministry is one.

Then in 5.1–4 the author turns to the official ministry: as a fellow-presbyter, he exhorts the presbyters to tend the flock of God and not to lord it over them. They are to exercise the oversight 'according unto God', $\kappa\alpha\tau\dot{\alpha}$ $\Theta\epsilon\acute{o}\nu$. The phrase is not very clear: does it only mean 'in godly fashion'? This sounds weak, more reminiscent of the author of the Pastorals. A stronger sense is 'as God did it', i.e. drawing them by the bands of love, as Christ drew us. If so, we have a fine reference to the

connection of Ephesians with Paul. It seems that the only source from which the alteration could have been derived is the Targum on Ps 68.19 (in Heb.). See Macpherson, *Ephesians, ad loc.* It appears to have been the traditional rabbinical interpretation of the passage. It is most unlikely that a 'Continuator' would have been acquainted with rabbinical traditions. This does not prove that Paul wrote the Epistle in its present form, but at least suggests that, if there was an editor, he was dealing with Pauline material.

[1] So also Massie; otherwise Godet, Goudge.

ministry as discharging Christ's task. The word for 'lord it over them' is κατακυριεύοντες, the same word as occurs in Mark 10.42, where it is contrasted with the method of the Incarnation, another link with our Lord's ministry. It is surely significant that the writer, who calls himself an apostle in 1.1, when speaking to presbyters describes himself as a fellow-presbyter. This suggests that there was not a hierarchical difference between apostle and presbyter. Thus, if we take these two passages together, we find a remarkable similarity to Paul's conception of the ministry, and even of the apostolate.

8

The Doctrine becomes Standardized

OUR CONCERN is with the doctrine of the relation of the ministry to the Church. We have now to trace the process by which the conception of the pioneer ministry which we find in the New Testament was gradually modified until it reached a state of standardization in Cyprian; and then how the Reformers raised again the question of the relation of the ministry to the Church, and went some way towards answering it in New Testament terms. But we should perhaps first sum up briefly our conclusions about the New Testament doctrine, so that we may be able to judge to what extent subsequent Christian thinkers were faithful to it.

We begin from the fact that the Remnant in the Book of Isaiah was to witness to the acts of God and to prophecy fulfilled. The apostles, whose nucleus was the Messiah with the Twelve, carried out exactly that function. They were not appointed as rulers over the future Church; they were intended to *be* the Church. They were the faithful Remnant, whose task it was after the resurrection to witness to the acts of God in Christ. This is in fact what we find them doing in the Book of Acts. In the beginning the earliest apostles *were* the Christian Church. This is what gave them their authority, and this is why their authority fades as the Gentile Church grows.

This does not mean, however, that the authority of the original apostles passed over to the growing Church by a sort of process of dissipation. We do find a ministry in the churches which Paul founded (the only area about which we have adequate records). Whatever Paul calls the ministers, whether *apostoloi*, *diakonoi*, or *episkopoi*, he and his fellow-workers did constitute an apostolic ministry for the Churches which they had founded. And Paul does give us a theology of the ministry, especially, though not exclusively, in the Corinthian Epistles. What he tells us is that it is the task of the ministry to live out the life of Christ in the Church and to be pioneers of the Christian life for the sake of the Church. But this is done only in order to enable the Church in its turn to live that life. We thus find the pattern: Christ—the ministry—the Church. But this does not mean that the ministry does nothing that the Church does not do: on the contrary, the purpose of the ordained ministry is to induce the whole Church to do what it does, i.e. what Christ does. We find therefore an apostolic, representative, pioneer ministry. The ministry does not come in between God and man, still less is it a substitute for the laity. It is rather what Christ is to all of us, a pioneer, a leader, an exemplar.[1] It must also be prepared to empty itself and efface itself as Christ did.

If the question is asked 'From where does the ministry derive its authority?', the answer seems to be that it gains its authority from the fact that it is the missionary, apostolic spearhead of the Church. In each area where they founded churches, Paul and his fellow-workers were the nucleus of the Church. In any case, the task of the ministry is always to be the pioneer in Christian living, in worship, in evangelism, in care for the flock. There is thus always a need for the ministry, for there is always a need for the nucleus of the Church, always perhaps a need for the faithful Remnant. According to this doctrine of the ministry, it is essential to the Church and yet not constitutive of the Church's existence; just as the Eucharist is essential to the Church and yet the Church is not constituted by the Eucharist. Ultimately it is the Incarnation that provides the link between ministry and Church, and the faithful Remnant that provides the form of the ministry.

As we might expect, this is an eschatological doctrine of the ministry. It was the faithful Remnant that was to witness to God's acts in the last days. So it is not surprising that in the period after the New Testament we find the relation of the ministry to the Church expressed in a way less profoundly connected with the Incarnation and the Remnant, until finally that relation becomes almost entirely external and the pioneer ministry is lost sight of—a process which we have called 'standardization'.

Clement does not have any theology of the ministry, though, as we shall see, he gives an account of the connection between the ministry and the apostles. In his *Letter to the Corinthians* XLII he derives the divine institution of the ministry from a text in the Old Testament, Isa. 60.17. In the RV it runs as follows:

> I will also make thy officers peace,
> and thine exactors righteousness.

Clement's version of this is as follows:

[1] Of course Christ is much more to each Christian also, his interior life, his Saviour, his daily bread. The ministry can only reproduce what we might call the exterior aspect of Christ. A similar distinction is made by Emil Mersch, S.J., in *The Theology of the Mystical Body*, ET, London, 1952, pp. 525 f.

καταστήσω τοὺς ἐπισκόπους αὐτῶν ἐν δικαιοσύνῃ
καὶ τοὺς διακόνους αὐτῶν ἐν πίστει.

This is not the version of the LXX as we have it, which uses ἄρχοντες for the first noun and ἐπίσκοποι for the second. We do not know whether Clement is quoting inaccurately from memory, or whether he had a version of the LXX which actually read what he writes. But it is hardly likely that Clement would have had recourse to so absurd a proof for the divine institution of *episkopoi* and *diakonoi* if he had known of any doctrine or tradition giving a more authoritative account of their origin.

It seems quite plain that Clement knows of only two orders in the ministry, bishop-presbyter and deacon. He refers to these two together in the chapter from which we have just quoted. Then in XLIII 4 f. he says that it would be a shame to thrust from office those who have unblameably offered 'the gifts of the episcopate' (τὰ δῶρα τῆς ἐπισκοπῆς), and goes on to say that happy are those *presbuteroi* who have died before this happened. Finally in LVII his injunction to them is: Submit yourselves to the presbyters'.[1] Only once does he use ἐπίσκοπος in the singular, and that is in referring to God as τὸν παντὸς πνεύματος κτίστην καὶ ἐπίσκοπον, 'the creator and bishop of every spirit'.

We have said that Clement does speak of the connection between the apostles and the ministry. The first mention is XLII 4:

So preaching everywhere in country and town, they appointed their firstfruits, when they had proved them by the Spirit, to be bishops and deacons unto them that should believe.[2]

It is interesting to notice here that it is the firstfruits who are appointed to the ministry; this shows that the thought of the pioneer ministry had not yet disappeared.[3] Clement comments on this appointment in XLIII 1:

And it is not surprising that those who had been entrusted in Christ with such a task by God should have appointed those mentioned above.[4] (My translation.)

Clement does not say that this appointment of bishops and deacons was a commandment received from our Lord. He seems rather to take the view which was taken later by Hooker and most other Anglican apologists of the sixteenth and seventeenth centuries, that episcopacy (in Clement's time

---

[1] Translations quoted from J. B. Lightfoot, *The Apostolic Fathers* (5 vols., 2nd ed., London, 1889–90; 1 vol., ed. J. R. Harmer, 1891), except where otherwise indicated.

[2] κατὰ χώρας οὖν καὶ πόλεις κηρύσσοντες καθίστανον τὰς ἀπαρχὰς αὐτῶν, δοκιμάσαντες τῷ πνεύματι, εἰς ἐπισκόπους καὶ διακόνους τῶν μελλόντων πιστεύειν.

[3] See p. 103, above.

[4] καί τι θαυμαστὸν εἰ οἱ ἐν Χριστῷ πιστευθέντες παρὰ Θεοῦ ἔργον τοιοῦτον κατέστησαν τοὺς προειρημένους.

episcopo-presbytery) was an apostolic institution, but not a divine injunction in origin.

In the next chapter, XLIV 2 f., he amplifies his statement:

Διὰ ταυτὴν οὖν τὴν αἰτίαν πρόγνωσιν εἰληφότες τελείαν κατέστησαν τοὺς προειρημένους, καὶ μεταξὺ ἐπιμονὴν δεδώκασιν ὅπως, ἐὰν κοιμηθῶσιν, διαδέξωνται ἕτεροι δεδοκιμασμένοι ἄνδρες τὴν λειτουργίαν αὐτῶν.

Lightfoot's translation is:

They appointed the aforesaid persons, and afterwards they provided a continuance, that if these should fall asleep, other approved men should succeed to their ministration.

There is some doubt about the important word ἐπιμονήν here. Gore[1] preferred the alternative reading ἐπινόμην, which he translated 'an additional injunction'. There is no doubt here a conception of succession, though Clement does not in this sentence specify how the succession is secured. He throws more light on this in the next passage:

τοὺς οὖν κατασταθέντας ὑπ᾽ ἐκείνων ἢ μεταξὺ ὑφ᾽ ἑτέρων ἐλλογίμων ἀνδρῶν, συνευδοκησῆς πάσης τῆς ἐκκλησίας κτλ.

Those therefore who were appointed by them, or afterward by other men of repute with the consent of the whole Church ... etc.

This is the passage which Gregory Dix in *The Apostolic Ministry* interpreted as proving the existence of a sort of episcopate existing side by side with the presbyterate during the 'tunnel' period. He understood the phrase ἐλλογίμων ἀνδρῶν to refer to what he called 'apostolic men', such as Timothy and Titus. And he assumed that the original apostles passed on their authority to these 'apostolic men', and that they in their turn lived long enough to pass it on to the first monarchical bishops. Now it may very well be that some of Paul's fellow-workers, who could be described as apostles according to the evidence we reviewed in the last chapter, did have an important voice (perhaps the deciding voice) in appointing the presbyter-bishops in the churches which they had evangelized. But this interpretation cannot legitimately be taken out of Clement's phrase ἐλλογίμων ἀνδρῶν. ἐλλόγιμος is a word which he uses elsewhere in his Epistle, and it seems to have no more distinctive meaning than 'respectable'. For example in LVII 2 and LVIII 2 he uses it of the respectable layman remaining quietly in his place, and in LXII 3, in a final word of compliment to the whole church in Corinth, he says that he knows he is writing to ἀνδράσιν πιστοῖς καὶ ἐλλογιμωτάτοις, which we might translate 'men of fidelity and the highest respectability'.[1]

In fact then, what Clement is saying in ch. XLIV is that the apostles ensured there always being in each church persons of suitable character to decide who was to be an *episkopos* or *diakonos*. He certainly believes that the ministry of his day was carrying out the function of the apostles (he uses λειτουργία in XLIV 2). So we have here the thought of a continuation of function, but not of a continuation of an order, bishop ordaining bishop and so on. The people whom he calls δεδοκιμασμένοι ἄνδρες 'men approved' are plainly the actual ministers. Those whom he calls ἐλλόγιμοι ἄνδρες might just as well be lay people, whose choice of men for the ministry Clement thinks was subject to the approval of the whole (local) church. So we may say that we find in Clement a conception of a continuance rather than of a succession; the ministry is still very closely associated in its appointment with the rest of the local church.

In the area of which Ignatius writes the monarchical episcopate was already established.[2] Ignatius has more to say about the ministry than Clement, and in his letters we meet something resembling Paul's doctrine of the ministry as intended to live out the life of Christ in the Church, or at least to represent Christ to the Church. Thus in *Ephesians* VI 1 he writes:

> For every man whom the master of the house sends into his household you must receive as you would him that sent him. So it is plain that you must regard the bishop as the Lord Himself.

There is a similar passage in *Philadelphians* V 1, where he says:

> προσφυγὼν τῷ εὐαγγελίῳ ὡς σαρκὶ Ἰησοῦ καὶ τοῖς ἀποστόλοις ὡς πρεσβυτερίῳ ἐκκλησίας.

> Taking refuge in the Gospel as in the flesh of Jesus, and in the apostolic writings as in the presbytery of the Church.

Lightfoot, no doubt rightly, claims that τοῖς ἀποστόλοις must be some part of the New Testament. The thought is that the Scriptures are to the whole Church what the presbytery is to the local church. Above each is God (or Jesus Christ) and the local bishop respectively. Connected also with this thought is his frequent comparison of God the Father to the bishop and the apostles to the presbytery, which we shall be considering below. We do not, however, in Ignatius seem to find the thought of the ministry, as such, showing forth Christ's sufferings. Ignatius represents himself, perhaps, as enduring vicarious suffering, but not apparently in his

---

[1] K. J. Woollcombe in *The Historic Episcopate*, p. 46, has a useful note on the meaning of ἐλλόγιμος, but has not apparently noticed that Clement uses it more than once.

[2] We must except his *Letter to the Romans*, where, most remarkably, there is no mention at all of a bishop.

capacity as bishop, since those to whom he writes are not under his jurisdiction. Thus in *Ephesians* XXI 1, he writes:

> I am a condemned criminal, you have obtained mercy;
> I am in peril, you are well established.

This is certainly an echo of I Cor. 4.10–13, but Ignatius does not echo Paul's irony in that passage. He seems to mean it quite seriously. In *Ephesians* XVIII he says: περίψημα τό ἐμὸν πνεῦμα τοῦ σταυροῦ. This is a difficult phrase. Does it mean 'My sufferings are dross compared with the cross?' He uses περίψημα again in *Ephesians* VIII 1, and ἀντίψυχον twice of himself (*Ephesians* XXI 1 and *Polycarp* VI 1). But both these words may have become fairly conventional by Ignatius' time.[1]

One of the things we miss in Ignatius as compared with Paul is the connection between the ministry of the ordained ministers and the ministry of the laity. There are certain hints, but they do not figure very prominently. Thus in *Ephesians* IV he has an elaborate metaphor: the bishop is the lyre, the presbytery are the strings, God gives the note, and the individual members of the church are to form themselves into a choir. If we press this figure, we find that the ministry is the instrument of the local church; but dare we press it? Somewhat clearer is *Polycarp* VI 1, where he refers to the whole church at Smyrna as ὡς Θεοῦ οἰκονόμοι καὶ πάρεδροι καὶ ὑπηρέται, which we may translate 'like stewards and assessors and ministers of God'. The use of the word οἰκονόμοι for the laity is interesting.[2] Paul uses it for the ministry in I Cor. 4.1. But unfortunately Ignatius does not develop the thought.

Ignatius insists on one thing which we do not find in the New Testament: he believes that the ministry is essential to the being of the Church. In *Trallians* III 1, having mentioned the bishop, presbyters, and deacons, he adds: χωρὶς τούτων ἐκκλησία οὐ καλεῖται, which apparently means, 'Without these the Church is not recognized'. Similarly in *Smyrnaeans* VIII he tells his readers that the valid Eucharist is that which is under the bishop, or whoever he entrusts it to. Wherever the bishop is, there let the people be, just as wherever Christ is, there is the Church. It is not lawful to baptize or hold an *agape* without the bishop. The ministry also represents the Church. He writes in *Magnesians* II:

> I have been counted worthy to see you (sc. the Magnesian church) in the person of your bishop, Damas, worthy of God, and the worthy presbyters Bassus and Apollonius, and my fellow-servant the deacon Zotion.[3]

---

[1] See pp. 61 f., above.
[2] Ignatius uses ὑπηρέται of the deacons in *Trallians* III.
[3] Cf. also *Trallians* I.

H

The bishop is thought of as a separate order, he is not just *primus inter pares* among the presbyters. This is plain in the musical metaphor we have noticed in *Ephesians* IV; the bishop is not just the most important string in the lyre; he is the frame, while the presbytery are the strings. This also appears from the frequent comparison of the bishop to God or Jesus Christ, while the presbytery is compared to the apostles. On the other hand, the two other orders are always closely associated with the bishop. Indeed, we might almost say that in Ignatius' letters the presbytery is as important as the bishop. It is not surprising to find T. M. Lindsay[1] claiming that Ignatius' nearest resemblance today is the presbyterian (or as he prefers to call it, conciliar) system of church government. He points out that in ten of the twelve references in Ignatius' letters to the three orders of the ministry, bishops and presbyters are mentioned together.

A link with Clement is that there does not seem to be any trace of what is meant today by succession in Ignatius' doctrine of the ministry. The quotation already referred to in *Ephesians* VI 1 about God sending a man into his household has no reference to the bishop as successor of the apostles. See also an interesting passage in *Philadelphians* I 1:

ὃν ἐπίσκοπον ἔγνων οὐκ ἀφ' ἑαυτοῦ, οὐδὲ δι' ἀνθρώπων κεκτῆσθαι τὴν διακονίαν τὴν εἰς τὸ κοινὸν ἀνήκουσαν, οὐδὲ κατὰ κενοδοξίαν, ἀλλ' ἐν ἀγάπῃ Θεοῦ πατρὸς καὶ Κυρίου Ἰησοῦ Χριστοῦ.

We may translate as follows:

And I know that this bishop received this ministry which concerns all of you, not of himself nor by men, not out of mere ambition, but in the love of God the Father and the Lord Jesus Christ.

This does not merely mean that their bishop was validly ordained, not self-appointed. It means that God in his love for the Philadelphians indicated him as their bishop. Succession as we understand it today seems positively ruled out. Indeed, if Ignatius thinks of anyone as successor to the apostles, it is the presbytery, not the bishop. He compares the bishop to God (or Christ) and the presbytery to the apostles in several places, e.g. *Magnesians* VI 1; XIII 2; *Trallians* III 1; *Smyrnaeans* VIII 1; and compare *Philadelphians* V 1. But even the presbyterate is not really thought of as the successor to the apostles; it is rather the contemporary image of, or parallel to, the apostles. The truth is that the conception of the 'apostolic succession' as later generations understood it had not yet occurred to anyone in the Church. Neither do we find in Ignatius Cyprian's notion

[1] *The Church and the Ministry in the Early Centuries*, London, 1902, pp. 196, 198.

of the bishops as corporately the ruling body of the Church. Thus in the quotation from *Philadelphians* V already referred to,[1] we have noted that the Scriptures are to the whole Church what the presbytery is to the local church, and above each is God and the bishop respectively. The bishop is the ruler of the local church; God (or Christ) is the ruler of the whole Church. The same conclusion follows from our quotation from *Smyrnaeans* VIII. Wherever the bishop is, there let the πλῆθος be, and by πλῆθος he must mean the mass of the faithful in any given place, the local church. In the same way, wherever Jesus Christ is, there is the ἐκκλησία, i.e. the whole catholic Church.

It does not seem that Ignatius thought of episcopacy as of divine institution. The nearest he comes to saying it is in *Ephesians* III 2, where he writes:

Concur with the purpose of God. For Jesus Christ our inseparable life is the purpose of the Father, as the bishops appointed throughout the ends (of the earth) are in the purpose of Jesus Christ.

Lightfoot paraphrases this: 'The bishops abide in the mind of Christ, just as Christ is the mind of the Father.' Ignatius does not seem to be saying anything more than that the bishops understand the mind of Christ. He is certainly not claiming that episcopacy as such expresses the mind of Christ. Another passage that might seem at first sight to claim at least an apostolic institution for episcopacy is *Trallians* VII:

. . . if you are inseparable from Jesus Christ and the bishop and the institutions of the apostles (τῶν διαταγμάτων τῶν ἀποστόλων).

Lightfoot suggests here that 'the institutions of the apostles' refers to the institution of episcopacy in Asia Minor by the apostle John. But the καί before it seems to rule this out. If the phrase referred to the episcopate, surely the 'and' would be unnecessary. If it refers to the ministry at all, it must refer to the presbyters and deacons. As we have seen, the presbyterate at least has a better claim to apostolic institution than has the monarchical episcopate. But in fact Ignatius is probably thinking of the moral teaching of the apostles.

Thus Ignatius, as compared with Clement, represents at once a deeper interpretation of the significance of the ministry and a slight development in thought about the ministry. He does try to relate the ministry to God on the one hand and to the Church on the other. But the relation is more static and less closely related to the Incarnation than what we find in Paul.

[1] 'Taking refuge in the Gospel as in the flesh of Jesus and in the apostolic writings as in the presbytery of the Church.'

On the other hand he does represent the ministry as in some sense constitutive of the Church, which we do not find in the New Testament. The
doctrine of the ministry had a considerable distance to travel before it
reached the form it takes in Cyprian's works, but in Ignatius' Epistles
it may be said to have started out on its journey.

The *Epistle of Barnabas*[1] has little to say about the ministry. The author
has a fine phrase which he uses to describe the Church as the faithful
Remnant: ὁ λαὸς ὃν ἡτοίμασεν ἐν τῷ ἠγαπημένῳ αὐτοῦ ('The people whom
God prepared for himself in his Beloved'; III 5). He has a strange theory
that the apostles before their call were greater sinners than any others,
apparently in order to prove that Christ did not come to call the righteous
but sinners (v 9). In v 8 he says that Christ gave the Twelve the authority
of the gospel (τὴν ἐξουσίαν τοῦ εὐαγγελίου). This seems to suggest that
they were primarily evangelists rather than rulers of the Church.

Altaner takes the view put forward by several others that there is some
connection between the *Epistle of Barnabas* and the *Didache*.[2] He would
date the latter some time before 150, though not, it seems, long before.
It is remarkable that in the *Didache* the presbyter-bishops still seem to be
the first order in the ministry (the deacons are the second). In xv 1 the
command is given:

> Appoint therefore for yourselves bishops and deacons (ἐπισκόπους καὶ
> διακόνους) worthy of the Lord.[3]

The name 'presbyter' does not occur in the *Didache*, and the command
(presumably to the local church) to appoint bishops and deacons suggests
that they were ordained locally, which of course makes any notion of
succession as understood by later generations unlikely. We find in the
Didache the same conception as in Ignatius that the ministry represents
God (IV 1):

> Remember him who speaks the word of God to thee day and night,
> and thou shalt honour him as the Lord; for where authority[4] speaks,
> there is the Lord.

These words probably apply primarily to the 'apostles', prophets, and
teachers who figure more prominently in the *Didache* than do the bishops
and deacons; but then no doubt the author believed such persons to be
quite as much members of the ministry as bishops and deacons. In fact
in xv he seems to commend the bishops and deacons to his readers'

[1] B. Altaner (*Patrologie*, 2nd ed., Freiburg, 1951) dates it between AD 116 and 140.
[2] *Op. cit.*, p. 38.
[3] Text in H. de Romestin, *The Teaching of the Twelve Apostles*, Oxford, 1884.
[4] κυριότης, cf. Jude 8.

attention on the ground that they fulfil the same office as the prophets and teachers.[1]

Our aim is not to provide a history of the doctrine of the ministry, but to show how Paul's dynamic doctrine of the pioneer ministry, deeply rooted in the doctrine of the Incarnation, began during the sub-apostolic age to harden into the doctrine of the apostolic succession as we find it in Cyprian. It will therefore be sufficient for our purpose if we take a glance at the work in which Cyprian set forth his doctrine of the Church, the *De Unitate Ecclesiae*. In ch. 5 he succinctly expresses his doctrine of the ministry:

Episcopatus unus est, cuius a singulis in solidum pars tenetur.

Blakeney translates: 'The episcopate is one—a joint property in which we all severally share.'[2] As we have noted, this is not Ignatius' doctrine; for him the bishop was the ruler of the local church, God or Christ was the ruler of the whole Church.

It is clear that Cyprian believed in the divine institution of episcopacy. In ch. 10 he refers to schismatics who 'of their own accord place themselves at the head of hasty conventicles without divine appointment, who constitute themselves leaders without any legitimate ordination, who arrogate to themselves the name of bishop, though no one has granted it to them'.[3] Again in ch. 19 he refers to sectarians as those 'who, despising the tradition of God, yearn for strange doctrines, and introduce teachings which have only a human origin'.[4] This language can only mean that he believed episcopacy to have been instituted by God himself.

In ch. 23 we find the nearest thing that Cyprian offers us to a proof of this doctrine:

God is one, and Christ is one, and his Church is one, and the faith one, and there is one laity joined together into the firm unity of the body by the glue of concord.[5]

This is simply based on the assumption that there can be only one ministry because there is only one Church. Cyprian does not stop to ask why Paul in Ephesians did not add 'one ministry' to his list of unities. Here,

---

[1] ὑμῖν γὰρ λειτουργοῦσιν (sc. οἱ ἐπ ίσκοποι καὶ διάκονοι) καὶ αὐτοὶ τὴν λειτουργίαν τῶν προφητῶν καὶ διδασκάλων.

[2] E. H. Blakeney, *Cyprian: De Unitate Ecclesiae*, London, 1928.

[3] My own translation. The Latin is: '*se ultro apud temerarios convenas sine divina dispositione praeficiunt, qui se praepositos sine ulla ordinationis lege constituunt, qui nemine episcopatum dante episcopi sibi nomen assumunt*'.

[4] My own translation. The Latin is: '*qui Dei traditione contemta alienas doctrinas appetunt et magisteria humanae institutionis inducunt.*'

[5] My own translation. The Latin is: '*Deus unus est, et Christus unus est, et una ecclesia eius, et fides una, et plebs in solidam corporis unitatem concordiae glutino copulata.*'

then, is the theory of the apostolic succession clearly set out, with more than a hint of Roman legalism to hold it together.

By Cyprian's time, therefore, Church and ministry have been distinguished and separated. The ministry now claims a direct descent from the apostles not *via* the Church, but *via* itself only. The logical conclusion of this is a doctrine of manual succession, and the obvious danger is sacerdotalism, whereby the ministry says in effect to the laity: 'You cannot continue without us, but we can continue without you'—though it is only fair to add that Cyprian never envisages the possibility of a ministry perpetuating itself outside the Church, and in an important sense he holds ministry, Church and Sacraments together. Such a development is not at all surprising, however, since the deepest teaching about the ministry in the New Testament is buried in the obscurest of Paul's Epistles, and the Church of the first three centuries was not conspicuous for its understanding of Paul's theology. Again, the very fact that the New Testament doctrine of the ministry was an eschatological one made it more difficult for those to grasp it who believed in an indefinite prolongation of the Church's existence. In effect, however, by the middle of the third century the conception of the pioneer ministry had entirely disappeared.

St Thomas Aquinas' discussion of Orders in his *Summa Theologica* is interesting, though he has nothing to say about the theological relation of the ministry to the Church, or about the priesthood of the whole Church. He admits[1] that in the New Testament priests and bishops are referred to under the same name, quoting I Tim. 5.17 and Acts 20.28. But he says that there always was a distinction in fact, since the bishops received their authority from the apostles, and the priests from the Seventy of Luke 10.1. It is interesting that in claiming an actual distinction between bishops and presbyters in the New Testament while admitting the common appellation he is anticipating the main thesis of the authors of *The Apostolic Ministry*; Aquinas however has left to later ages the task of proving this thesis.

Aquinas has one fine discussion about invalid orders. He relates the contingency of a man being made bishop and then finding that he had never been baptized. He concludes that such a man would have to be baptized, then reordained and reconsecrated, and all his ordinations up till then would have to be regarded as invalid. But he adds:

> Yet it may piously be believed that as regards the ultimate effects of the sacraments the High Priest will supply the defect, and that He would not allow this to be so hidden as to endanger the Church.[2]

[1] St Thomas Aquinas, *The Summa Theologica*. ET by the Fathers of the English Dominican Province, II 2.6 (Vol. 14), 1922, Qu. 184, Article 6, p. 167.
[2] *Ibid.*, III 5 (Vol. 19), 1922, Qu. 35, Article 3, p. 15.

Here surely is something like the ecumenical outlook!

Later Aquinas discusses the episcopate,[1] and concludes that in one sense the episcopate is not an order, that is, in the sense in which an order is a Sacrament. The reason seems to be that the episcopate adds nothing to the priest's power in the Eucharist. But he adds that the episcopate is an order in one sense, 'since in hierarchical actions a bishop has in relation to the mystical body a higher power than the priest'. We would have been grateful for a fuller exposition of the relation of the ministry as a whole to the Church. But perhaps the very fact that Aquinas left so much undetermined meant that later theologians had more room in which to manoeuvre.

[1] *Ibid.*, Qu. 40, Article 6, p. 69.

9
Reappraisal

THE REFORMATION was in part at least a rediscovery of biblical doctrine. Among the doctrines rediscovered or reconsidered, the doctrine of the ministry did not at first take a prominent place, except in so far as the biblical basis of the doctrine of the Papacy had to be criticized. But it was inevitable, as time went on and the Reformers found themselves driven to organize 'evangelical' churches in opposition to the unreformed church, that they should have to face the question: what is the ministry, and what is its relation to the Church? Luther, because he was the first in time, was the first to try to answer this question. In certain ways his answer was the least definite of all the doctrines of the ministry that the Reformation inspired, and to this day it could be said of Lutheranism generally that it does not possess a distinctive doctrine of the ministry. On the other hand, his very vagueness, as we shall see, enabled him to recapture some insights about the New Testament doctrine of the ministry which Calvin, perhaps because of his very passion for definiteness, missed.

Luther made a valiant effort to connect the priesthood of the ministry with the priesthood of the whole Church. Obviously one of the features of the Church situation in Western Europe at the time of the Reformation was the conviction in the minds of many Christians that the ministry had, so to speak, captured the Church. The official ministers claimed that they alone had the right to decide what the Church should believe or practise, and anything that seemed to be incompatible with Scripture was defended on the bare word of authority: 'We are content that these things are consonant with Scripture. It is not for anyone else to challenge them.' It is not surprising therefore that we find Luther striving to make the ministry more responsible to the Church and reasserting the priesthood of the whole Church over against the priesthood of the ordained ministry.

Luther claims that many of the promises given by our Lord to the apostles were in fact given to the whole Church. For example he maintains that the power of the keys was given, not to Peter alone, but to the Church as a whole. In 'An Open Letter to the Christian Nobility' he writes:

Although they allege this power was given to Peter when the keys were given to him, it is plain enough that the keys were not given to Peter alone, but to the whole community.[1]

Again in 'The Babylonian Captivity of the Church' he tries to vindicate the priesthood of the whole Church and the representative nature of the ordained ministry:

> If they (Luther's opponents) were forced to grant that as many of us as have been baptized are all priests without distinction, as indeed we are, and that to them was committed the ministry only, yet with our consent, they would presently learn that they have no right to rule over us, except in so far as we freely concede it (he then quotes I Peter 2.9). Therefore we are all priests, as many of us as are Christians. But the priests, as we call them, are ministers chosen from among us, who do all that they do in our name. And the priesthood is nothing but a ministry, as we learn from I Cor. 4.1.[2]

A little later he continues:

> We are all priests, and there is no difference between us; that is to say, we have the same power in respect to the Word and all the sacraments. However, no one may make of this power except by the consent of the community or the call of a superior.[3]

Luther is still uncertain about how ministerial authority is conveyed, but he is here feeling his way towards a closer relationship between Church and ministry.

In a sermon on 'The Right of a Christian Congregation' Luther reverts to the priesthood of the Church, a priesthood conferred on all Christians in baptism:

> We conclude, then, that where there is a Christian congregation that has the Gospel, it not only has the right and power, but is in duty bound, according to the obedience it pledged to Christ in Baptism, to withdraw from the authority which our Bishops exercise today.[4]

Luther goes on to say that there must be preachers of the word; the present bishops will not give the people any preachers; therefore in virtue of the priesthood conferred in baptism the congregation must call them. Luther is in fact appealing from the authority of the ordained priesthood to the authority of the priesthood of the Church. As this exposition stands, it would lead to what was later called Congregationalism, a system which is

[1] All quotations are from Martin Luther, *Works* (ET), The Philadelphia Edition Philadelphia, 1931; this quotation is from Vol. I, p. 75.
[2] Vol. II, p. 279.   [3] *Ibid.*, p. 283.
[4] 'The Right and Power of a Christian Congregation or Community to judge all Teaching, and to Call, Appoint, and Dismiss Teachers, Established and Proved from Scripture', Vol. IV, p. 79.

very different from the polity actually adopted by Lutheranism. But his appeal to baptism as that which confers authority in the Church differentiates him from men like John Owen. Indeed, this emphasis on baptism is typical of Luther, and should in itself be a sufficient refutation of the common 'catholic' calumny that his concentration on justification by faith left no room for the Sacraments, and that they therefore proved something of an embarrassment to him.[1]

Combined with this courageous attempt to relate the ministry more closely to the Church was a real insight into the nature of *diakonia* in the New Testament. Luther emphasizes as Calvin does not that the essence of ministry is service, not rule. In his 'Treatise on Christian Liberty' he writes thus:

> Injustice is done these words 'priest', 'cleric', 'spiritual', 'ecclesiastic' when they are transferred from all other Christians to those few who are now by a mischievous usage called 'ecclesiastics'. For Holy Scripture makes no distinction between them, except that it gives the name 'ministers', 'servants', 'stewards' to those who are now proudly called popes, bishops, and lords, and who should by the ministry of the Word serve others and teach them the faith of Christ and the liberty of believers. For although we are all equally priests, yet we cannot all publicly minister and teach, nor ought we if we could.[2]

Again in a work called 'Secular Authority' he says:

> What then are priests and bishops? I answer, Their government is not one of authority and power, but a service and an office; for they are neither higher nor better than other Christians. Therefore they should not impose any law or decree on others without their will and consent; their rule consists in nothing else than in dealing with God's Word, leading Christians by it, and overcoming heresy by its means.[3]

In one place Luther rediscovers something very like the apostolic function of the ministry which we have found in Paul. It occurs in the sermon referred to above on 'The Right of a Christian Congregation':

> Now you will say: 'But unless he has been called to do this he dare not preach, as you yourself have repeatedly taught.' I reply: Here you must consider the Christian from a double point of view. On the one hand, when he is in a place where there are no Christians, he needs no other call than the fact that he is a Christian, inwardly called and anointed by God; he is bound by the duty of brotherly love to preach to the erring heathen or non-Christians and to teach them the Gospel, even though no one call him to this work.[4]

[1] It is distressing to find this hoary fallacy repeated by implication in so recent a work as the *Oxford Dictionary of the Christian Church*, ed. F. L. Cross, London, 1957; see art. on Baptism.

[2] Vol. II, p. 325.   [3] Appendix to Vol. III, p. 262.   [4] Vol. IV, p. 80.

He then cites the examples of Stephen, Philip, and Apollos, who, he claims, were not commissioned as apostles. This is very like Paul's doctrine of the apostolic ministry as the nucleus of the Church. We notice the reference to 'anointed by God', which no doubt indicates baptism.

It was Luther, apparently, who originated the definition of the Church, so popular among Reformed Christians, that the Church is where the word of God is preached and the Sacraments duly performed. In fact we find a fuller definition of the Church, though one based on this formula, in a work called 'On the Councils and the Churches'.[1] Here we find the marks of the Church according to Luther. He details seven: the preaching of God's word; the sacrament of baptism; the holy Sacrament of the altar; the public use of the keys (i.e. discipline); the consecration and calling of ministers; public prayers and praise, in which he includes the use of the Psalms and the Creeds; and seventhly suffering. He has quite a lot of comment to make about the fifth mark of the Church, the calling and consecration of ministers. He says that the first four marks demand a ministry in order to administer them: 'The whole group cannot do these things, but must commit them, or allow them to be committed, to someone.' Luther then proceeds to face the question: from where does the authority of his preachers come? He begins by saying that the present hierarchy is incapable of preaching the word or administering the Sacraments rightly (he refers especially to the Eucharist). Then he adds:

> Now if the apostles, evangelists, and prophets have ceased, others must have arisen in their stead, and must continue to arise until the end of the world, and therefore apostles, evangelists, and teachers must continue, by whatever names they may be called, who are occupied with God's Word and work. . . . It was said above about the other four points of the great, divine, holy possession whereby the holy Church is made holy, that you ought not to be concerned about who they are from whom it is received. So here too you ought not to ask who he is that gives it to you, or who has the official position. It is all given, not to him who has the office, but to him who through his office is to give it,[2] except that of course he can get it with you if he will. If he is in office and is tolerated by the assembly, let that be enough for you.

Here is the typical Lutheran conception of the gospel creating the Church, but here also the Sacraments are added. It is certainly refreshing to find the Church put before the ministry instead of the ministry before the Church; and one does feel that Luther is trying to find his way back to Paul's doctrine: the ministry derives its authority from the fact that it is

---

[1] Vol. V, pp. 269 f.
[2] This looks like an adumbration of a theory of the Sacrament being valid only *in usu*, but we may not press Luther's words here.

the Church *in nucleo*. But this passage is too vague and antinomian to constitute a doctrine of ministerial authority and succession. We feel the need for some of Calvin's definiteness.

It would probably be true to say of Luther, as it certainly is of Calvin, that he did not consciously desire to originate a completely new ministry. Luther only began ordaining others when the supply of regularly ordained priests began to run out. His first ordination was in 1525 in Wittenberg.[1] In any case he would no doubt have maintained that the authority given to every Christian in baptism authorized them, acting as the local Christian church, to ordain to the ministry in certain circumstances. It does not seem likely that Luther (still less Calvin) would ever have accepted as a minister anyone who had never received any authority from any body of Christians. Both these Reformers were in an unprecedented situation: church authority as constituted in their day had, they believed, to be repudiated. From where were they to draw authority for the ministry in future? It is to Luther's credit, not to his discredit, that he fell back on the Church as constituted in the sacrament of baptism. He does not offer us a carefully worked out doctrine of the ministry, as does Calvin; what we find in Luther is rather a number of profound insights.

We find Calvin's exposition of his doctrine of the Church and ministry in the fourth book of the *Institutes*.[2] Unlike Luther, he had a very clear and definite doctrine of the ministry. He believes that in Matt. 18.15–20 our Lord formally transferred jurisdiction from the Sanhedrin to the apostles as the first ministers in his Church, and that this jurisdiction now resided in the ruling elders.[3] He also brings in Eph. 4.1–16 as the charter of the Church's ministry. He says:

> Let that passage be diligently pondered, and there will be no doubt that Paul there meant to give a complete representation of that sacred and ecclesiastical government to which posterity has given the name of hierarchy.[4]

In this list we find five functions named: apostles, prophets, evangelists, pastors, and teachers. But Calvin claims that the first three were only temporary (or at least non-successive[5]) offices; only pastors and teachers were intended to be permanent offices in the Church's ministry. The difference between pastors and teachers is that the former administer

---

[1] My information comes from P. Z. Strodach, in Luther's *Works*, Vol. VI, pp. 234 f.
[2] All references are to John Calvin, *Institutes of the Christian Religion*, ET (Calvin Translation Society), Edinburgh, 1846, Vol. III.
[3] Book IV, ch. 11.1, p. 228.   [4] Ch. 6.10, p. 118.
[5] He says that God may from time to time raise up apostles, prophets, and evangelists in his Church still.

discipline, while the latter merely teach.[1] He identifies 'pastor', 'presbyter', and 'bishop' as all indicating the same office in the New Testament, no doubt rightly. There is to be only one pastor in each church, but he is to be assisted by the 'teachers'. Thus in the early Church Calvin would identify the bishop with his 'ruling pastor' and the presbyters with his 'teachers'. This means that Calvin, normally regarded as the great champion of Presbyterianism, can highly approve of what Cyprian says about episcopacy. Calvin maintained that the system of Church government which he expounds was preserved intact in the early Church till AD 400 and later, and was only obscured with the rise of the lord bishop, or bishop with secular office, in the Dark Ages.[2]

The consequence of this doctrine is that Calvin nowhere seriously considers the relation of the ministry to the Church. He assumes that our Lord gave his rule and authority to the ministry, so the relation of the ministry to the Church does not really come within his purview. In one place he asks the question: why has God appointed a ministry?[3] Calvin points out that the work of the ministry could have been carried out by angels. But he thinks that God appointed a ministry for three reasons: to show his condescension towards us, employing men as his ambassadors; to train us in humility, since we may have to listen to men inferior to ourselves (Calvin shows a keen appreciation of the average educated layman's outlook here!); thirdly, to cherish mutual charity by making us dependent on the ministry. In none of these reasons do we find any hint of the function of the ministry as expressed in such passages as I Cor. 4.9-14. Indeed this language suggests that Calvin considers the ministry essential to constitute the Church. No doubt he does regard it as essential to the Church, but he does not make it constitutive of the Church. We find in the *Institutes* that Calvin, like Luther, thinks of the Church as constituted by pure doctrine and the right administration of the Sacraments. He proves this by a gloss on Eph. 2.20: the Church, he says, is founded on the *doctrine* of the apostles and prophets:

> Paul declares that the Church is not founded either upon the judgements of men or the priesthood, but upon the doctrine of the Apostles and Prophets.[4]

Calvin is far more strict than Luther is about the conditions necessary for ordination. He considers that only those whom he calls 'pastors', 'bishops', or 'ruling elders' have authority to ordain, and that the

---

[1] For this exposition see ch. 3.4, pp. 61 f.   [2] See ch. 11.6, p. 234.
[3] Ch. 3.1, pp. 57 f.   [4] Ch. 2.4, p. 48.

'presbyters' or 'teaching elders' do not possess this authority. He is therefore compelled to interpret 'the laying-on of hands of the presbytery' in I Tim. 4.14 as meaning, not that the presbyters laid hands on Timothy, but in the sense of 'the laying-on of hands when I made you a presbyter'— a truly remarkable translation![1]

It does not seem that Calvin, any more than Luther, had the intention of starting a new ministry. On the contrary, since he held that those who were called 'bishops' in his day had usurped the right of ruling the Church from those who were called 'priests' in his day, he must have maintained that he was only recovering the old ministry. He seems to envisage the same Church as continuing with the necessary reforms enacted in it, much as happened in Geneva when he himself carried out his reformation there. In this spirit, he does recognize in one place that the vestiges of the Church remain in the old unreformed church.

> Still, as in ancient times there remained among the Jews certain special privileges of a Church, so in the present day we deny not to the Papists those vestiges of a Church which the Lord has allowed to remain among them amid the dissipation. . . . He . . . first preserved baptism there as an evidence of the covenant—baptism which, consecrated by his lips, retains its power in spite of human depravity; secondly he provided by his providence that there should be other remains also to prevent the Church from utterly perishing. . . . In one word, I call them churches inasmuch as the Lord there wondrously preserves some remains of his people, though miserably torn and scattered, and inasmuch as some symbols of the Church still remain—symbols especially whose efficacy neither the craft of the devil nor human depravity can destroy.[2]

Calvin therefore has less reason than Luther to be concerned about the authority of his ministers: he had restored to them the authority which God had always meant them to have, that was all.

Occasionally Calvin says something which suggests that the Church as well as the ministry may be the source of authority; once he suggests that in Old Testament times there was a true Jewish church, which consisted of the prophets. The priests' church was the false one: 'It cannot be denied, that the Jews had a true Church under the prophets.'[3] This might suggest the thought that the reformed church was a sort of prophetic Remnant, starting afresh on the basis of the word of God. But he does not actually draw this conclusion. In matters of discipline, however, Calvin was quite ready to admit that authority lay with the whole Church, not with the ministry only. Of excommunication he writes:

[1] Ch. 3.16, p. 72.
[2] Ch. 2.11 f., pp. 53 ff.   [3] Ch. 9.6, p. 181.

The Lord testifies that such judgement of the faithful is nothing else than the promulgation of his own sentence, and that what they do on earth is ratified in heaven.[1]

Again he applauds Cyprian for having associated both clergy and laity with him in his judgement of disciplinary cases.[2] Finally, we may make another quotation from chapter 12:

> The legitimate course to be taken in excommunication, as shown by Paul, is not for the elders alone to act apart from others, but with the knowledge and approbation of the Church, so that the body of the people, without regulating the procedure, may, as witnesses and guardians, observe it, and prevent the few from doing any thing capriciously.[3]

Thus on the question of the relation of the Church to the ministry Calvin must be regarded as a supporter of the traditional view: our Lord instituted a ministry to which he committed all rule and authority (or nearly all rule and authority) in the Church. On the other hand, Calvin's scriptural proofs for the institution of the ministry will not stand the test of modern methods of assessing biblical evidence, and probably a great many Presbyterian scholars would admit this today. The fact that there are still many today on the 'catholic' side of Christendom who maintain that their theory of the ministry is the scriptural one is not an indication that their scriptural proofs are any more compelling than Calvin's; it is rather a sign that they set more store by the ministry as constitutive of the Church and are therefore more reluctant than Presbyterians are to admit that their theory cannot be proved from the New Testament.

The Anglican Reformers did not have to devise a new form for the ministry, as did both Luther and Calvin. Their task was rather that of defending a continuance of the old form, purged and simplified. This meant that they were precluded from any profound insights about the relation of the ministry to the Church, such as Luther gained from the very fact that he had to reconsider the whole question from the beginning. On the other hand Anglicanism did not have, and never has had, a distinctive doctrine of the ministry, and this on the whole was an advantage in dealing both with Roman and with Genevan dogmatism.

Bishop John Jewel in his famous *Apology*[4] has no hesitation at all in saying that the Church of England has cut itself off from the Church of Rome. But, he says, it has not cut itself off thereby from the true Church.[5] It is remarkable that he uses the same analogy as Calvin does, that there

---

[1] Ch. 11.2, p. 230. [2] Ch. 11.6, p. 234. [3] Ch. 12.7, p. 254.
[4] ET by Lady Anne Bacon, 1564, ed. R. W. Jelf, London, n.d. (*c.* 1859).
[5] Part IV, ch. 9.3, pp. 71 f.

was always a faithful Remnant in the Old Testament period (p. 76). He expresses this perfectly clearly:

> We have renounced that church, wherein we could neither have the word of God sincerely taught, nor the Sacraments rightly administered, nor the Name of God duly called upon.[1]

Then he specifically discusses the question of succession, and in particular papal succession.[2] He points out that succession does not in itself guarantee purity, quoting the example of Manasseh who succeeded Hezekiah, and Caiaphas as Aaron's successor. What is really striking is that nowhere does he use the argument: 'We have preserved the episcopal succession, and therefore have not departed from the Church.' His appeal is always, as in Luther's and Calvin's works, to the word of God. He does however write as follows:

> Furthermore, we believe that there be divers degrees of ministers in the Church; whereof some be deacons, some priests, some bishops, to whom is committed the office to instruct the people, and the whole charge and setting forth of religion.[3]

But he does not draw any doctrinal conclusions from his belief in the threefold ministry, so his attitude is very much that of the Preface to the Ordinal in the Book of Common Prayer. The Church of England intends to preserve the three orders of the ministry, but does not officially pass any judgement on those who have the ministry in another form.

Hooker's view of episcopacy is peculiar to himself: he could neither reject it as non-scriptural, nor could he agree with the traditional view that it was instituted by our Lord. He outlines a theory that it was devised by the apostles as a remedy against disunity. In Book VII of the *Ecclesiastical Polity* he gives the impression of being definitely on the 'catholic' side:

> Which [sc. the sacred regiment of bishops] to have been ordained of God, I am for mine own part even as resolutely persuaded, as that any other kind of government in the world whatsoever is of God.[4]

But presently we realize that this is not the same as saying that Christ instituted episcopacy. A little later he writes:

> The same word [sc. bishop] in ecclesiastical writings being applied unto church governors, at the first unto all and not unto the chiefest only, grew in short time peculiar and proper to signify such episcopal authority alone as the chiefest governors exercised over the rest.[5]

[1] Part V, ch. 15.3, p. 111.   [2] Part VI, ch. 20, p. 144.   [3] Part II, ch. 2.1, p. 21.
[4] Book VII, ch. 1.4, p. 329. (Page references are to the Oxford edition of 1845.)
[5] Ch. 2.2, p. 332.

This is more like the view defended in *The Apostolic Ministry*, that there were degrees of *episkope* in the New Testament Church. Later still[1] Hooker puts forward his theory that the apostles founded colleges of presbyter-bishops, but that this occasioned disputes, so one was picked out from the rest in each place, on the model of the Jerusalem church, to rule over them. This is to treat episcopacy as an apostolic ordinance rather than as something directly instituted by Christ.

In ch. 11 we find some hints that this derivation of episcopacy from the apostles was not regarded by Hooker as conclusively proved:

> Albeit[2] the Scripture did no way insinuate the same to be God's ordinance, and the Apostles to have brought it in, albeit the Church were acknowledged by all men to have been the first beginner thereof a long time after the Apostles were gone; yet is not the authority of bishops hereby disannulled, it is not hereby proved unfit or unprofitable for the Church.[3]

A little later he tells us that his own opinions had changed in favour of the 'catholic' view:

> Now, although we should leave the general received persuasion held from the first beginning, that the Apostles themselves left bishops invested with power above other pastors; although, I say, we should give over this opinion and embrace that other conjecture which so many have thought good to follow, and which myself did sometime judge a great deal more probable than now I do, merely that after the Apostles were deceased, churches did agree among themselves for preservation of peace and order to make one presbyter in each city chief over the rest, and to translate unto him that power by force and virtue whereof the Apostles, while they were yet alive, did preserve and uphold order in the Church, exercising spiritual jurisdiction partly by themselves and partly by evangelists, because they could not always everywhere themselves be present— . . . etc.[4]

The apodosis naturally is that even so we are not justified in rejecting episcopacy. We notice that the view towards which Hooker has eventually inclined is not that our Lord instituted episcopacy, but that the apostles did. Hooker's proof of episcopacy from Scripture is no worse than Calvin's proof of Presbyterianism from Scripture; indeed we might say that it is rather better than Calvin's as being less dogmatically put forward. It is *mutatis mutandis* very like the proof of episcopacy from Scripture put forward by modern Anglo-Catholics, and we can say of it what we say of

---

[1] Ch. 5.1, pp. 340 f.
[2] 'Albeit' here means not 'although', but 'supposing for the sake of argument'; see also the next quotation, where 'although' is used in this sense as well.
[3] Ch. 11.2, p. 382.   [4] Ch. 11.8, p. 385.

I

that: it will seem convincing to those already convinced on other grounds. It will not convince others.

No doubt because Hooker defended the 'catholic' view of the origin of the ministry and the threefold order of the ministry as included in the Elizabethan settlement, he does not look very deeply into the question: what is the function of the ministry? Here he is like Calvin, in that he seems to think the primary function of the ministry is that of rule.

> Hereupon we hold that God's clergy are a state which hath been and will be as long as there is a Church upon earth, necessary by the plain word of God himself; a state whereunto the rest of God's people must be subject as touching things that appertain to their souls' health.[1]

Again in Book VI, we read:

> I therefore conclude that spiritual authority is a power which Christ hath given to be used over them which are subject unto it for the eternal good of their souls, according to his own most sacred laws and the wholesome positive constitutions of his Church.[2]

Here all the emphasis is on the ruling function of the ministry: we miss any reference to the ministry as service, such as Luther so finely rediscovered.

In one respect Hooker falls short of both Luther and Calvin. He does not seem to give the laity any part at all in selecting or ordaining the clergy. His sole reference to this is his statement to the effect that the part of the laity in assigning their sphere of work to the clergy (not in ordaining, for they have none) is exercised by patrons.[3] He was committed to defending the whole of the Elizabethan settlement between church and state, the unfortunate compromises as well as the permanent principles.

Although we can trace a resemblance between Hooker's position with regard to the origin of the ministry and that of modern Anglo-Catholics, in one respect he is entirely different from them. He deliberately refuses to unchurch non-episcopal churches. The passages in which he makes this clear are well known, but must be quoted. The first is as follows:

> In which respect for mine own part, although I see that certain reformed churches, the Scottish especially and the French, have not that which best agreeth with the sacred Scriptures, I mean the government that is by Bishops, inasmuch as both these churches are fallen under a different kind of regiment; which to remedy it is for the one altogether too late, and too soon for the other during their present afflictions and trouble: this their defect and imperfection I had rather lament than exagitate, considering that men often times without any fault of their

[1] Book III, ch. 11.20, p. 344.
[2] Book VI, ch. 2.2, p. 238.   [3] Book VII, ch. 14.12, p. 404.

own may be driven to want that kind of polity or regiment which is best, and to content themselves with that, which either the irremediable error of former times, or the necessity of the present hath cast upon them.[1]

He puts it even more clearly in Book VII:

> There may be sometimes very just and sufficient reason to allow ordination made without a bishop. The whole Church visible being the true original subject of all power, it hath not ordinarily allowed any other than bishops alone to ordain; howbeit, as the ordinary course is ordinarily in all things to be observed, so it may be in some cases not unnecessary that we decline from the ordinary ways. . . . Another extraordinary kind of vocation is, when the exigence of necessity doth constrain to leave the usual way of the Church, which otherwise we would willingly keep: where the Church must needs have some ordained, and neither hath nor can have possibly a bishop to ordain: in cases of such necessity, the ordinary institution of God hath given oftentimes, and may give, place. And therefore we are not simply without exception to urge a lineal descent of power from the Apostles by continued succession of Bishops in every effectual ordination.[2]

However this power of exception may be applied in particular cases, it is quite clear from this passage that Hooker could not have held episcopacy to be of the very *esse* of the Church. Indeed we can trace in this passage the possibility of a more profound approach to the doctrine of the ministry. Hooker says that the whole Church visible is the original subject of all power, and he infers that in certain circumstances the Church may deviate from the rule of episcopal ordination. According to strict 'catholic' theory this would be impossible, for the Church does not possess the ministry. We are reminded here of Luther's bold resort to baptism as that which ultimately gives authority to the ministry. But neither the circumstances of the time, nor Hooker's cautious temper of mind, made it easy for him to pursue this insight to its logical conclusion.

The last Reformer whose works we consider lived nearly a hundred years later than Hooker. In certain ways John Owen (1616–83) comes nearer to the New Testament than any other Reformer. And yet he too at some points is still held by the 'catholic' conception of the ministry. We may begin by noting that John Owen strongly emphasized Luther's intuition that the nature of the ministry is one of service. Indeed in this respect he comes closer to the New Testament teaching even than Luther does, for he connects the ordained ministry with our Lord's ministry. For example, in his 'Discourse on Spiritual Gifts'[3] he says that Christ's

---

[1] Book III, ch. 11.17, p. 340.   [2] Book VII, ch. 14.11, p. 402.
[3] John Owen, *Works*, ed. W. H. Goold, Vol. IV, London and Edinburgh, 1852, p. 490.

going down into the lower parts of the earth, i.e. his humiliation in the Incarnation, is the 'fountain and origin of the ministry of the church'. In another work he makes the fine assertion that the ministry is 'a branch that grew out of the grave of Christ'.[1] In the 'Discourse' quoted above Owen claims that the ministry has the rule in the Church, but that this rule is spiritual, not secular or coercive, and its end is 'merely and solely the edification of the church'.[2] Again, in 'The True Nature of a Gospel Church' he mentions 'a compassionate suffering with all the members of the church' as a qualification for the ministry, and he quotes II Cor. 11.29.[3] This is very like Paul's conception of the ministry as living out Christ's life in the Church. Finally in this connection we may quote an admirable summary of the purpose of the ministry which we find later on in the same work:

> The especial design of the rule of the church in its government is, to represent the holiness, love, compassion, care, and authority of Christ towards his church.[4]

On the other hand, Owen is very firmly on the side of Calvin and the 'catholic' conception of the purpose of the ministry when he comes to define the source from which the ministry derives its authority. He will have nothing to do with any theory that suggests the ministry gains its authority from the Church. God does use the Church as the instrument by which this power is conveyed, but this does not mean that the Church itself possesses ministerial power or authority. We quote the 'Discourse on Spiritual Gifts':

> He (Christ) doth it (makes ministers) by giving power unto his church in all ages to call and separate unto the work of the ministry such as he hath fitted and gifted for it. . . . Hence all the acting of the church in this matter is nothing but an instituted means of conveying authority and office from Christ unto persons called thereunto. The church doth not give them any authority of its own or resident in itself; but only in a way of obedience unto Christ, doth transmit power from him unto them who are called. Hence do they become ministers of Christ. . . . Some would have ministers of the gospel to receive all their authority from the people that choose them, and some from the bishops that ordain them, and whence they have theirs, I know not.[5]

By 'the church' John Owen meant the local congregation,[6] both elders and laity taking part in the laying on of hands. This view of ministerial authority is expanded in a passage in 'The True Nature of a Gospel Church':

---

[1] *Ibid.*, Vol. IX, 1851, 'The Ministry the Gift of Christ', p. 441.
[2] *Ibid.*, Vol. IV, pp. 514 f.   [3] *Ibid.*, Vol. XVI, 1853, p. 87.
[4] *Ibid.*, p. 135.   [5] *Ibid.*, Vol. IV, p. 494.   [6] *Ibid.*, Vol. XVI, p. 55

The Lord Jesus Christ having instituted and appointed officers, rulers, or leaders in his church . . . to look unto the discharge of all church duties among the members of it, to administer and dispense all its privileges, and to exercise all its authority . . . etc.[1]

The ministers are in no sense representatives of the Church, but of Christ.

It was because of this somewhat 'sacerdotal' view of the ministry that Owen did not allow unordained men to administer the Sacraments, thereby differing in a remarkable way from the practice of many modern Congregationalists. See 'The True Nature of a Gospel Church', and notice the following passage, where he asks the question: suppose a church has not got a pastor, may it delegate the administration of the Sacraments to some one member of the church for the time being?[2] He answers that it may not:

If the church may delegate or substitute others for the discharge of all ordinances whatsoever, without elders or pastors, then it may perfect the saints, and complete the work of the ministry without them, which is contrary to Eph. 4.11, 12, and, secondly, it would render the ministry only convenient, and not absolutely necessary to the church, which is contrary to the institution of it.[3]

To complete this picture, we may quote another passage some pages later. He definitely rejects the view of those who believe that

all church power or authority is seated in the community of the brethren or body of the people; and they look on ministers as . . . acting the authority of the church by a mere delegation, and not any of their own received directly from Christ.[4]

In this respect John Owen, Dean of Christ Church in the seventeenth century, and William Temple, Archbishop of Canterbury in the twentieth, appear to join hands.[5]

There is however one great flaw in John Owen's doctrine: all that he says of the relation of the ministry to the Church he means to apply to the local gathered congregation only. He did not believe in any visible catholic Church. He makes this quite clear in his Preface to 'The True Nature of a Gospel Church':

We know of no catholic visible church that any pastors are ordained to.[6]

In fact he seems to believe in an invisible catholic Church and a visible local congregation. We must regret this, as in this respect he was something less than faithful to the New Testament. All that Paul tells us about

---

[1] *Ibid.*, p. 28.   [2] *Ibid.*, p. 17.   [3] *Ibid.*, p. 80.
[4] *Ibid.*, p. 112.   [5] See p. 143, below.   [6] *Op. cit.*, Vol. XVI, p. 4.

the ministry is told in the context of a local church situation, but his conception of the Church as the Remnant, and what he says about the Church as a whole in such passages as I Cor. 12 and Eph. 4, make it plain that the local church is the representative of the whole Church. It does not in itself completely exhaust the meaning of the whole. We should however be grateful to Owen for his contribution to the thought of the Reformers about the relation of the ministry to the Church, and we should surely regret that, owing to social and political circumstances, his theology became canalized as the possession of one body of Christians only. He is in fact a sort of bridge between Luther and Calvin: he has Luther's insight into the function of the ministry, and Calvin's emphasis on the ministry as the sole repository of the Church's authority. And, as we have seen, he does in some ways remind us of the 'catholic' theory of the ministry in his virtual exclusion of the laity from any exercise of the Church's authority. It is true that his method of perpetuating the authority of the Church in the ministry is quite different from the 'catholic' one. He has no use at all for continuity in time: authority always comes vertically from Christ, the local church (laity as well as elders) being the *ad hoc* vehicle by which the authority is conveyed. But he is as firm as any Ultramontanist that Church authority belongs to the ministry, and to the ministry alone.

10

The Modern Debate

THE REFORMATION caused a reappraisal of the doctrine of the relation of the Church to the ministry. It did not produce a standard doctrine on this subject, nor did it solve many questions about the ministry. But it meant that in future the 'catholic' doctrine of the ministry would not go unchallenged, and would have to vindicate itself as scriptural if it was to be accepted by Reformed Christians. The only place, however, where Reformed Christians still maintained a form of the ministry continuous with that of the mediaeval church was England.[1] Consequently it is in England that the debate about the origin and form of the ministry has been most acute. Two developments in the nineteenth century gave this debate fresh impetus: the first was the Tractarian Movement, with its revival of the 'catholic' theory of episcopacy in its strictest form. The second was the rise of historical criticism of the New Testament, which meant that a great many arguments on both sides had to be reconsidered, or at least restated. We must remind ourselves, however, that in this work we are not primarily concerned with the question of ministerial succession, around which the debate has raged hottest. We are interested in defining the relation of the ministry to the Church.

In examining questions which have exercised English theologians during the last hundred years, it is usually profitable to see what F. D. Maurice had to say on the subject under consideration. Unfortunately, however, Maurice seems to have written little of lasting value on the precise subject that concerns us. We find in him the same *a priori* approach that we find later in Gore and in the authors of *The Apostolic Ministry*. He seems to assume that, because the apostles were given authority by our Lord, and because the bishop in the second century is found possessing the greatest authority in the Church, the apostles must somehow or other have deliberately passed on their authority to the bishops. One quotation therefore will suffice:

[1] I am aware that, strictly speaking, Sweden could also be put in this category, but owing to historical circumstances the question of the ministry does not seem to have been hotly debated there.

But supposing it were calmly represented . . . that, according to the doctrine that has always prevailed in the Church, the episcopate does contain in it the administration of the sacraments, the delivery of absolution, the preaching of the Gospel, the ministering to the sick and poor—all the functions in short which were at any time committed by our Lord to his immediate disciples; and that the bishops have, and ought to believe they have, all needful powers for performing these functions: secondly, that their connection with previous ages and with the first Apostles is maintained expressly as a witness of the permanent constitution of the Church, and therefore of the continued abiding of Christ in it, and of each bishop in each case being his servant and the receiver of gifts and powers directly from him—they [Maurice's imaginary interlocutors] may begin perhaps to view the whole subject differently. . . . They may ask themselves with some anxiety whether there be any reason to expect that an order will be introduced by signs and wonders which seems to be already in being, whether there be anything to justify them in standing aloof from the body of Christ's universal Church, and in not submitting to those whom he has himself placed over it.[1]

Maurice's style is not very lucid, and it is not easy to decide what exactly he believes about the relation of the Church to the ministry, but the following points seem to stand out: Maurice believes that our Lord gave ministerial authority over the Church to his apostles, and that they have handed this authority on to the bishops, not *via* the Church but directly. It seems to be full authority; there does not seem to be any authority left for anyone else. The episcopate *seems* to be essential to the Church, since those who do not accept it are described as 'standing aloof from the body of Christ's universal Church'; indeed a claim is here made for episcopacy which we have not previously encountered: the episcopate is a witness to Christ's continued presence in the Church. This may be mostly rhetoric, but if taken to its logical extreme would seem to imply that episcopacy (not just the ministry, but episcopacy as such) is a sort of sacrament of the Holy Spirit. Finally Maurice seems to suggest that episcopacy was deliberately instituted by our Lord. In this respect Maurice is what he is not in most other respects, typical of one school of theologians in Anglicanism. The Tractarians and their successors exalt episcopacy as such to a higher position than do any other theologians in Christendom; they make it more essential and central to the Church's life than do either Roman Catholics or Orthodox. We cannot help feeling that this verges on idolatry and is not characteristic of a balanced and catholic theology, but is rather a product of local historical circumstances.

[1] F. D. Maurice, *The Kingdom of Christ*, ed. A. R. Vidler, London, 1958, Vol. II, pp. 139 f.

In 1897 a book by F. J. A. Hort called *The Christian Ecclesia* was published posthumously. It represents just what one would have expected from so great a scholar, a careful examination of the New Testament evidence about the Church. It is chiefly remarkable from the point of view of this study because Hort clearly states one of the principal points on which we have insisted in earlier chapters, that the apostles represent not the rulers of the Church, but the Church itself.[1]

> In virtue of this personal faith vivifying their discipleship, the Apostles became themselves the first little Ecclesia, constituting a living rock upon which a far larger and ever enlarging Ecclesia should very shortly be built slowly up.

This conclusion is confirmed by Hort's consideration of the institution of the Eucharist. He writes:

> If they [the Twelve] represented an apostolic order within the Ecclesia, then the Holy Communion must have been intended only for members of that order, and the rest of the Ecclesia had no part in it. But if, as the men of the sub-apostolic age and subsequent ages believed without hesitation, the Holy Communion was meant for the Ecclesia at large, then the disciples sat there that evening as representatives of the Ecclesia at large.[2]

Hort goes on to draw the natural conclusion that the Church as a whole is the true heir to the mission of the apostles,[3] and, we may conclude, of all other promises and commands given to the apostles by our Lord, such as those related in John 20.21–23; 21.15–17.

We may give one other quotation, as it exactly agrees with the conclusions reached earlier on in this work:

> It would seem then that they themselves [the apostles] constituted the foundation in the sense which the Gospels led us to recognize, the chosen band of intimate disciples, the first rudimentary Ecclesia, on which the Ecclesia of Palestine was first built, and then indirectly every other Ecclesia, whether it had or had not been personally founded by an Apostle.[4]

Hort does not however link up the apostolic band with the faithful Remnant of the Old Testament, and he has not traced out the genuinely apostolic character of the New Testament ministry as reflected in St Paul's Epistles.

We now turn to two books written within a few years of each other, and written with very much the same purpose, to prove by examination of the

---

[1] *Op. cit.*, p. 17.
[3] *Ibid.*, p. 32.
[2] *Ibid.*, p. 30.
[4] *Ibid.*, p. 167.

scriptural and sub-apostolic evidence that the episcopate was the legitimate heir of the apostles' ruling authority, and that this was God's intention. We shall examine both books with a special interest in any light they throw on the relation of the ministry to the church.

R. C. Moberly's book, *Ministerial Priesthood*[1] is chiefly valuable for a very careful and theological statement of a representative or ministerial doctrine of priesthood, over against the Roman Catholic doctrine of a vicarial priesthood on the one hand and the Free Church denial of any ministerial priesthood on the other.[2] On p. 95 Moberly writes:

> It is an abuse of the sacerdotal conception, if it supposed that the priesthood exists to celebrate sacrifices or acts of worship in the place of the body of the people or as their substitute.

And here on p. 242 is a most careful statement of Christian priesthood:

> The Christian Priest does not offer an atoning sacrifice on behalf of the Church: it is rather the Church through his act that, not so much 'offers an atonement', as 'is identified on earth with the one heavenly offering of the atonement of Christ'.

Moberly even glances at the picture of the priestly life which Paul gives in I Cor. 4,[3] but he draws no theological conclusions from it and contents himself with remarking that the dominant idea here is 'the unreserved offering, the total self-dedication . . . joy only in completeness of utter sacrifice'.

With so scriptural a conception of ministerial priesthood, we might expect that Moberly would outline a theory of ministerial authority that would relate ministry to Church more integrally than does the 'catholic' doctrine. But he seems to be prevented from doing this by the assumption on which the book is founded: it must be shown that Church authority is passed on within the ministry without reference to the rest of the Church. On p. 68 Moberly discusses this very question of the relation of the ministry to the church. He denies that the ministry is the intermediary between the Body and its life, or that the ministry confers life on the Body.[4] 'The ministers', he says, 'are the organs of the Body, through which the Body expresses itself in particular functions of detail.' But Moberly adds that this does not mean the Body can dispense with these organs, or even that 'the authority of the ministers to minister is derived from, or is con-

---

[1] All quotations are from the second edition, London, 1899.

[2] This is emphatically not to suggest that modern Free Churchmen would deny a ministerial priesthood; but it has to be remembered that sixty years ago Free Church theology was very much under the influence of Liberalism and individualism, and also that Moberly was evidently not in close personal touch with those Free Churchmen whose views he opposed.

[3] *Ibid.*, pp. 284 f.   [4] Contrast Maurice as quoted on p. 136, above.

ferred by, the mere act or will of the Body'. And he quotes Gore to the effect that 'the ministry is the instrument as well as the symbol of the Church's unity'. That the ministry is the symbol of the Church's unity we can readily agree, but that the ministry is the instrument of the Church's unity is not the doctrine of the New Testament. As we have seen, the ministry, like the Eucharist, is an expression of the unity already given in baptism. It does not constitute the Church as baptism does. Again, in Moberly's language we seem to detect that use of what A. P. Herbert has called 'witch-words'[1] which are so frequently met with in the writings of this school of theologians: the authority of the ministers, Moberly says, is not conferred by a 'mere act' of the Body. But authority is, apparently, conferred by a mere act of the bishop. All are agreed that ministerial authority is conferred by Christ. The question is: is it conferred by Christ through the Church or not? Moberly seems to be saying that it is conferred by Christ through the ministry apart from the Church.

Moberly elaborates his theory on p. 106, where he distinguishes three possible views of how the divine commission can be conveyed: (a) directly by God's call; (b) by the Church, but by any means the Church chooses; (c) by those who have themselves received it from duly authorized persons. Naturally he decides in favour of the third view. There is indeed a sense in which it is the only possible view: the authorized ministers must be duly authorized. But Moberly is not justified in proceeding to draw the conclusion that the episcopate is the only duly authorized ministry. The New Testament, as we have seen, offers no support for this. Again, we can claim that at the time of the Reformation the Church was divided: there was no agreement among Western Christians as to what the duly authorized commissioning body of the Church was. In countries where the historic episcopate was not retained, such as Denmark, Germany Switzerland, and Scotland, it is not justifiable to say that the Church did not have authority to appoint ministers. The ministry is the instrument of the Church, but the Church is not dependent on the ministry for its very existence, or rather the ministry is the Church in its pioneer, apostolic aspect, and hence the ministry cannot be lost by mere failure of succession. This is the difficulty which we always encounter with the 'catholic' doctrine of the ministry. It first separates the ministry from the Church, and then delivers the Church bound hand and foot into the hand of the ministry. The relation between the two is external, not integral; legal, not theological.

---

[1] By this he means tendentious epithets: e.g. 'intoxicating liquor' for wine. A.P.H. himself suggests 'lethal vehicles' for motor-cars.

As we might expect, we find that much of Moberly's argument in favour of the authority of the apostles in the New Testament, and of the transmission of that authority to the second-century episcopate, is based on the argument from silence. Thus on p. 136 we read: 'Nothing comes into existence on a basis independent of the apostolate.' We might ask: who founded the church in Rome? We may presume that Moberly would not have attributed this to either Peter or Paul, so the only possible answer compatible with Moberly's theory is: it was founded by some person or persons unknown, who must have been commissioned by the apostles. But here is sheer conjecture, unless he be willing to accept Andronicus and Junias in Rom. 16.7 as members of the original apostolic body. We encounter the same combination of *a priori* assumption with *argumentum e silentio* in Moberly's treatment of the evidence to be gleaned from Clement of Rome. Thus on p. 183 he argues that, though there is no hint of any higher authority than the presbyterate in Clement's *Epistle*, it must be implied there, and he finds the bishops, as do several of his successors in this school, in the ἐλλόγιμοι ἄνδρες of I Clement XLIV 2 f.[1] Moberly's argument is very simple: these men were either presbyters or bishops. But they were not presbyters, as that would not explain the existence of bishops such as we find elsewhere at this period. Therefore they were bishops.[2]

Charles Gore's book, *The Church and the Ministry*, came out at about the same time as Moberly's and uses very much the same arguments.[3] On p. 71 of this work Gore gives some more general considerations on the subject of the apostolic succession; he maintains that, unless there is an apostolic succession, it is impossible to persuade the average Christian that sacramental grace really comes from outside and from above. If so, it is remarkable that the first Christian missionaries of whom we read in the New Testament do not seem to have encountered this difficulty: we do not find them appealing to the authority of the ministry as a proof of the reality of their ministrations. In fact they do just the reverse; see II Cor. 12.12; Rom. 15.18 f. But, even assuming that this difficulty exists in the minds of some Christians, why should a doctrine of the apostolic succession be necessary in order to prove the reality of divine grace? Sacramental grace comes to us through the Church; why is the heredity and claim of the Church not sufficient guarantee, if guarantee is needed? Even according to Gore's theory the apostolic succession does not seem to be necessary in order to convince men of the reality of baptismal grace; why then should it be necessary in the case of the Eucharist?

---

[1] See pp. 111 f., above.   [2] *Op. cit.*, p. 189.
[3] We quote however from the 5th edition, London, 1913.

Gore's arguments to prove the continuity of the apostolate through to the time of monepiscopacy are no more satisfactory than Moberly's. He is anxious to prove that Paul exercised a catholic jurisdiction, not only one extending to the churches he founded.[1] We have seen reason to doubt this on the basis of such passages as II Cor. 10.13–16; Rom. 1.11 f.; 15.20. Gore also discusses the significance of the episcopate in Ignatius' *Epistles*, and he claims that throughout the period from the death of Paul to the writing of Ignatius' *Epistles* there was an episcopal office, distinct from the presbyterate, which nevertheless bore the name of πρεσβύτερος as well as of ἐπίσκοπος. He sums it up thus:

The bishops then in Ignatius succeed to an authority which had been apostolic and had never belonged to the presbyters.[2]

This is precisely the point for which the evidence is lacking. The evidence would in fact seem to admit of two possible views: (*a*) The apostles gave their authority to the local presbyterate (whose members could also be called ἐπίσκοποι), and from this presbyterate the second-century form of monepiscopacy developed. But in this case the word 'apostles' must be very liberally interpreted, to include, for example, such men as Andronicus and Junias. (*b*) The apostles did not regularly give authority to any one set of ministers. The presbyterate developed locally, and from it monepiscopacy arose.

The conception of the pioneer, apostolic ministry which we have traced in Paul's writings is compatible with either view. The doctrine of the apostolic succession is, strictly speaking, compatible with the first view, though not with the second. Gore, like Moberly, manages to smuggle some sort of bishops into the church in Corinth as we find it in Clement's *Epistle*.[3] But he only achieves this by interpreting the phrase οἱ ἡγούμενοι in chs. I and XXI as referring to bishops in contradistinction to presbyters. Even so, this argument proves too much, for it indicates, if it is true, more than one bishop in Corinth at the time, but a college of bishops at this time is exactly what this school of theologians argues against. It also leaves us with the mysterious situation that Clement, writing to a church where the laity had driven out the clergy, never once mentions the bishop either by name or by office, but contents himself with two obscure references to the bishop in the plural. On the whole Gore is not at his best in this book. Moberly, though his historical arguments are no more convincing than Gore's, is a far more persuasive and convincing advocate of his view, and is far more aware of the need to provide a theological account of the relation of the ministry to the Church.

[1] *Op. cit.*, p. 217.   *Ibid.*, p. 277.   [3] *Ibid.*, p. 292.

We now pass to two writers of the earlier part of this century who represent a return to Hort's position; they do not claim any more for the episcopate than the historical evidence warrants, but they do not for that reason reject episcopacy. A. C. Headlam, writing in 1920, deliberately reaffirms Hort's conclusion as the only one that will fit the evidence. He writes:

> They (the apostles), sometimes with others, sometimes without, are the Church in embryo, the nucleus from which it grew, the seed which was to develop, and as the Church they received directions which are intended for the Church of the future. Authority is given to the Church.[1]

We also give three quotations about episcopacy which are relevant to our purpose:

> We may believe that an Apostolic ministry is an important part of Church life, but we have no ground in Scripture for making it the one thing that matters.

> We cannot therefore say that any form [of the ministry] is essential to entitle it to be called a Church, nor are we entitled to say that any particular Christian society has no claim to be considered a part of the Church because it has not a particular form of the ministry.

> The Early Church held that the bishops were the successors of the Apostles, but there is no evidence at all to shew that it considered that they held that position because they had received grace by transmission from the Apostles. They were the successors of the Apostles because they had been appointed by the Church to perform those functions which the Apostles had performed.[2]

These statements are true, but they are largely negative. Headlam does not elaborate a theology which connects the ministry with the Church. The attraction of the 'catholic' view is that it does provide a link between Church and ministry, even though it must be criticized as an external and legal connection. We may guess that the 'catholic' theory will continue to attract many, despite the weakness of the historical evidence, until it is realized that the New Testament itself provides a link between Church and ministry more integral and more closely related to the Incarnation than anything which the 'catholic' theory offers.

It is a great misfortune for our understanding of the theology of the ministry that O. C. Quick did not live longer. He might have written something more solid and authoritative on the ministry than he was actually able to do. But even his relatively brief account of the ministry in *The Christian Sacraments* goes some way towards supplementing Head-

---

[1] *The Doctrine of the Church and Christian Reunion* (Bampton Lectures), 2nd ed., London, 1920, p. 37.   [2] *Ibid.*, pp. 215, 242, 265.

lam's deficiency. His criticism of the 'catholic' (or, to be more exact, the Tractarian) theory of the ministry is extremely acute. He reduces it to an absurdity:

> We are required to accept the intolerable paradox that a man who has ordination in some hole-and-corner fashion from a wandering bishop deprived of all office and jurisdiction is fully and validly ordained, whereas one who has received the solemn authorization of one, say, of the great Presbyterian communions is not ordained at all. This seems contrary to reason, if authority is really of the essence of orders.[1]

Quick has put his finger on the great weakness of the 'catholic' theory: the ministry is completely divorced from the Church. Quick's own conclusion about orders is most interesting: authority is of the essence of orders, therefore, as long as the Church is divided, all orders are to that extent lacking in full authority.

Finally, we turn to a group of five theologians who might all be described as being still living influences, indeed three of them are still living and joining in the debate from time to time by their writings. The first is William Temple. He is surely one of those people, like Maurice, whose utterances on any subject one cannot afford to ignore. And yet, like Maurice in this instance also, his theory proves strangely unsatisfactory and ill-considered when we examine its implications. What Archbishop Temple said is as follows:

> When we go back to the first records of the Church we find neither a Ministry which called people into association with it, nor an undifferentiated fellowship which delegated powers to a Ministry; but we find a complete Church, with the Apostolate accepted as the focus of its administration and authority. When the Lord's earthly ministry was ended, there was found in the world as its fruit and as means of its continuance this Body, in which the distinction of Ministry and Laity is already established. The Apostles were in no sense ministers of the Laity, they were ministers of Christ to the laity, and to the world waiting to be won. They took steps for the perpetuation of the ministry, and it has descended to ourselves. So when I consecrate a godly and well learned man to the office and work of a Bishop in the Church of God, I do not act as a representative of the Church, if by that is meant the whole number of contemporary Christians; but I do act as the ministerial instrument of Christ in His Body the Church. The authority by which I act is His, transmitted to me through His apostles and those to whom they committed it; I hold it neither from the Church nor apart from the Church, but from Christ in the Church.[2]

[1] *Op. cit.*, London, 1927, p. 143.
[2] Quoted in E. J. Bicknell, *The Thirty-nine Articles*, 3rd ed., revised by H. J. Carpenter, London, 1955, p. 332. It is part of Temple's presidential address to the Convocation

This is in fact a very definite statement of the 'catholic' view of the relation of the ministry to the Church, and shows up in a remarkable fashion the weaknesses of that view. We may first point out the historical difficulties inherent in it: 'the distinction of the Ministry and the Laity is already established' when we first have any record of the Church, we are told. This means, we may presume, that the Twelve (plus Paul? plus James?) were the ministry and the rest the laity. But surely ministry (*diakonia*) is not restricted to the Twelve in the New Testament. Is it then perhaps that the Twelve had in their hands all authority? But even this is extremely doubtful. Except that the Twelve were the nucleus of the Church, it is very difficult to say what else they had exclusively to themselves.

Again, Temple says that the Apostolate (he does not define how many, but presumably a limited number) 'took steps for the perpetuation of the ministry'. This is precisely the debatable point, the unproved assumption on which the whole 'catholic' theory of the ministry depends. What steps did they take? Except for Paul, the only possible way in which the ministry of the other apostles could have been described as being perpetuated was in the presbyters of the Jerusalem church in Acts. But to describe these presbyters as successors to the apostles is absolutely fatal to the 'catholic' theory of the ministry. That is why everyone who tries to find evidence for the 'catholic' theory has to invent or discover a set of bishops (who were also called presbyters) to carry on the essential succession from the apostles to the bishop of the second century. Even when we turn to Paul, about whom we know so much more, it is not easy to say exactly what steps he took to perpetuate the ministry of the apostles. He certainly appointed local ministers, who were called bishops or presbyters or both. But it is just this category of minister whom the 'catholic' school of theologians is most unwilling to describe as recipients of full apostolic authority. They only seem to have local authority, so some others must be found to carry on the universal authority through the 'tunnel' period till the time of Ignatius at earliest. So recourse must be had to such figures as Timothy, Titus, and even perhaps Clement, who are described as 'apostolic men', not exactly apostles and not exactly bishops, but useful to bridge the gap. So Temple's simple statement about the apostles perpetuating their ministry does in fact beg a whole encyclopaedia of questions.

Great as are the historical difficulties inherent in Temple's account of

of Canterbury in May 1943. The last sentence is quoted with approval in the *Lambeth Conference 1958* report, London, 1958, Part 2, p. 88. This is perhaps not the only instance in which the Lambeth Fathers have given commendation to a view whose implications they did not stay to examine very closely.

the ministry, the theological difficulties are even greater: 'When I conse-
crate a godly and well learned man to the office and work of a Bishop ...
I do not act as a representative of the Church, if by that is meant the whole
number of contemporary Christians; but I do act as a ministerial instrument of Christ in His Body the Church.' Is it possible to represent Christ
without representing the Church? Surely we have here the possibility of a
dangerous divorce between Christ and the Church, between Christ's
authority and the Church's authority.

One thing at least is clear: Temple's theory is incompatible with
Moberly's carefully expounded theory of representative or ministerial
priesthood. Temple denies that he represents the Church militant. What
then is the office and function of a bishop? We in the Church of South
India have deliberately adopted and willingly put into practice the historic episcopate because we believed that the bishop is the fittest representative of the whole Church. Those who have previously worked in non-
episcopal churches have often borne testimony to the fact that they now
find in the historic episcopate a means by which the ministry and authority
of the whole Church is exercised and represented. Indeed the main difference that union has brought to the Christian coolie in his remote village
is that now from time to time he meets one who represents to him not just
the Christians in the area in which he lives, but all the Christians in the
diocese, and beyond that too. We rejoice in our possession of the episcopate because we believe it to be representative of the whole Church. But
if we are to believe the exponents of the 'catholic' view, we are mistaken.
The bishop, it seems, has no integral connection with the Church as we
know it; he has been appointed by Christ, without reference to the Church,
to exercise authority in the Church. He has been given an authority which
does not belong to the rest of the Church and which the rest of the Church
can neither give him nor take away from him.

Temple's language in the passage quoted above, in which he claims an
authority transmitted to him from the apostles independently of the Church,
underlines a fundamental difficulty which this view of the ministry encounters. As Daniel Jenkins well expresses it 'One of the most misleading
implications of the Catholic doctrine of the apostolic succession is that it
must be taken for granted that the only possible successors of the apostles
are the ministers of the Church.'[1] The same weakness is clearly illustrated
in E. L. Mascall's book, *The Recovery of Unity* (quoted above p. 12), when
he writes, 'The bishop himself has received his full apostolate from those
other bishops who together represent the Apostolate of the universal

---

[1] *The Protestant Ministry*, London, 1958, p. 34.

K

Church.'[1] 'Represent' here seems to mean 'constitute'. Perhaps only in a Western situation could anyone so easily persuade himself that the bishops only had the apostolate of the Church. In a missionary situation such as one finds in Asia and Africa today it is much more obvious that the apostolate belongs to the whole Church and therefore must be exercised by every individual Christian as well as by the ministry. The very latest demonstration of this attitude is provided by Dr Farrer in his new Foreword to *The Apostolic Ministry* (already quoted on p. 10). Dealing with alternative theories about the origin of the ministry to his, he sums them all up in the words, 'There is no apostolic ministry because all are apostles.'[2] This seems to be a simple *non sequitur*. If the Church is apostolic, there must be some sense in which all Christians are apostles. The truth is that the authors of *The Apostolic Ministry* wholly fail to convince us that they believe in an apostolic Church at all. The ministry has monopolized the apostolate of the Church.

It is interesting to compare with Temple a modern Roman Catholic writer, Emil Mersch. In his monumental work, *The Theology of the Mystical Body*,[3] Fr Mersch does have something to say of the relation of the ministry to the Church. At first sight it looks as if he gives a very important function to the Church as a whole:

> The Vatican Council declares that the Church is the custodian and teacher of revealed truth.[4]

A little later on we read:

> The Church is Christ and Christ is God. When the Church as such speaks, we need not pursue our investigations further.

But we soon realize that when he speaks of the Church he really means the ministry: it is the ministry that is the custodian of revealed truth; when 'the Church as such speaks', it is in fact the ministry (to be exact, the Bishop of Rome) that speaks. So we are not surprised to read:

> The authority possessed by ecclesiastic superiors is that possessed by Christ in His sacred humanity.[5]

The ministry in fact seems to have entirely eclipsed the rest of the Church. The climax is reached when he says:

> Even when superiors are wrong, and even, as can happen, when they are responsible for their own error, the subject does the will of Christ in obeying them.[6]

[1] *Op. cit.*, pp. 173 f.   [2] *Op. cit.*, p. xviii.   [3] ET, London, 1952.
[4] *Op. cit.*, p. 527.   [5] *Ibid.*, p. 537.   [6] *Ibid.*, p. 544.

On the other hand, Mersch is obviously aware of the need of connecting the ministry with the Church in a more integral manner, and he does strive to find some sort of a connection. He writes:

> The invisible Christ establishes a mystical unity between the superiors and the body of the faithful.[1]

Here we suspect that mysticism is called in to repair the deficiencies of theology. Later however Mersch concedes more than Temple does:

> The other sacraments make men members of the Church, holy orders makes a man a representative of the whole Church. . . . Holy orders joins a member to the body that he may perform the actions of the body.[2]

Temple seems to have more or less repudiated this idea, as far as the rite of ordination is concerned at least. Mersch, as we see, has a place for it, though it is not easy to see how a man can be a representative of the body if he does not gain his authority through the body and is not responsible to the body.

It must also be said that Mersch does strive to clear a space for a priesthood of the laity. He says that there is a derived priesthood of the laity. This consists in 'certain deficient participations by which (Christ's) members share in His sacerdotal power in a measure suitable to their position; this participation varies with the degree of their membership'.[3] He later further defines this priesthood as 'a universal power of sanctification that is truly their own; the power and the duty of Catholic prayer (*sic*), of Catholic edification, and of intercession for all men by way of merit and supplication'. He finally adds a word to the effect that their task comprises 'redeeming the world and evangelizing the earth'.

Fundamentally Mersch and Temple agree about the relation of the Church to the ministry: it is an external, legal relation. The ministry is given and perpetuated without reference to the Church. The Church is indeed the object of the ministry's activities, but there is no internal relationship. In fact it would hardly be unfair to say that neither Mersch nor Temple possess a theology of the Church-ministry relationship at all. The two are given separately by God, and Calvin's account of why God gave a ministry[4] would be no more absurd in the context of Mersch's book or Temple's address than it is in the *Institutes*. If it were clear from Scripture that God had given a ministry unrelated to the Church in this way, we might accept the 'catholic' account as the best to be had. But since this is not the witness of Scripture, we must reject the 'catholic' account because of its theological deficiencies.[5]

[1] *Ibid.*, p. 537.   [2] *Ibid.*, p. 577.   [3] *Ibid.*, p. 563.   [4] See above, p. 125.
[5] I have already discussed Bishop Kirk's important book, *The Apostolic Ministry*, in chapter seven and elsewhere.

There is one more modern theologian of the 'catholic' school whose work we must examine. E. L. Mascall's book *Corpus Christi*[1] is chiefly valuable for his interesting discussion of the doctrine of our Lord's presence in the Eucharist. He goes far towards establishing an understanding on the subject between Roman Catholic and Reformed theologians. But the earlier part of the book is devoted to a discussion of orders, in the course of which he puts forward some remarkable views about the relation of the ministry to the Church. Mascall does not deal with the scriptural evidence. On pp. 12 f. he assumes without proof that 'the visible organ by which the Church's unity is expressed and maintained is the Apostolate, instituted by Christ in the Twelve and expanded through the centuries into the universal Episcopate'.[2] Starting from this most doubtful assumption, he then presses on to try to show that, unless this view of the episcopate is accepted, it is next to useless to adopt the episcopate at all as a system of church government. He quotes Archbishop Gregg as follows:

> If it [the episcopate] represents merely the result of evolution upwards out of the presbyterate, and if it represents anything less than a devolution downwards from the Apostolate, it is hard to see any vital reason why it should not rank with any other experiment in administration which happened to justify itself on utilitarian grounds.[3]

This is a particularly clear specimen of the use of 'witch-words': the development of the episcopate from the presbyterate is described as 'merely an evolution upwards'; the development which the writer approves is called 'a devolution downwards'. There is no reason *a priori* why either view should have a moral advantage over the other, but these propaganda labels are attached to them. Again, the phrase which Dr Gregg applies to the episcopate regarded solely as a development from the presbyterate would apply with equal force to the Apostles' Creed, the Canon of the New Testament, and the early liturgies. All these could be described as in their time 'an experiment which happened to justify itself on utilitarian grounds'. None of them can be traced back to the apostles, and all of them were (quite unjustifiably) claimed as apostolic in origin by Church leaders in later times. Presumably Dr Gregg does not believe that the apostles composed the Apostles' Creed, yet he accepts that Creed on its own merits. As far as scriptural and historical evidence goes, the episcopate is on precisely the same level as Creed, Liturgies, and Canon. We accept the latter because they have been handed down from the early Church, are not contrary to Scripture, and have commended them-

---

[1] London, 1953.   [2] *Op. cit.*, pp. 12 f.   [3] *Ibid.*, p. 16.

selves in the experience of the universal Church. We have no right to pretend that they go back to the apostles.

Mascall next brings forward a new argument, this time drawn from the experience of the younger churches:

> To accept the historic Episcopate without insisting on any theory about it can, in practice, only mean accepting it in the form which, in the course of history, it has come to take. And that is to destroy all hope of correcting the abuses with which it has become infected. . . . It is, in this connection, perhaps relevant to point out that in the mission field it is the low-church Anglican societies which have tended to reproduce overseas the customary features of twentieth-century English ecclesiastical organization—to treat Anglicanism as a matter of all or nothing —while the Catholic-minded societies have shewn themselves ready to abandon any customary Anglican features other than those which, on the basis of theological doctrine, they have believed to be essential to the Church's life.[1]

Those who are not uncritical admirers of the 'catholic-minded societies' will perhaps suspect that such societies have sometimes been guilty of teaching to their converts as unquestioned dogmas views about the episcopate (and other matters also) which most informed Anglicans would rather characterize as unfounded speculations. But, apart altogether from the question of missionary policy, Dr Mascall's contention is surely disproved by the very existence of the Church of South India. Here is a church which has deliberately accepted the historic episcopate 'without insisting on any theory about it'. According to Dr Mascall's thesis, the episcopate in the Church of South India should exhibit 'all the abuses with which it has become infected' in the course of history. Exactly the reverse is the fact: observers of all shades of opinion are agreed that the episcopate in CSI is more like the episcopate of the second and third centuries AD than is the episcopate in some other bodies in which it has been continuously preserved since before the Reformation. We see the Anglican bishops in North India still struggling to rid themselves of the character of senior ICS officials, with which they were too much invested in the time of the British Raj; we see the bishops of the Methodist Episcopal Church in India still trying to carry out a function which strikes the outsider as more like that of a top executive in an American business firm. But in CSI we have been able to a considerable extent to break free from these traditions just because we have accepted the historic episcopate as a fact, and have not committed ourselves to unproved (not to say disproved) theories. What we have in effect done is to restore as far as we can the

[1] *Ibid.*

episcopate of the second century. In the second century the doctrine of the apostolic succession as expounded by 'catholic' theologians today had not yet been invented. It would therefore be quite absurd to make it compulsory in CSI. Those missionaries who do found churches in Asia or Africa and teach their converts the doctrine of the apostolic succession as *de fide* are not really being 'catholic-minded'. They are in fact impairing the value of the gift they are handing on by treating the ministry as something which in fact it is not, the constitutive element in the Church. Fortunately however the time must eventually come when every missionary society hands over the direction of the Church and the Church's tradition to indigenous leadership; and there is every reason to believe that Church leaders in Asia and Africa will be well able to make up their own minds as to what is, and what is not, essential to the being of the Church.

But Dr Mascall's crowning argument is still to come.

> There is, on the one hand, the doctrine that ordination is an act (whether divinely instituted or humanly invented) by which one of the constituent parts of the Church militant, to the extent to which it is competent to do so, authorizes one of its members to perform on its behalf certain functions which any Christian is in principle already capable of performing. And there is, on the other hand, the doctrine that ordination is an act by which the universal Apostolate, most of whose members are not on earth at all, acting through its earthly part, incorporates a new member into itself. This view, it must be stressed, does not mean that the Apostolate is a kind of inner ring which operates in isolation from the Church as a whole. It is an organ within the Church; ordination therefore takes place in the setting of the Church's liturgy in the presence of all the faithful.[1]

This is calling in the unseen world to redress the balance of the seen with a vengeance! The episcopate, it seems, is not only continuous from the apostles in the Church militant, but also continues to exist in heaven. Even in heaven we cannot do without bishops! There is every indication that Dr Mascall means this remarkable opinion to be taken seriously, so it must be seriously criticized. We may notice first of all that we are still not provided with any theological account of the relation of the ministry to the Church. On the contrary, the exclusive hold of the ministry on Church authority is now dignified by the addition of an eternal dimension. Mascall repudiates the conception of the apostolate as an 'inner ring', but that is in fact precisely what it is according to his theory. It is difficult to see why according to his theory the setting of the liturgy is essential for the validity of the rite.

[1] *Op. cit.*, p. 23.

Again we may ask: why stop at ordination? If the acts of the episcopate on earth are really the acts of the episcopate in heaven, presumably any episcopal act has eternal validity. If therefore a bishop excommunicates someone from the Church on earth, presumably he is excommunicated from the Church in heaven also. But this is a claim which, I believe, not even the Pope makes. As we have observed before, exaggerated emphasis on the episcopate in isolation from the Church leads to conclusions which out-Romanize Rome.

A further difficulty arises: if orders are still valid in heaven, what is their significance? There are no sacraments in heaven, so what is the priest or bishop to do with his orders?[1] Mascall tries to meet this difficulty. He suggests that in heaven there may be a ministry which consists in being what one is ordained to be, the organ of Christ's pastoral oversight of his sheep. He also suggests that the ministry in heaven may in some way be exercised through worship: 'For the worship of heaven is an organic, symphonic, differentiated and corporate worship.'[2] A theory that can only be given meaning by means of a speculation which is by its very nature totally unverifiable is not one that will commend itself to those who do not hold it already on other grounds.

Perhaps we may be permitted to suggest one more objection to this remarkable theory. If the apostolate never ceases, but is continued into the next world, what of those members of it who have not attained to heaven but to hell? If orders are as indelible as all that, it seems illogical to conclude that merely because a bishop is suffering eternal punishment he should be considered as having lost his orders. If we follow the conclusions of certain mediaeval pessimists, indeed, most of the apostolate must be in hell. It is a distressing thought that the authority conferred in consecration may be just as much infernal in its origin as supernal.

Dr Mascall uses the analogy of the Blessed Trinity to explain the nature of ministerial priesthood:

> We can see how congruous it is that, in addition to the apostolic and priestly character of the whole Church as *corpus Christi*, there should be an apostolic and priestly character that inheres in the ordained ministry alone.[3]

If we are to draw an analogy between the Trinity and Christian priesthood, let us draw it out fully. Presumably Christ's priesthood,

---

[1] Incidentally, Mascall seems to have St Thomas Aquinas against him here. See *Summa Theologica* III 5 (ET, Vol. 19, p. 6), Qu. 34, Article 4. Thomas concludes that order is conveyed by sensible signs, sensible signs are not found among angels, hence order is 'a sacrament among men but not among angels'. But in heaven we are ὡς ἄγγελοι ἐν τοῖς οὐρανοῖς, see Mark 12.25.

[2] *Op. cit.*, p. 27. [3] *Ibid.*, p. 32.

corresponds to the Father, the Church's priesthood to the Son, and the priesthood of the ordained ministry to the Spirit. But the Spirit proceeds from the Father and the Son (or perhaps better still 'through the Son'); surely therefore it is even more congruous that the derived priesthood of the ministry should be mediated through the priestly body, the Church?

Disastrous as are the consequences to which the 'catholic' theory of the relation of the Church to the ministry leads, it has one great advantage: it is a definite theory, and it does provide one with a means of deciding among the various ministries possessed by the divided Church today. In a divided Christendom, it is at least better than no doctrine of the ministry. The existence of schism in the Church urgently presents the question of a theological justification for the ministry. Indeed, in a divided Church only those can afford to have no doctrine of the ministry who do not care about the visible structure of the Church. Unjustifiable schisms are much more frequent than justifiable ones, and if the unjustifiable schismatic ordains men to the ministry, we must be able to say why we do not accept such ordinations. Of course the 'catholic' theory has its own difficulties in connection with schism: the Tractarian would maintain that, because episcopal succession was retained at the time of the Reformation in England, the Church of England did not go into schism from the catholic Church. The Roman Catholic is quite certain that it did. Most Orthodox theologians would probably describe both the Church of England and the Church of Rome as being in schism from the true Church. But, as compared with the chaotic variety of belief and practice about the ministry which is found in the other reformed churches, the 'catholic' theory seems neat and clear.

Does this mean that none except the 'catholic' school of theologians has produced any other theory of Church and ministry in modern times? It is certainly true, as we have already noticed, that most Presbyterians today have abandoned Calvin's claim to have discovered the true form and doctrine of the ministry in the New Testament. But it is not precisely true to say that no one else has produced any theory of the ministry. There have been attempts to discuss the relation of the Church to the ministry from the side of non-episcopalian theologians. We will deal with two here. The first is Daniel Jenkins' *The Gift of the Ministry*.[1] This book contains many interesting and stimulating ideas which the author has not stayed to work out very fully. Perhaps he may do so in some subsequent book. He is obviously inspired by John Owen, whom he quotes to very good effect.

[1] London, 1947.

In particular he reverts to the idea of the ministry as service, that fundamental conception in the New Testament, so unhappily ignored by almost everyone except Luther from Cyprian to Hooker. Jenkins most acutely points out that the key text for the ministry is Mark 10.45.[1] Again he makes the excellent point that, though the rule of the ministry does in a sense reproduce the rule of God on earth, it does so in much the same way as our Lord showed his rule on earth, in the form of a servant.[2] His exposition of the role of the minister as 'representative man' is not far away from Paul's profound conception of the pioneer ministry.[3] He actually quotes I Cor. 4.9–13, and emphasizes most rightly that the proper place for the minister is on the frontiers of faith.[4] If 'catholic' theologians, instead of merely commending Mr Jenkins for the points in which he seems to approximate to their views, had been inspired by his book to work out a theology of the relation of the Church to the ministry, the debate on the ministry might have taken a new lease of life. It may still do so: we must cease from picking over the historical evidence, which will in any case never give a decisive answer, and must face the far more profound question which Jenkins asks: what do we really mean by the ministry?

The other book is T. F. Torrance's *Royal Priesthood*,[5] all the more interesting because written by a member of the committee that produced the recent report on methods by which the Church of England and the Church of Scotland might be brought into relations of communion. The book does not give a full exposition of the doctrine of the ministry, but rather, like Jenkins' book, contains a number of insights that should not be neglected in any adequate doctrine of the ministry. His main point is that in the New Testament the ministry is first and foremost the corporate ministry of the Church. Thus he quotes I Cor. 4.10 of the Church[6] and points out that the Church, being baptized with Christ's baptism, assumes like him the form of a servant and dies.[7] A little later he insists that, as the ministry within the Church is primarily corporate, the ministry of the ordained minister is also primarily corporate; and he quotes with approval J.A.T. Robinson: 'All that is said of the ministry in the New Testament is said not of individuals nor of some apostolic college or "essential ministry", but of the whole Body, whatever the differentiation of function within it.'[8] This hardly seems to allow for what Paul has to say about the ordained ministry. We get the same impression from what Torrance says about the

---

[1] *Op. cit.*, p. 20.   [2] *Ibid.*, p. 27.   [3] *Ibid.*, pp. 59–62.   [4] *Ibid.*, p. 62.
[5] London and Edinburgh, 1955.
[6] By mistake or misprint he calls it II Cor. 4.10.
[7] *Op. cit.*, p. 34.   [8] *The Historic Episcopate* ,p. 14.

apostolate;[1] the apostles, he says, are the foundations of the Church:
'In this sense there can be no talk of apostolic succession, for the Apostolate
cannot be transmitted.' This is an assertion commonly met with from
those who, quite rightly, oppose the 'catholic' attempt to show that there
was some form of apostolic ministerial authority passed on to bishops or
others. But it will hardly stand the test of comparison with what Paul
writes about the work of himself and his companions. The apostolic task
is passed on to the apostolic Remnant in each new area.

We give two more quotations: the first underlines a conclusion to
which we came in an earlier chapter:

> The historical succession of ecclesiastical representatives is not identical
> with the real succession of the corporate participation of the Church
> in the ministry of Christ, and can only point to it and signify it.[2]

To put it in other words, the ministry is an expression of the Church's
unity, but it does not itself constitute that unity.

The other quotation deals with the Eucharist, and is complementary
to the last one:

> The sacrament of the Lord's Supper clearly presupposes a prior unity,
> but that unity is given in Holy Baptism through which we are incor-
> porated into the Body of Christ. . . . For a church to refuse the Lord's
> Supper to those who are baptized into Christ and incorporated into
> His One Body would seem to amount either to a denial of Baptism or
> to attempted schism within the Body of Christ.[3]

This is a conclusion to which we seem to be reasonably led by our previous examination of the place of the Eucharist.

Thus we can claim that, though the Reformed tradition has not yet
produced a clear doctrine of the relation of the Church to the ministry, a
beginning has been made, and the materials exist for a more fruitful
exchange with the 'catholic' school of theologians in the future.

---

[1] *Op. cit.*, pp. 27 f.   [2] *Ibid.*, p. 41.   [3] *Ibid.*, p. 105.

II

The Church Catholic and Apostolic Today

WE HAVE already asserted that the doctrine of the relation of Church to ministry as we have traced it in the New Testament does not entitle us to pass judgement concerning validity or invalidity on any of the forms of ministry possessed by the Church today. But the whole purpose of this work will have been frustrated if it does not enable us to draw some conclusions about the nature of the various ministries found in the Church. At least we can say something about how we are to frame a satisfactory doctrine of the ministry today.

We may say this much to begin with: the ministry must be related to the Church at every point, not just in its historical origin. The only authorization which the ministry possesses is that in some sense or at some point it is the Church, not in the 'catholic' sense that it speaks instead of the Church and does everything in the Church, leaving the laity as a largely passive body; but rather that the ministry leads the way in doing what the Church must do, and acts as the Church must act. It begins by being the Church, and its function is only fulfilled when the part of the Church in which it works is growing and active and taking upon itself the responsibilities which the ministry originally wielded. This does not mean that the functions of the ministry gradually devolve upon laymen, but that it must be constantly striving to raise up and increase the local ministry in the place where it is at work. In other words, in a situation where the Church is divided or static the task of the ministry cannot be adequately carried out. We shall be reverting to this point later.

Another point follows from this one: the ministry is originally the Church *in nucleo*, the faithful Remnant whose task is to gather others and lead them also in carrying on the ministry of the Messiah. Therefore the ministry must not be represented as doing anything that the Church cannot, or should not, do. If we think of any of the distinctive functions of the ministry, we must say that the ministry only carries them out as the representative of the Church, and that if any minister claims to do them on his own responsibility and not as acting on behalf of the Church, he is wrong and is moving towards schism. It is not the priest who celebrates the Eucharist, but the priest and the local church, and the local church celebrates through him. This applies still more obviously to baptism. If it is objected that no reference is made to Christ, we must answer that of course Christ is the real author of all these actions: in the Eucharist, Christ offers the Church to the Father, and only in that offering can the Church by the priest's action offer itself. Christ baptizes; but he does so in the Church and through the Church. If any minister claims to by-pass the Church, and says that he is acting as a direct representative of Christ and not also at the same time as a representative of the Church, he is giving way to a subtle form of pride and speaking more like a Gnostic than an orthodox Christian.

This point holds for all ministerial acts without exception: the pastoral work of the ministry is the work of the Church building itself up in love (Eph. 4.16). There is no danger of Pelagianism here: this work is the same thing as Christ building the Church up, but it is the work of Christ in and through the Church. When the priest pronounces absolution, he does not do so as a direct representative of God speaking to the individual. He does so as God's representative *in the Church*: all sin is not only an offence against God, but it also damages the Church: if one member suffer, all the members suffer. Part of the Church's ministry is to declare God's forgiveness in Christ to those who have sinned. Christ is injured in all his members by the sin of Christians. Sin is not a purely individual affair, and neither is forgiveness. The same must hold for ordination also: when Paul appointed members of the household of Stephanas to the ministry, he did not do so as one who held a commission direct from Christ to dispose of his authority as his fancy took him. He did it as a representative of the first church in Corinth passing on the apostolic commission to the firstfruits of his own apostolic work. It is the Church that ordains, or rather Christ ordains through the Church. It is not enough to say, as Temple says, that Christ ordains in the Church, making the Church merely the environment of the act, not the instrument. Ordination is the means whereby the faithful Remnant in one place extends its borders, sends forth apostles who will themselves be the faithful Remnant in the place to which they are sent. It should always be regarded as a sending forth, an outward-looking act, not merely a means of maintaining the fabric. We know of no ordination in the New Testament save that which takes place in a local situation: the same is true of the Eucharist. But those who ordain in the Church at any time are not merely representatives of the local church: they are the local church representing the whole Church. They may be called presbyters or bishops, but they are at the same time apostles. Unless those who ordain are thought of as thoroughly identified with the people of God as visible and present in the place where the ordination takes place, it is not ordination as understood in the light of St Paul's doctrine of the ministry. The tendency to represent those who ordain as not being in any way responsible to the Church on earth is fundamentally unscriptural; it avoids the scandal of the particular, the shocking thought that the ministry bears the authority of Christ given through the visible, divided, sinful Church which we know on earth.

These considerations should enable us to understand something more of what the apostolicity of the Church means. The apostolicity of the Church consists in being the Church, and that means being the apostolic Remnant: 'The Church is the mission.'[1] The apostles were not something else plus the Church or over the Church: they were the first Church, and hence the Church is apostolic in as far as it carries out the task which the original apostolic Remnant carried out, proclaims the redemptive acts of God in history, witnesses to prophecy fulfilled, lives out the self-emptying ministry of Christ in the world. For this purpose a ministry is necessary, but to predicate apostolicity of the ministry apart from the Church is meaningless by New Testament standards. The ministry is only apostolic in as far as it carries out its task of leading the Church into the Church's apostolic task. To imagine that there can be a certain quality of apostolicity belonging to the ministry because of some characteristics or pedigree which it possesses in itself apart from the rest of the Church is a disastrous error. We cannot make a satisfactory judgement about any given ministry existing in the Church today unless we first make a judgement about the body of Christians in which that ministry operates. It is not the ministry which constitutes the Church, but the Church the ministry. To take an example, we are not justified in saying of the Abyssinian Church, 'It is a true part of the Church because it has preserved the apostolic succession', and of the Church of Scotland, 'It is not a church at all because it has not preserved episcopacy'. This is to judge the Church by its ministry, and in effect to subordinate the Church to the ministry.

We have already suggested[2] that the task of the ministry cannot be fully carried out in a situation where the Church is dwindling or static. The ministry is the apostolic mission of the Church: its task is essentially pioneer, it is the spearhead of the Church. This is peculiarly true of the

---

[1] Dr M. A. C. Warren's great dictum.   [2] See above p. 155.

Church in the New Testament, both because the New Testament Church was set in a missionary situation, and because the New Testament writers were so conscious of living also in an eschatological situation. The function of the ministry was to carry on the apostolic task of the Church while there was yet time in a world over which the powers of evil still held rule. Paul in I Cor. 4 thinks of the ministry as playing out its part on a vast world stage, angels and men looking on. It is therefore not at all surprising that the New Testament doctrine of the ministry comes to life more plainly in the younger churches than in the West. Indeed it might be said that the mere fact of being the only church in a large area where Christians are in a small minority imposes a certain catholic pattern upon almost any body of Christians.

This is a point which deserves some elaboration, since it is extraordinarily difficult for Christians in a 'Christendom' situation to realize. We unconsciously assume that we will find reproduced in Asia the full complement of competing denominations which we are used to as the normal pattern in the West. In fact of course nothing like it can be maintained east of Suez. In India at any rate every denomination can point to several areas in which it is quite literally the only church. If anyone living in those areas wishes to be a Christian, he must belong to that denomination, for there is no other form of Christianity available. In such a situation every denomination that is not completely given over to the sectarian spirit takes on some of the lineaments of the catholic Church, whether it deliberately intends so or not. To take an actual instance: Congregationalism in England has many of the characteristics of a sect rather than a church. The average Congregationalist minister feels himself responsible only for the members of his congregation, not for all the Christians in the area where he ministers. One of the consequences of this is that in England many Congregationalists are casual about the Sacraments, do not insist on baptism, and feel themselves justified in dispensing with doctrinal standards. If people want a sacramental religion and emphasis on doctrine, they can go to some other church.[1] But, in many areas of South India before 1947, the South India United Church, mainly Congregationalist in origin, was the only church and was responsible for all the Christians in the area where it worked.[2] The consequence was that in all

---

[1] These remarks are not intended to apply to Congregationalism as a whole, or to the original tradition of Congregationalism: high regard for the Sacraments and a deep understanding of Christian doctrine are the marks of Congregationalism as understood by such men as Bernard Manning, Nathaniel Micklem, and J. S. Whale. Nor would I wish to imply that the Church of England's attitude to either Sacraments or doctrine is always impeccable.

[2] In 1947 it entered the Church of South India.

those points wherein some Congregationalists in England were lax, the SIUC was strict. Baptism and the Lord's Supper were unfailingly administered, doctrinal standards were definitely maintained, church discipline was not ignored, ordination to the ministry was definite and regular, a strong central administration was established. A definite understanding about admitting full church members from other denominations was arranged with most of the other non-Roman Catholic denominations in South India. This was not because the leaders of the SIUC were powerfully affected by a desire to return to traditional practices repudiated by their brethren in England, but simply because the SIUC had to maintain the burden of being the catholic Church (because the only church) in many areas.

There is a further theological implication of this undeniable feature of the life of the younger churches: we have seen good reason to believe that in the New Testament the local church consists of all the Christians living in any given area. We leave aside for the moment the question of heresy: obviously there must come a point where doctrinal aberration grows so great as to destroy the catholicity of a body of Christians. But the examples we have in mind are well within the fold of doctrinal orthodoxy. None but a determined bigot, for instance, would characterize as heretical bodies the four churches that joined together to form the Church of South India, whatever might be said of schism. If therefore we find all the Christians in one place without exception in one church, and that church administers the Sacraments duly and preaches sound doctrine, we are simply not entitled by scriptural standards to refuse it the title of church because of the form of its ministry or its alleged lack of authorization. Surely, if catholicity means anything, it means the quality of including all Christians. A church with the most impeccable pedigree for its ministry, and unassailably orthodox doctrine, is yet lacking in catholicity if it only includes a small minority of the Christians actually living within the area where it is situated. Unless one is determined to make the ministry the *sine qua non* of the Church's existence, any church that includes all the Christians in a given area must be the catholic Church in that area (excluding for the moment, as we have explained, the supposition of heresy). But we have seen very good reason to make baptism, and not the ministry, that which constitutes the church. If therefore the catholic Church is there, its ministry must be sufficiently authorized. The alternative is to divide the ministry from the Church in a way which we have already repudiated. Thus it follows that in this very important aspect of catholicity many of the younger churches are better off than our denominations in the West.

A virtual recognition of this state of affairs was conceded by all the orthodox non-Roman Catholic churches in India long before there was any thought of union. It is not generally realized in the West that the acceptance of comity itself carries certain implications. According to the arrangement known as comity, each denomination agrees to confine its evangelistic activities to a certain area, and not to try to set up churches in those areas where the other consenting denominations are working. A natural corollary of this is that when a member of one denomination moved to another area where another denomination was working, he was normally recommended to the clergy of that denomination. For example, before union, if an Anglican moved to an area where only Methodists were found, he was urged to attend the Methodist Church and was often recommended to the local Methodist minister. This included of course his becoming, while he was in that area, a communicant member of the Methodist Church. Any other policy indeed would have been suicidal. If the Anglicans had said: 'Do not join the Methodists, as they are not really a church at all', in nine cases out of ten they would have been saying in effect: 'Cease the practice of Christianity altogether.' In other words, each denomination proceeded on the assumption that where there was only one denomination at work, that denomination was the Church, and therefore was the catholic Church. The Anglican was not told: 'Join the Methodists in your new station, but do not communicate with them'; that would have been tantamount to saying: 'Go on practising Christianity, but not sacramental Christianity.' Very naturally Anglicans, faced with the alternative of urging their converts who had moved to non-Anglican areas to cease the practice of normal Christianity or of accepting the other denominations as the catholic Church in their respective areas, chose the latter course.

'Are we to conclude, then, that the Methodist or Congregationalist churches are sects in England but the catholic Church in India?' The most honest answer which an Anglican can give to this question is, Yes. And we can give scriptural warrant for such an answer:[1] the primary meaning of apostolicity when applied to the Church is twofold. It consists in maintaining the witness of the apostles and in carrying out the mission of the apostles. In India and many other parts of Asia we find bodies of Christians which have come into existence because Methodists and Congregationalists from England have carried out that apostolic task

---

[1] We can also compare the attitude of the great majority of Anglican writers in the seventeenth century, who regarded English Dissenters as sectarians but recognized Presbyterians on the continent as possessing true churches with valid Sacraments.

in parts of India and the rest of Asia which Anglican missionaries have not been able to reach. There is no question here of schisms or sects or rival denominations. There were, for example, no Christians of any description whatever in Medak in Hyderabad State before the Methodists began work there. Subsequent history gives us no justification for suggesting that if the Methodists had not begun work there Anglicans would eventually have stepped in. The Methodists built up a church there that was entirely orthodox by any reasonable standard of doctrine, a church which carefully administered and highly reverenced the two gospel Sacraments, and which ordained a well-trained ministry. Their Eucharistic life was in fact stronger than that of some parts of the Anglican Communion.[1] If St Paul's doctrine of the pioneer ministry means anything, the Methodist ministry in that area was sufficiently authorized: they had carried out the apostolic mission of the Remnant, they had built up a church themselves in a hitherto unevangelized area, they had taught that church itself to undertake the apostolic mission and to reach out to evangelize the people round them. The only grounds on which one can deny them the title of Church (and in that context it can only mean the catholic Church) is that their ministry is not regular. But we have already seen that we are not justified in Scripture in making the ministry constitutive of the Church.[2]

It must be admitted that defenders of the 'catholic' doctrine of the ministry are very often prepared to make a concession here, a concession in practice at least, though not perhaps in theory. 'God', they say, 'does perhaps include these ministries within his uncovenanted mercies. We do not deny that his grace is vouchsafed to them and that the Sacrament of the Eucharist is celebrated through them. But we are not on that account justified in recognizing them.' This sounds like saying that, though God recognizes them, we may not; or, as someone has well put it, God breaks his own rules in a slightly reprehensible way. The truth is that in a divided Church we must be prepared for anomalies, and recognize that perhaps God is leading us into a way of repairing our divisions through the experience of the younger churches which, by their very missionary situation, are able to teach us something about how the catholic Church would function in an undivided Christendom.

[1] There are some parts of Northern Ireland, for example, where, though the Eucharist is celebrated every Sunday, the majority of the members of the Anglican Church never communicate at all from year's end to year's end.
[2] At this point in the argument I have sometimes met this objection: 'I do not wish to pass judgement on such ministries; but I would never accept them myself.' In the context this seems to be tantamount to saying: 'They may be all right for the Anglican coolie, who has no choice, but well-bred churchmen in England can afford to condemn them.'

What we have in fact been arguing for is a sort of local apostolicity and catholicity belonging to the Church where in any given area it comprises all Christians. This thought finds a certain amount of support in the seventeenth chapter of St John's Gospel. In vv. 1–10 we find the thought frequently repeated of the showing forth of God's glory: in v. 1 God is to glorify the Son, and the Son will glorify the Father. In v. 4 the Son has glorified the Father, and in v. 5 the Father is asked to glorify the Son. We must understand the word 'glorify' in the Fourth Gospel as meaning 'show forth the full character'; that is why the glory of the Father is shown forth supremely on the Cross. Then in v. 6 our Lord declares that he has manifested the Father's Name to 'the men who thou gavest me out of the world'. This must refer to the disciples, and to the disciples as representing the Church, not just the ministry. The 'manifesting of the name' is the same as the glorifying. As Charles Wesley so finely writes: 'His nature and his Name is love.' In v. 10 we find the Son glorified 'in them', that is in the disciples, the faithful Remnant. This leads on to the mission of the Remnant in v. 18:

> As thou didst send me into the world,
> even so sent I them into the world.

The Greek is ἀποστέλλω. Dodd à propos v. 6 quotes Heb. 2.12:

> I will declare thy name unto my brethren,
> in the midst of the congregration will I sing thy praise.[1]

This is itself a quotation from Ps. 22(21).22, where the LXX uses ἐκκλησια for 'congregation'. Dodd thinks that the quotation is echoed in John 17.6 also. In that case the reference of both v. 6 and v. 10 to the whole Church, and not to the ministry only, is perfectly clear.

Then in v. 20 the circle is enlarged to include all believers:

> Neither for these only do I pray, but for them also that believe on me through their word.

And in v. 23 the thought of v. 10 is applied to the future Church:

> I in them, and thou in me, that they may be perfected into one;
> that the world may know that thou didst send me.

This does not mean that in the previous verses our Lord was thinking of the ministry, and only now does he turn to the Church; but that previously he was thinking of the Church in the Upper Room, and now he enlarges his vision to include the whole Church of the future. This

---

[1] *Interpretation of the Fourth Gospel*, Cambridge, 1953, p. 96 n. 2.

Church is to be one in order that the world may know that the Father has sent the Son. The unity of the Church, in fact, shows forth the apostolate of the Son. But in v. 18 the apostolate of the Son is realized in the apostolate of the Church. The conclusion is inevitable that the apostolate of the Church is marred by its visible disunity. It seems therefore to follow quite clearly that in any given locality the Church is to that extent apostolic so far as it remains one, visibly united, so visibly that the outside world can see it to be one (v. 23). To say, as in effect the 'catholic' school of theologians says, that the apostolic part of the Church remains one through the episcopate, is simply an evasion of the issue. To call one part of the divided Church more apostolic than another, simply on the grounds of the form or authorization of the ministry, is to reduce the meaning of that word 'apostolic'. It is a quality that belongs to the Church, not to the ministry considered independently of the Church.

Now that we have reached this point, we are perhaps in a position to do justice to the reformed doctrine of the Church in some of its aspects. Luther, rebelling against the institutional church of his day, was compelled to work out a new definition of the Church to vindicate his organizing an 'evangelical' church in opposition to Rome. It is to his credit that he did not in fact embrace a doctrine of a purely invisible church. He originated instead the well known reformed definition. We quote from the Confession of Augsburg, Article VII:

> They teach that the one Holy Church will remain for ever. Now this Church is the congregation of the saints in which the Gospel is rightly taught and the sacraments rightly administered. And for that true unity of the Church it is enough to have unity of belief concerning the teaching of the Gospel and the administration of the sacraments.[1]

Calvin accepts essentially the same definition when discussing the nature of the Church.[2] He distinguishes the sense in which the word is used in Scripture: 1. It means all the elect and sanctified in heaven and earth. 2. It means the totality of persons either believing in one God or baptized on earth. The wideness in which the second sense could be interpreted is startling; strictly speaking it would include Muslims as well. But in section 9 he elaborates his definition. Wherever the word of God is sincerely preached and wherever the Sacraments are administered according to the institution of Christ, there is the Church. See also his remarks about the old, unreformed church quoted above on page 126. Here is his definition of the catholic Church:

[1] H. Bettenson, *Documents of the Christian Church*, Oxford, 1943, p. 295.
[2] *Institutes*, Book IV, ch. 1.8–9, pp. 20 f.

With regard to the general body we must feel differently; if they have the ministry of the word, and honour the administration of the sacraments, they are undoubtedly entitled to be ranked with the Church, because it is certain that these things are not without a beneficial result.

We may also compare the definition of the Church in Article XIX of the Thirty-nine Articles:

The visible Church of Christ is a congregation of faithful men, in which the pure Word of God is preached, and the Sacraments be duly administered according to Christ's ordinance in all those things that of necessity are requisite to the same.

The Church is where the gospel is preached and the Sacraments rightly administered: so said the Reformers. We have maintained that the Church carrying out its apostolic task creates the ministry. The ministry is the pioneer Church. Again, the preaching of the gospel creates the Church in each new unevangelized area; those who accept the gospel are baptized. Their daily Christian life is maintained and strengthened by the Sacrament of the Eucharist. Hence this reformed definition of the Church is really entirely faithful to Scripture: the New Testament sees the Church as constituted by water and the word (Eph. 5.26). The faithful Remnant proclaims the apostolic message of God's acts in Christ and prophecy fulfilled; those who accept it are baptized, and there is the Church. To say 'the Church consists of all who have been baptized' is true, but it gives a somewhat static picture of the Church. In the New Testament the Church is not content to remain passive, it is actively pursuing its mission of preaching, baptizing, breaking the bread. Again, to say 'the Church is where . . . ' does give the local church its proper place. The danger in this definition lies in the suggestion it conveys that the Church is a series of isolated units, outcrops of Christianity in a dark world. It does not necessarily imply that all the places where the gospel is preached and the Sacraments duly administered are joined together in one catholic Church.

On the other hand, when we turn to the 'catholic' school for definitions of the Church, we find at once that the definition is almost entirely in terms of the ministry. The Roman Catholics would say that the catholic Church consists of all those who accept the authority of the Bishop of Rome. Tractarians would say that the Church consists of all those who are under episcopal government. We have seen sufficient reason to conclude that the Church is not constituted by the ministry, and therefore should not be defined in terms of the ministry. The definition of the Reformers does safeguard the apostolic mission of the Church, and is not at all incompatible with the conception of a catholic Church. The fatal tendency in all 'catholic' definitions is that they divide perfectly orthodox Christians into two groups, catholic Christians, who are full members, and 'non-catholic' Christians, who are not. The real objection to 'non-catholic' Christians from the 'catholic' point of view is that their ministry is not authorized. Admittedly 'catholics' also tend to bring charges of heresy against 'non-catholics', but non-Roman Catholics should not take these charges seriously. The ecumenical movement (not to mention the Church of South India) has shown that, as far as fundamental doctrinal issues are concerned, there is no reason to think that the division between Anglican and most non-episcopal Christians in contact with the World Council of Churches need be ultimate.[1] The Church is where the gospel is preached and the Sacraments duly administered: wherever you find Christians doing that, there is the catholic Church. We note that the reference to both gospel and Sacraments answers the objection that immediately occurs: 'Do you accept any congregation of Christians as the catholic Church without any qualification?' There must be a doctrinal safeguard; heresy can un-church. Nor need we accept all forms of the ministry as equally well authorized. The ministry commissioned by the leaders of an unjustified schism cannot be considered as equally well authorized with all other ministries. But orthodox schism does not separate from the catholic Church. So perhaps the only modification we need make in the Reformer's definition is the introduction of the word 'catholic' before 'Church'. If we do not use this word, it will become the prerogative of 'catholics' and will become inextricably associated with some one form of the ministry. Once we abandon the conception of the ministry being constitutive of the Church, we can begin to understand why the Reformers had to search for a more satisfactory definition of the Church; and we can admit that they have at least pointed the direction in which we must begin to look for one.

The definition of the Reformers, as we have seen, was arrived at in a period when a large part of Western Christendom felt itself compelled to rebel against constituted church authority. This inevitably brought up the question: assuming that there are circumstances in which Christians are justified in repudiating the authority of the constituted ministry, where are they to find authority for a more satisfactory ministry? As we have observed, only Luther faced this problem fully; Calvin believed that the authorized ministry was already there in the presbyterate. Hooker was

---

[1] We must, it seems, make an exception for the Baptists. But perhaps events in North India or Ceylon may in time eliminate this exception, at least as far as those Baptists affiliated to the World Council of Churches are concerned.

defending a ministry which, as far as the passing on of authority was concerned, was continuous with the old one. Luther however did have to make something of a new start, and he went back to the only certain authority that could be appealed to once he had repudiated the authority of the ministry as constituted in his day. He went back to the authority of the Church as given in baptism. Once grant that Luther was justified in breaking away at all, and it is hard to see how he could have done better. If Moberly had taken his admirable doctrine of representative priesthood seriously, he too would have arrived at this conclusion. The priesthood of the ministry is mediated through the priesthood of the Church; both are derived from Christ's priesthood. As we have seen, in the New Testament all ministry is one.

Of course as soon as it is suggested that the ministry can be authorized by any means except the episcopate, as for example by falling back on the authority of the Church conferred in baptism, the objection occurs: How does the Church exercise such authority? How does the priesthood conferred in baptism exercise its authority? To that there can be no completely satisfactory answer, given Luther's circumstances. The only satisfactory answer is: through the ministry, the authorized representatives of the Church. But what is to be done if the ministry has gone astray and is misleading the Church? Once again, Luther's solution seems to be the only possible one in the circumstances: he fell back on the authority of the Church, exercised through the local church. Both Calvin and Hooker were better off in this respect: Calvin succeeded in securing the united action of something like a national church, at least the church of a semi-independent town-state. Hooker could appeal to the decision of a whole national church. When Luther was faced with the problem of authorizing the ministry, the political situation was not sufficiently clear for him to be able to appeal to the authority of the church of a whole province. He fell back on what is the unit of the Church in the New Testament, the local church. We must remember also that such a possibility is not repudiated by Hooker himself; he believes that the whole Church has authority to dispense with episcopal ordination if need be, and he is very much inclined to justify, or at least condone, the instances of such action which he saw on the Continent and in Scotland in his day. The reasonable conclusion therefore seems to be that there are circumstances in which it is justifiable to repudiate the authority of the constituted ministry, and in such circumstances it is necessary to appeal to the authority of the priesthood conferred in baptism.

We have been trying to decide from where authority for the ministry should be looked for by those who repudiate the traditional form of the ministry. But we only did so in order to vindicate to some extent Luther's action, and to show that the New Testament basis of the ministry is the right one to fall back on in such circumstances. We are not faced with such circumstances today. The question today is rather: how are we to unify the many ministries which have sprung up as a result of the Reformation? We have concluded that these ministries are for the most part still ministries of the catholic Church and that the possession of a non-episcopal ministry does not necessarily exclude the body that possesses it from the catholic Church. Some might therefore gain the impression that our object is to advocate a Ronald Knoxian 'reunion all round'. Let all ministries be recognized by everyone as equally authorized, and all will be well! Such is not the aim of this work. In the New Testament there is only one ministry, and the present anomalous condition of the divided Church can only be mended when there is once again only one ministry recognized by the catholic Church throughout the world. The ministry does not constitute the Church, but it is the prime means of expressing the Church's unity, and that unity cannot be satisfactorily shown forth until there is only one universally recognized ministry.

The New Testament, we have concluded, does not give us the means of deciding between the various forms of the ministry now found in the Church. There were apostles, none apparently with an authority that exceeded the bounds of the Church which he had founded; and there was a local ministry, whether we call it a presbyterate or an episcopate. Later, in the Pastorals, we find a definite order of deacons.[1] This does not correspond exactly with any form of the ministry to be found in any denomination today, nor can we expect it to, since plainly the form of the ministry as we see it in the New Testament is still in process of development. Indeed, as far as the New Testament evidence is concerned, it would be more accurate to reverse Streeter's dictum and say: 'Nobody has won and none shall have prizes.' Does this mean, then, that the form of the ministry in the Church today is a matter of indifference, and that one form is as good as another—whether we adopt the centralized Roman system, or the Anglican concept of constitutional episcopacy organized in autonomous provinces, or the conciliar system of Presbyterianism, or the loose congregational system of the Baptists? Such a conclusion does not necessarily follow. We cannot concede to any one form of the ministry the distinction of having been instituted by our Lord or by the first apostles; we cannot even say that any one system found in the Church

---

[1] I assume that they were published in their present form between AD 95 and 105.

today at least reproduces what was found in the New Testament Church. But we can bring forward certain considerations based on the New Testament which may help us to decide what should be the form of the ministry in the one undivided Church.

The first consideration is one which we have referred to already: in the New Testament there was only one ministry universally recognized, and this was the case for many years after the New Testament period. If then there is any one form of the ministry which is more likely to be accepted by all Christians, or most Christians, it should have a preference. This would seem to suggest that the best form of the ministry in the future is likely to be some version of episcopacy: it is already the form of the ministry found among the great majority of Christians, and the indications are that a good many Christians who do not at present have an episcopal form of government would be willing in certain circumstances to accept it. We in the Church of South India can say quite honestly that we have adopted episcopacy as the necessary path along which we must advance to union, and after ten years' experience of it we now value it for its own sake. This shows, at least, that in order to use an episcopal form of ministry fully and adequately it is not necessary to believe that it is the only legitimate form. And indeed, if episcopacy has a certain prior claim because of its universality, it must not be commended on wrong grounds. On the contrary, where episcopacy is made the *sine qua non* of the Church's existence it is not so likely to be of value, too much weight is laid upon it, and claims are made for it that give it an exaggerated and perverted place in the economy of the Church. If there is anything like an undivided Church in the future, episcopacy no doubt is the form which the ministry will bear in that Church, but it will be a very personal and pastoral form of episcopacy, very closely related to the presbyterate, and not magnified into an hierarchical body on which the Church depends for its very existence. The office of bishop is quite sufficiently dignified and impressive in itself: it does not need to be buttressed by doubtful historical and theological theories.

The second consideration has already been hinted at.[1] Paul and his companions in the mission came to each new place which they evangelized as apostles, that is, as representatives of the faithful Remnant, the whole Church of the Messiah. They may have been originally sent from Antioch, but we do not receive the impression that they regarded themselves as representatives merely of the Christian congregation in Antioch. Consequently, if we are to be faithful to the principles of the New Testament conception of the ministry, we should wish to have a form of the ministry

[1] See p. 86, above.

where this representative character is sufficiently expressed. There can be little doubt that episcopacy, better than any other form of the ministry, expresses the fact that the ministry represents the whole Church. The bishop we take to be the representative of the great Church, bearing its authority in a special degree, and empowered by it as its representative. This is of course true of the episcopate properly used, not of the Celtic bishop, for instance, who seems to have been a mere functionary in the abbot's entourage. Still less is it true of the mediaeval prince-bishop; and it is very little true either of the modern suffragan bishop, who is really more representative of the *Zeitgeist* of modern bureaucracy than a satisfactory representative of the Church.

This representative character of the episcopate properly understood can be well illustrated from the experience of the Church of South India. In Dornakal Diocese, for example, at the time of union in 1947, the Christian population consisted of roughly fifty thousand from the Anglican Church on the eastern side of the diocese, and fifty thousand from the Methodist Church on the western side. Because both these churches had previously observed comity, there were few if any places in the diocese where an ex-Anglican and an ex-Methodist congregation were found side by side. In these circumstances the bishop was the obvious and necessary bond of union: it was he who was engaged all the time in travelling throughout the two areas, representing in his own person as no one else could the greater Church beyond and the new-found unity.

Perhaps a personal experience may be relevant in this connection. While on furlough, I attended an interdenominational missionary conference in South Wales. Among the other speakers was a young Indian presbyter from one of the dioceses in the Church of South India which is almost entirely SIUC by tradition, i.e. Congregationalist. At this conference a number of Welsh Congregationalist ministers held a keen discussion with the Indian clergyman in my hearing. They asked him in particular how it was that he, a Congregationalist by tradition, could accept the authority of a bishop. His answer was most interesting: 'We do not,' he said, 'look on our bishop as an administrator, or a tyrant, or a master. We look on him as a father, and naturally we ask for, and act on, the advice of our father in God.' This, surely, is the true relation of a bishop to his flock, personal, not legal; integral, not coercive. If Christian relationships break down, there must be, and there is, a legal constitution. But the deepest relationship (may we not say 'the theological relationship'?) is not legal but personal, spiritual in the Pauline sense of a relationship depending on God in the first place. In pre-union days all the non-Anglican churches had an office not unlike that of the bishop in some respects, 'superintending missionary or minister'. It is most significant that the bishop is not generally looked on as the old superintendent in a new guise. He is the bearer of an authority which is not that of mere power and position; his is a spiritual office, and the fact that he has been consecrated to it makes it both easier for the flock to accept his authority and for himself to avoid the danger of self-importance. But for us in the Church of South India the bishop does not come as some strange new official authenticated direct from God without reference to the rest of the Church. He comes bearing the authority of the great Church because he has been given this authority by the Church. As far as uniting the Church is concerned, a ministry which is not responsible to the Church is useless.[1]

If this approach to the problem of reunion is the right one, it will follow that we should not concern ourselves with authenticating already existing ministries, but with introducing one ministry accepted by all. This is the method which we have employed in the Church of South India: from the time of union all ordinations are performed by the bishop or by the bishop in presbytery,[2] but all ministers recognized at the time of union by the uniting churches continue to be recognized as presbyters in the united church. This has caused difficulties among some Anglicans; they would prefer to see all ministers co-opted into one ministry at the time of union by some act of mutual commissioning or recognition. Indeed such a ceremony is planned in the proposed scheme of union in North India and Pakistan and also in Ceylon. In the case of the North India Scheme we must recognize that special difficulties are caused by the fact that one of the uniting churches already has bishops who are not in the historic succession. In effect, however, it is far more important from the point of view of the Church in India that it should have fully integrated union within its own borders than that it should have relations of full inter-communion with this or that world-denomination. From the point of view

---

[1] Daniel Jenkins, in his latest book on the ministry, itself largely a reproduction of his earlier book discussed on pp. 152 f., does not seem to be much impressed by the argument adduced in favour of episcopacy in the foregoing paragraphs. He writes (in *The Protestant Ministry*, 1958, p. 63): 'The fact that they [sc. Anglican bishops] are encouraged to believe that they carry the official unity of the Church round with them wherever they go does often seem to make them reluctant to examine the possibility that they themselves may be hindrances to unity and barriers in the way of the free flow of experience and fellowship from one Christian community to another.' This criticism must not be denied out of hand, but it is possible that Mr Jenkins in his critique of episcopacy has concentrated too much on the bishops of the Church of England, and not enough on episcopacy as seen in other parts of the Anglican Communion, and even outside it.

[2] The bishop alone lays on hands for the ordination of deacons; in ordaining presbyters the bishop and presbyters together lay on hands. In the consecration of bishops either method may be followed.

of theology and history, internal organic union among different denominations in one country is catholic union. Even the fullest relations with any one denomination must mean something less, for no one denomination represents the whole catholic Church.

We are living in a time when the ecumenical movement is bearing fruit in two ways: it is causing a great reassessment of traditional theological positions, so that sometimes a man's foes prove to be those of his own household—and that in every denomination. And it is actually causing organic union to take place between previously separated denominations in some parts of the world. It is therefore urgently necessary that a sincere effort be made to find out whether the New Testament really has a doctrine of the relation of the ministry to the Church, and, if so, how it should affect our church relations today. This book is offered mainly as an attempted contribution to that task.

INDEX OF NAMES

INDEX OF BIBLICAL REFERENCES
OLD TESTAMENT

APOCRYPHA AND INTERTESTAMENTAL LITERATURE

NEW TESTAMENT